GW00691764

ZAGATSURVEY®

25TH ANNIVERSARY

2005

LONDON
NIGHTLIFE

Local Editor: Jeremy Hazlehurst

Editor: Yoji Yamaguchi

Published and distributed by
ZAGAT SURVEY, LLC
4 Columbus Circle
New York, New York 10019
Tel: 212 977 6000
E-mail: londonnightlife@zagat.com
Web site: www.zagat.com

Acknowledgments

For their help on this book, we thank John Adams IV, Kathy Batt, Todd Cote, Phil Cusick, Tom Erikson, Elgy Gillespie, Dema Grim, Nicholas Helfrich, Jeanne Kearsley, Heejin Kim, Amy Marr, Kevin Odle, Pat Ryan, Steven Shukow, Nick Tangborn, Jonathan Urquhart, Amy Ventura, Craig and Vivienne Von Wiedorhold, Mike "Guitar" Wolf and Carolyn Wolff, as well as the following members of our staff: Betsy Andrews, Reni Chin, Anuradha Duggal, Griff Foxley, Schuyler Frazier, Jeff Freier, Katherine Harris, Natalie Lebert, Mike Liao, Dave Makulec, Robert Poole, Daniel Simmons, Kelly Sinanis and Sharon Yates.

Contents

About This Survey

Here are the results of our *London Nightlife Survey,* covering 866 bars, pubs and clubs in London and its surrounding areas. By surveying a large number of local nightlife denizens, we think we have achieved a uniquely current and reliable guide. We hope you will agree.

What started 25 years ago as a hobby involving 200 friends rating local restaurants has come a long way. Today we have more than 250,000 surveyors and have branched out to cover entertaining, golf, hotels, movies, music, nightlife, resorts, shopping, spas, theater and travel in over 90 countries. Our *Surveys* are also available on wireless devices and by subscription at zagat.com, where you can vote and shop as well.

Eight hundred thirty-nine people participated in our inaugural *London Nightlife Survey* in 2003. For this book an additional 1,557 people took part. This year's crowd go out an average of 2.4 times per week, amounting to roughly 195,000 nights out per year. In contrast to our *2005 London Restaurant Survey,* where our respondents' mean age is 42, the average age of the participants in this *Survey* is 35. The breakdown: 31% are in their 20s; 44%, 30s; and 25%, 40s or above. As far as we can tell, younger people drink more than they eat, while the opposite is true of their elders. We suspect there is a metabolic change that occurs before people reach the age of 40.

In any event, we want to thank all of our participants. Since this book is based entirely on their ratings and comments (which we show in quotation marks), it is really "theirs."

We are especially grateful to our editor, Jeremy Hazlehurst, a London freelance journalist who has contributed to the *Times, Daily Telegraph* and *Independent on Sunday.*

To help guide you to the places that best fit your needs, we've prepared a number of lists. See Most Popular (page 9), Top Ratings (pages 10–15) and Best Buys (page 16). In addition, we have provided 42 handy indexes.

To join this or any of our upcoming *Surveys,* just register at zagat.com. Each participant will receive a free copy of the resulting guide when published. Your comments and even criticisms of this guide are also solicited. There is always room for improvement with your help. You can contact us at londonnightlife@zagat.com. We look forward to hearing from you.

New York, NY
3 September, 2004

Nina and Tim Zagat

What's New

Smoke Signals: As this book goes to press, debate is raging over a proposed ban on smoking in bars and pubs under consideration by the government. Not surprisingly, advocates on both sides of the argument are presenting conflicting data to bolster their positions. Among our surveyors, a majority (54%) favour such a regulation. Over one-third (37%) say they would go out more if venues were smoke-free, while only 11% said less.

Sojourning Beyond Soho: Though a plurality of surveyors still salute Soho as their top nightlife neighbourhood, other areas are snapping at its grungy heels. This year the Fitzrovia/Marylebone area has been shaping up as a credible alternative for an upmarket night in central London, with such swanky new openings as Crazy Bear, Salt Whisky Bar and Wax. Farther afield, Dusk and Iniquity in Battersea, Bar Sia in Wimbledon, the Balham Kitchen and Bar, and Atlantic 66 and Brixton Bar & Grill in Brixton are tempting even die-hard northerners to venture (shhh) south of the river.

Gastro-A-Go-Go: While there have been rumblings in the media about the death of the gastro-pub, recent activity tells us otherwise – witness new additions like Waterloo's Anchor and Hope, Borough's Hartley's Pub & Dining Rooms and Medcalf in Clerkenwell, and the transformation of the Cat & Mutton in Hackney from a traditional pub to a purveyor of Modern British cuisine. Nowadays it seems like you can hardly set foot in a local boozer without tripping over a pan-fried calf's liver.

Easterly Winds: Undoubtedly the hottest upscale opening of the year was Alan Yau's (of Hakkasan fame) dim sum and tea bar, Yauatcha, an infusion of the East into beery old Soho. Not to be outdone, Yau's younger brother, Gary, has opened his own posh production, the Bali-themed Taman Gang in Mayfair. Elsewhere, the former West Street in Covent Garden has been reintroduced as East@West, offering cocktails and a tasting menu with an Asian flair.

Coming Back: Perhaps the most eagerly awaited new opening in coming months is the metamorphosis of Terence Conran's Mezzo into the London version of Cuba's legendary El Floridita, a favourite of Papa Hemingway and the purported cradle of the daiquiri. Meanwhile, plans are in the works to relaunch the Bluebird Club in Chelsea with a return to its '20s roots.

Cheers: In sum, London's nightlife seems to be reinventing itself as we write. There's only one appropriate response to all the exciting new things happening here – cheers!

London, England   Jeremy Hazlehurst
3 September, 2004

Ratings & Symbols

Name, Address, Tube Stop/Rail, Phone Number* & Web Site

Zagat Ratings

Credit Cards

A	D	S	C
▽ 23	5	9	£2

TIM & NINA'S PUB ⊅

Exeter St., WC2 (Covent Garden), 020-7123 4567;
www.zagat.com

☑ With a late licence till 5 AM, this "grotty yet, well, grotty" Covent Garden pub/dance club has become the destination of "ravers", "punks", "tacky American tourists" and "errant MPs" who dig the "so-uncool-it's-cool" vibe and "dirt-cheap" "unreal" ale; though the service is "dismal" and the DJs are stuck in a "bad '80s groove", the "sticky floors" keep punters riveted till the "very bitter" end.

Review, with surveyors' comments in quotes

Nightspots with the highest overall ratings and greatest popularity and importance are printed in CAPITAL LETTERS.

Before reviews a symbol indicates whether responses were uniform ■ or mixed ☑.

Credit Cards: ⊅ no credit cards accepted

Ratings: Appeal, Decor and Service are rated on a scale of **0** to **30**. The Cost (C) column reflects surveyors' estimated price of a typical single drink.

A	Appeal	D	Decor	S	Service	C	Cost
23		5		9		£2	

0–9 poor to fair	**20–25** very good to excellent
10–15 fair to good	**26–30** extraordinary to perfection
16–19 good to very good	▽ low response/less reliable

For places listed without ratings or a numerical cost estimate, such as a newcomer or survey write-in, the price range is indicated by the following symbols.

I	below £3	**E**	£5 to £7
M	£3 to £4	**VE**	more than £7

---

* When calling from outside the U.K., dial international code +44, then omit the first zero of the number.

Most Popular

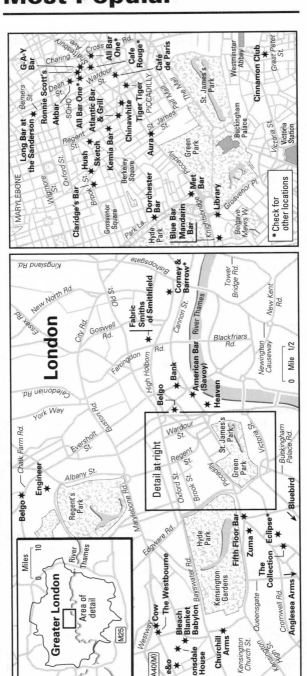

Most Popular

1. Eclipse	22. Churchill Arms
2. Blue Bar	23. Corney & Barrow*
3. Chinawhite	24. Kemia Bar
4. Zuma	25. Fifth Floor
5. All Bar One	26. Akbar
6. Mandarin Bar	27. Hush
7. Tiger Tiger	28. e&o
8. Claridge's Bar	29. Lonsdale Hse.
9. Fabric	30. Westbourne*
10. Annabel's	31. Bank
11. Café Rouge*	32. Collection
12. Café de Paris	33. Aura
13. Atlantic B&G	34. Cinnamon Club*
14. Sketch	35. Heaven*
15. Anglesea Arms (SW7)	36. Met Bar
16. Beach Blanket	37. Ronnie Scott's
17. Smiths/Smithfield	38. Engineer
18. Long Bar	39. G-A-Y Bar*
19. Dorchester Bar	40. American Bar (WC2)
20. Library*	41. Bluebird*
21. Belgo	42. Cow*

It's obvious that many of the places on the above list are among the most expensive, but London night-owls also love a bargain. Were popularity calibrated to price, we suspect that a number of other places would join the above ranks. Thus, we have listed 50 Best Buys on page 16.

---

* Indicates a tie with place above

Top Ratings

Top lists exclude places with low voting

Top Overall Appeal

28 Royal Oak (SE1)
26 Library
Plan B
Wenlock Arms
25 Sultan
Dove
Ling Ling
Holly Bush
Ye Olde Mitre*
Jerusalem Tavern
Claridge's Bar
24 Kemia Bar
Purple Bar*
Grenadier
Rivoli Bar/Ritz
Zuma
Blue Bar
Milk & Honey
Dragon
Ain't Nothin' But

Annabel's
23 Cargo
Just Oriental
Windows Bar*
Ronnie Scott's
Trafalgar Tavern
Jazz Cafe
Baltic
Chinawhite
Star Tavern
Dorchester Bar
Herbal
Gordon's
Lamb
Well*
American Bar (W1)
Mandarin Bar
Draper's Arms
Dukes Hotel Bar
e&o

By Special Appeal

After Work
25 Ling Ling
Jerusalem Tavern
23 Baltic
Gordon's
Lamb

Beer Specialist
28 Royal Oak (SE1)
26 Wenlock Arms
25 Sultan
Dove
Jerusalem Tavern

Cocktail Experts
26 Library
25 Ling Ling
Claridge's Bar
24 Kemia Bar
Purple Bar*

Comedy Clubs
23 Comedy Store
22 Troubadour Cafe
21 Bedford
20 Madame JoJo's
17 Jongleurs/Bar Risa

Commuter
25 Jerusalem Tavern
23 Gordon's
22 Smiths/Smithfield
Maket Porter
21 Lamb Tavern

DJ Bars
26 Plan B
24 Dragon
23 Cargo
Herbal
Hoxton Sq. Bar

Eastern
25 Ling Ling
24 Zuma
23 Chinawhite
e&o
22 Akbar

Expense-Accounters
26 Library
25 Ling Ling
Claridge's Bar
24 Purple Bar
Blue Bar

Top Appeal

Fine Food Too
- **25** Dove
  Ling Ling
  Claridge's Bar
- **24** Kemia Bar
- **23** Cargo

Gastro-Pubs
- **23** Well
  Draper's Arms
  Westbourne, The
- **22** Bull's Head
  Approach Tavern

Gay
- **20** Shadow Lounge
  Yard Bar
  Heaven
  King William IV
  Freedom

Group-Friendly
- **23** Cargo
  Jazz Cafe
- **22** Fabric
- **21** Eclipse
  Albion

Grown-Ups
- **26** Wenlock Arms
- **25** Dove
  Ling Ling
  Ye Old Mitre
  Claridge's Bar

Hen Party
- **23** 25 Canonbury Ln.
- **22** Cross
  Julie's
  Player
  Lonsdale Hse.

Hotel Bars
- **24** Rivoli Bar
  Ritz Hotel
- **23** Windows Bar
  Hilton Park Lane
  Mandarin Bar
  Mandarin Oriental
  Dukes Hotel Bar
  Dukes Hotel
- **22** Long Bar
  Sanderson Hotel

Irish
- **21** O'Hanlon's
- **20** Porterhouse
- **19** Toucan
- **18** O'Conor Don
  Filthy MacNasty's

Jazz Clubs
- **23** Ronnie Scott's
  Jazz Cafe
- **22** Bull's Head
- **21** 606 Club
- **17** Dover St.

Late Licence
- **26** Library
  Plan B
- **25** Ling Ling
- **24** Zuma
  Blue Bar

Latin
- **22** Kick
- **20** La Perla
- **19** Barcelona Tapas
  Lomo
- **18** Amber

Lesbian
- **19** Candy Bar
- **18** Sanctuary Soho
- **15** Kudos
  Astoria
- **14** Office

Live Music
- **26** Wenlock Arms
- **24** Kemia Bar
  Dragon
  Ain't Nothin' But
- **23** Cargo

Meat Markets
- **23** Chinawhite
- **22** Player
- **21** Eclipse
  Scala
  Prince Bonaparte

Newcomers/Unrated
- Anchor and Hope
  Crazy Bear
  Medcalf
  Salt Whisky Bar
  Yauatcha

Top Appeal

Stag Party
23 Comedy Store
22 Cross
Player
21 Sosho
Bedford

Suits
24 Milk and Honey
Annabel's
23 Baltic
Gordon's
American Bar (WC2)

Trendy
26 Plan B
25 Ling Ling
24 Milk & Honey
Dragon
23 Cargo

Wine Bars
23 Gordon's
22 Cellar Gascon
Julie's
21 Cork & Bottle
20 Tea Rooms/Artistes

By Neighbourhood

Belgravia/Knightsbridge
26 Library
24 Grenadier
Zuma
Blue Bar
23 Star Tavern

Bloomsbury/Fitzrovia
25 Ling Ling
24 Purple Bar
23 Lamb
22 Long Bar
21 Villandry

Brixton/Clapham
26 Plan B
21 Bread & Roses
20 Tea Rooms/Artistes
Calf
Lavender*
Windmill on Common*

Camden Town/Primrose Hill
23 Jazz Cafe
21 Lansdowne
20 Bartok
Engineer
19 Head of Steam

Chelsea/South Kensington
21 Eclipse
FireHouse
Apartment 195
606 Club
20 Builder's Arms

City/Clerkenwell
25 Ye Olde Mitre
Jerusalem Tavern
23 Well
George Inn
Twentyfour

Covent Garden
22 American Bar
Na Zdrowie
Light Bar
21 End
Freud

Hampstead
25 Holly Bush
20 Spaniard's Inn
Flask
King William IV
18 Freemasons Arms

Islington
23 Draper's Arms
25 Canonbury Ln.
21 Albion
Social
Duke of Cambridge

Mayfair/St. James's
25 Claridge's Bar
24 Rivoli Bar
Annabel's
23 Just Oriental
Windows Bar*

Notting Hill
23 e&o
   Westbourne
22 Julie's
   Lonsdale Hse.
21 Eclipse

Piccadilly
24 Kemia Bar
23 Chinawhite
   Gordon's
   Comedy Store
21 Cork & Bottle

Putney/Richmond/
Wandsworth/Wimbledon
25 Sultan
21 Eclipse
   Duke's Head
20 Putney Bridge
   Old Ship
   White Swan*

Shoreditch/Hoxton
26 Wenlock Arms
24 Dragon
23 Cargo
   Herbal
   Hoxton Sq. Bar

Soho
24 Milk & Honey
   Ain't Nothin' But
23 Ronnie Scott's
22 Player
   Akbar

South Bank/Borough/
Southwark
28 Royal Oak (SE1)
22 Oxo Tower
   Market Porter
21 Founder's Arms
19 Anchor Bankside

Top Decor

28 Ling Ling	Lamb
27 Purple Bar	Princess Louise
26 Rivoli Bar	**22** Jewel
25 Library	Warrington*
Claridge's Bar	Lonsdale Hse.
24 Just Oriental	Holly Bush
Sketch	Chinawhite
Kemia Bar	George Inn
Blue Bar	Light Bar
Ye Olde Mitre	Opium
American Bar (WC2)	SO.UK
Royal Oak (SE1)	Cross
Baltic	Dukes Hotel Bar
Zuma	Old Bank
Long Bar	Isola
Pasha	Cargo
23 Plan B	**21** Beach Blanket
Black Friar	Dorchester Bar
Cinnamon Club	Akbar
Mandarin Bar	Bed*
Jerusalem Tavern	Annabel's

Dramatic Interiors

Blue Bar	Light Bar
Crazy Bear	Ling Ling
Elysium	Purple Bar
Kingly Club	Sketch

Old London

George Inn	Royal Oak (SE1)
Grapes	Trafalgar Tavern
Hoop & Grapes	Ye Old Cheshire
Jerusalem Tavern	Ye Olde Mitre

Outdoors

Albion	Putney Bridge
Coach & Horses (SW1)	Spaniard's Inn
Flask (N6)	Sun Inn
Prospect/Whitby	Windmill on Common

Romance

Bartok	Library
Claridge's Bar	Rivoli Bar
Dove	Soho
Gordon's	Twentyfour

Views

Anchor Bankside	Putney Bridge
Old Ship	Trafalgar Tavern
Old Thameside	Twentyfour
Oxo Tower	Windows Bar

Top Service

25 Library
Dukes Hotel Bar
24 Royal Oak (SE1)
Wenlock Arms
Claridge's Bar
Dorchester Bar
Plan B
American Bar (W1)
Sultan
23 Annabel's
Rivoli Bar
Sekforde Arms*
Swag & Tails*
American Bar (WC2)
Milk & Honey
22 Draper's Arms
Na Zdrowie*
O'Conor Don
Seven Stars*
21 Mandarin Bar
Player
Blue Bar

Cellar Gascon
Potemkin*
Artillery Arms
Head of Steam
Lab
Boisdale
Pasha*
20 Baltic
Purple Bar
Pride Spitalfields
Zuma
Bonds
Jerusalem Tavern
Cinnamon Club
Bull's Head (SW13)
Captain Kidd*
Guinea*
Lamb Tavern*
Lyceum Tavern*
Salisbury Tavern*
Thirst*
Ye Olde Mitre*

Best Buys

More Rounds for Your Pounds

1. Royal Oak (SE1)
2. Sultan
3. Wenlock Arms
4. Artillery Arms
5. Ye Olde Mitre
6. Head of Steam
7. Sekforde Arms
8. Pride Spitalfields
9. O'Hanlon's
10. Jerusalem Tavern
11. Market Porter
12. Bread & Roses
13. Princess Louise
14. Holly Bush
15. Compton Arms
16. Ship & Shovell
17. Coach & Horses (SW13)
18. Lamb Tavern
19. Founder's Arms
20. Dove
21. Buckingham Arms
22. Fox & Anchor
23. Black Friar
24. Camden Head
25. Old Ship (Richmond)
26. Coat & Badge
27. Albion
28. Star Tavern
29. Westminster Arms
30. City Pride
31. Hen & Chickens
32. Bricklayer's Arms (EC2)
33. Bedford
34. Cittie of Yorke
35. Trafalgar Tavern
36. King's Head Theatre
37. Hamilton Hall
38. Spread Eagle
39. Blue Anchor
40. Bradley's
41. Hare & Billet
42. Flask
43. Old Bank
44. Flask, The
45. Warrington
46. Bishop's Finger
47. Hand in Hand
48. Bricklayer's Arms (EC2)
49. George Inn
50. Bull's Head (SW13)

Nightlife Directory

Abbaye
16 | 14 | 15 | £5

55 Charterhouse St., EC1 (Farringdon), 020-7253 1612
■ A "nice variety" of 32 beers "on draught and in bottles", a "stylish" "traditional Belgian cafe" setting (with an "outside terrace for seating in summer") and a "relaxed atmosphere" make this Clerkenwell bar/restaurant a "welcome change from the trendy-trendy", attracting "lots of businessmen and their paychecks"; while wallet-watchers warn it's "not for the tight-fisted", others find it "great value."

Abbey Road Pub & Dining Room
17 | 16 | 17 | £4

(fka Salt House)
63 Abbey Rd., NW8 (St. John's Wood), 020-7328 6626
◪ The new management decided to give this cocktail lounge/restaurant in St. John's Wood the Oriental makeover (think black walls and floors), leaving some wondering "why is it so dark?"; there's still "good food" and a "nice patio", and in the end it continues to draw a "hip crowd."

Abigail's Party
16 | 18 | 15 | £6

25-27 Brewer St., W1 (Piccadilly Circus), 020-7434 2911; www.abigailsparty.com
◪ "Delightful hospitality", "good food and drinks", a "refreshing" ambience and "trendy decor" make this "classy", "cosy", "name-on-the-door type" "private bar" in Soho a "home from home" for "beautiful people"; despite "crazy prices" and its "members' club" policy, the "cramped" space can get "very crowded on weekends."

Abingdon
18 | 17 | 16 | £5

54 Abingdon Rd., W8 (High St. Kensington), 020-7937 3339
■ You "go for the people and the atmosphere" at this "smart" South Ken "gastro-pub", a "favourite local" spot serving "decent" drinks and "reliable" Modern British fare in a "cool" yet "unpretentious" setting; "friendly service" and "comfortable booths and sofas" help make it a "cosy dating place", but while it's "great before 6 PM", insiders caution it can get "too busy at peak times."

Adelaide
13 | 10 | 13 | £3

143 Adelaide Rd., NW3 (Chalk Farm/Swiss Cottage), 020-7722 3777
■ A "favourite haunt of Australian expats" and a "nice Sunday chillin'" spot, this "charming" gastro-pub that's "conveniently" located on Primrose Hill offers a menu of "good, uncomplicated" Thai cooking; in the summer you can tuck into barbecue fare or just have a pint in the "large beer garden."

ad lib
18 | 17 | 19 | £8

246 Fulham Rd., SW10 (South Kensington), 020-7376 7775; www.adlib246.com
■ Libertines love the "crazy, sexy cool" of this "funky" Chelsea boîte that's "bumping on most nights" with a crowd

quaffing "brilliant" libations like the "yummy mojitos" and nibbling on Thai fare in a "cosy" modern space, when they're not gyrating to the "funky soul grooves" spun by DJs; alas, it "can be tough to get in."

Admiral Codrington   18 | 16 | 16 | £4
17 Mossop St., SW3 (South Kensington), 020-7581 0005
■ Though it's "very Chelsea" ("posh totty", "Hugo on his mobile, etc."), boosters boast this "hangout" is "one of the best bars in South Ken", and despite going "upmarket" it's "retained a pub feel" that's right for a "lazy Sunday afternoon booze-up"; added to the bar is a "fantastic restaurant" that does a "great brunch", where "children are welcome during the day" (it's "pet-friendly", too); in the summer, the "retractable roof" and "cute terrace" come into play.

Admiral Duncan   15 | 13 | 16 | £3
54 Old Compton St., W1 (Leicester Sq.), 020-7437 5300
◩ A "classic" "old-skool gay bar" on Soho's Old Compton Street, this pub attracts a "good-looking" crowd "without a lot of pretence" that makes for a "relaxed", "friendly" atmosphere; mutineers moan the "boring" scene "full of camp old men" "needs an update", though, and complain that it also attracts morbid types who come only to "see it for the nail bomb story" (a 1999 attack that killed three).

Africa Bar ⇩   16 | 17 | 15 | £8
Africa Ctr., 38 King St., WC2 (Covent Garden/Leicester Sq.), 020-7836 1976
■ The Covent Garden venue below the Africa Centre, where Soul II Soul and others cut their teeth in the late '80s, is "still kicking after all these years" with African music, theatre and poetry (and beers) on offer; "friendly" punters and a "cool atmosphere" that's "true to its name" will "take you right back" to the sub-Sahara.

AIN'T NOTHIN' BUT   24 | 16 | 14 | £3
20 Kingly St., W1 (Oxford Circus/Piccadilly Circus), 020-7287 0514; www.aintnothinbut.co.uk
■ It "feels like you're in a small blues bar somewhere down south in the USA" at this "simple" but "brilliant" "raunchy late-night dive" in Soho where "very good live bands" churn out "toe-tapping" tunes in a "tiny" space that's "always packed to the hilt" with a "boozy crowd"; the drinks, though, ain't nothing but "expensive", "even by W1 standards."

AKA   20 | 20 | 15 | £5
18 West Central St., WC1 (Holborn/Tottenham Court Rd.), 020-7836 0110; www.akalondon.com
■ For those who "want more than a pub but not a massive clubbing session", this "funky, trendy" next-door sibling of The End is a "safe bet" for a "midweek pickup" or "pre-club" drinks, with DJs spinning "banging tunes" in a "loft"-like space housed in a former post office; the atmosphere

is "civilised" and "relaxed", with a somewhat "older crowd" "keeping things under control."

AKBAR   22 | 21 | 17 | £8
Red Fort Restaurant, 77 Dean St., W1 (Tottenham Court Rd./ Piccadilly Circus), 020-7437 2525; www.redfort.co.uk
■ Tucked below Red Fort (the upscale Indian where Tony Blair gets his takeaway), this "exotic", "Raj-themed" bar is a "great retreat" serving some of the "best cocktails in town", though the "expensive" menu may make it more appropriate for a "sharpener" or "after-dinner drinks", and the "crowd's a little old to be hip"; still, with its "dark, sensuous" "carved niches" and "alcoves" with "lots of pillows", it's a "winner" when you want to "impress a date."

Albion   21 | 15 | 16 | £3
10 Thornhill Rd., N1 (Angel), 020-7607 7450; www.thealbion.net
■ When you "want to feel like you're in the countryside in central London", "away from all the hustle and bustle", fans recommend this pub set in an ivy-clad former coaching inn "on the backstreets of Islington", where "great pub food" (especially the "Sunday roasts") and "friendly service" come with a rustic setting warmed by a fireplace in the winter; there's also a "large", "shady" "beer garden" that's "nice in the summer."

Alexandra Pub, The ⌦   16 | 14 | 16 | £3
14 Clapham Common Southside, SW4 (Clapham Common), 020-7627 5102
■ Though it may look "forbidding" on the outside, this Clapham "boozer" is really a "relaxed", "olde, traditional pub" where a "welcoming and sociable" crowd gathers for a "proper pint" under the watchful eyes of "portraits of Prime Ministers"; it can also get "lively", and with "lots of space", it's a perfect site for "parties."

Alexandra/Smart Alec's   15 | 14 | 15 | £3
33 Wimbledon Hill Rd., SW19 (Wimbledon), 020-8947 7691; www.youngs.co.uk
☑ "Bang in the middle of Wimbledon", this "traditional" "high street pub" with a wine bar annexe and a "lively" roof garden "caters to all walks of life" – for some, it's a "friendly old local" serving Young's, while the enoteca is a "nice venue" (albeit "quite expensive"); still, detractors demur on the "noisy", "smoky" "suburban" scene; N.B. no relation to the Clapham establishment.

ALL BAR ONE   12 | 13 | 13 | £4
84 Charing Cross Rd., WC2 (Leicester Sq./Tottenham Court Rd.), 020-7379 8311
48 Leicester Sq., WC2 (Leicester Sq.), 020-7747 9921
197 Chiswick High Rd., W4 (Turnham Green), 020-8987 8211
36-38 Dean St., W1 (Leicester Sq.), 020-7479 7921
1-2 Chicheley St., SE1 (Waterloo), 020-7921 9471

(continued)
ALL BAR ONE
2-4 The Broadway, N8 (Finsbury Park), 020-8342 7871
103 Cannon St., EC4 (Cannon St./Monument), 020-7220 9031
15-16 Byward St., EC3 (Tower Hill), 020-7553 0301
18-20 Appold St., EC2 (Liverpool St.), 020-7377 9671
93 Charterhouse St., EC1 (Barbican/Farringdon), 020-7553 9391
◪ "If you prefer 'nice and light' to 'dark and dingy'", the "bright, clean, minimal" "leather couches"–and–"bleached wood" style of this "dependable" group beckons; a popular "after-work" "meeting place", it's always full of "suits" and "20–30-year-old up-and-comers", and the over-21 age limit "keeps the kids out"; "boring", "bland, bland and more bland" howl hecklers of this "Milton Keynes of chain pubs" that's "like Ikea, only more expensive."

Almeida
20 | 18 | 19 | £4

30 Almeida St., N1 (Angel/Highbury & Islington), 020-7354 4777;
www.almeida-restaurant.co.uk
■ A "wonderful wine list", "good French country" fare and "fabulous" "star-spotting" possibilities attract "local trendy drinkers" in Islington to this "small", "quiet" bar attached to the famed Almeida for a "pre-dinner or pre-theatre" tipple; the service is "attentive but not overbearing", and the decor is "pleasant", if somewhat "clinical."

Alphabet
19 | 17 | 15 | £5

61-63 Beak St., W1 (Oxford Circus/Piccadilly Circus),
020-7439 2190; www.alphabetbar.com
■ A "very Soho media joint", Amber's "shabby chic" sibling is a popular way to "kick off an evening in the West End" say fans who quaff "fab cocktails" in a "modern", minimalist space with two levels (including a "cool basement") furnished with "posh couches"; a "trendy" crowd and "sexy barmen" give it a "nice vibe", though it can be "very busy and quite noisy", and "ridiculous at weekends"; while it's "a bit on the expensive side", it's "worth the money."

Al's Bar Café
13 | 9 | 11 | £3

11-13 Exmouth Mkt., EC1 (Angel/Farringdon), 020-7837 4821
■ In keeping with the Clerkenwell spirit, this pub known for "cheap" "Czech beer" and other brews is "getting cool and trendy", and a "hip" ambience fills the "stark", "weirdly cosy" space; but it's "still quirky and good", drawing an "odd mix of people", from *Guardian* scribblers to local scallies.

Amber
18 | 19 | 19 | £5

6 Poland St., W1 (Oxford Circus), 020-7734 3094;
www.amberbar.com
■ "Lively, trendy fun" in the form of "great cocktails", Iberian tapas and DJs spinning Latin tunes awaits at this "quality" Soho sibling of the nearby Alphabet; while the bi-level space is a "fantastic party venue", the "intimate" booths also make

it "ok" as a "quiet spot to meet for drinks" (be sure to "get there early" to secure one), and it's a great "fallback option" that's "surprisingly easy to get into on weekends"; the only peeve – it "needs a later license."

AMERICAN BAR
22 | 21 | 23 | £9

Savoy Hotel, The Strand , WC2 (Charing Cross), 020-7836 4343; www.savoy-group.com

■ "Live the dream in the 1930s" at this "classic" "old favourite" in the Strand's Savoy Hotel that's "forever cool without trying to be", offering up "seriously composed", "near-perfect" drinks in a "stylish", "sedate" setting for "grown-ups"; for an "upscale" experience with a "real sense of occasion", "bring someone nice" and "make that cocktail last."

AMERICAN BAR
23 | 24 | 24 | £9

Connaught Hotel, 16 Carlos Pl., W1 (Bond St.), 020-7499 7070; www.savoy-group.com

■ Nestled in the back of the Connaught Hotel in Mayfair, this "smart and serious" watering hole resembles an "old-fashioned" "gentlemen's club", with "dark, rich" oak-panelling and oil paintings; "great drinks" and "discrete", "attentive" service help foster a "relaxed atmosphere" that's ideal for a "one-on-one", though critics caution they can get "snotty" if you show up too casually attired.

Anchor and Hope, The
– | – | – | I

36 The Cut, SE1 (Waterloo/Southwark), 020-7928 9898

The "delights of the kitchen" attract a "good, friendly crowd" to this "great new gastro-pub" run by graduates of The Eagle and St John in the rather "grim surroundings" of Waterloo; it follows the gastro-blueprint of Brit fare ("they like their offal") and proper beer served in a spartan setting of plain tables and chairs; be prepared to wait, because it takes no bookings and can get "very busy."

Anchor Bankside & Southwark Premier Lodge
19 | 17 | 13 | £3

Premier Lodge Southwark, 34 Park St., SE1 (London Bridge), 020-7407 1577; www.premierlodge.com

■ "The history! the view! the atmosphere!" crow cronies of this "wonderful", sprawling South Bank pub that looks onto St. Paul's and the City, with five bars and a restaurant, plus two outdoor terraces facing the Thames that are perfect for "long summer evenings"; while the "hordes of tourists" from the nearby Tate Modern and Globe Theatre may "lessen its charm", for locals it's "fantastic out of season."

Anexo
– | – | – | M

Turnmills, 61 Turnmill St., EC1 (Farringdon), 020-7250 3401; www.anexo.co.uk

With its Gaudí-esque mosaics of lizards, grapes and vines, this annexe to the Turnmills club brings a bit of southern sunshine to grey old Clerkenwell, especially in the summer when the French windows open onto the street; there's Mediterranean fare to go along with the "jugs of cocktails", and DJs help make it a fine pre-club option.

Angel, The — 16 | 11 | 15 | £3

61 St. Giles High St., WC2 (Tottenham Court Rd.), 020-7240 2876
■ For a "quiet corner away from frantic Oxford Street and Covent Garden" or a pre-theatre tipple, this "lively, friendly", slightly "scruffy" "old pub" is a popular option, offering "cheap", "good English beers" of the Sam Smith's variety and "no music"; still, it can get "noisy", especially on Fridays and Saturdays, when it's often "packed."

Anglesea Arms — 21 | 16 | 15 | £3

35 Wingate Rd., W6 (Ravenscourt Park), 020-8749 1291
■ "Thirtysomething" gourmands gush the "awesome food" at this Shepherd's Bush gastro-pub "beats the hell out of almost every restaurant", while oenophiles extol the "great selection of wines by the glass"; a "grown-up ambience" fills a space that's "like my living room, only better", and thanks to a no-booking policy "it's always full and buzzy", which can sometimes translate into an "endless wait."

ANGLESEA ARMS — 20 | 15 | 17 | £4

15 Selwood Terr., SW7 (South Kensington), 020-7373 7960
■ A "cosy backstreet pub" perfect for those "Saturday afternoons", this Chelsea stalwart has "plenty of history" (the Great Train Robbery was purportedly plotted here), as well as "lovely ales" and "decent grub" served up in the "old English" setting; there's also "great people-watching" on "sunny, warm days" when resident "hooray Henrys" and "Sloany Ponies" mix with "tourists" and Aussie "expats" on the terrace.

ANNABEL'S — 24 | 21 | 23 | £11

Private club; inquiries: 020-7629 1096
◪ Time may have "stopped in the mid-'80s" at this Mayfair members-only place, but it's "still going strong", "oozing old money, confidence and good manners from every pore", with "staff who are keen to please", which is why it remains a "long-time favourite" for "over-40s", "royalty and celebs"; there are plenty of "wanna-be '60s playboys" and "fathers and daughters", but a "younger, more eclectic crowd" is "revitalising" the scene, and loyalists insist there's "no better place for a drink, dinner or dance in style."

Antelope — 20 | 15 | 15 | £3

22-24 Eaton Terr., SW1 (Sloane Sq.), 020-7824 8512
■ Wags quip this "very British" Belgravia pub has "been around since Noah's Ark", but admirers consider it "one of the best watering holes in the area", with an "old-fashioned" ambience that's "cosy" and "charming" (though those in-the-know warn "it's always packed by 6 PM"); it's "nicely

located" on a "backstreet", and in the summer you can "observe the locals" from an outdoor pew.

Apartment 195
21 | 19 | 20 | £9

195 King's Rd., SW3 (Sloane Sq.), 020-7351 5195;
www.apartment195.co.uk

■ A bar where you "can have a civilised conversation", this "stunningly, gorgeously, deliciously wonderful" King's Road "secret" is a "great launching pad for a night out", attracting a "sophisticated" crowd of "beautiful people" that gathers over "creative, tasty" cocktails mixed by an "all-lady staff" in a "relaxed", "clublike" atmosphere; oak panelling, "interesting artwork", Victorian bay windows and chandeliers grace the "stylish" three-room space.

Appogee
∇ 19 | 16 | 18 | £4

3 Leicester Pl., WC2 (Leicester Sq.), 020-7437 4556

■ This "lovely little" spot is a high point in Leicester Square say fans who appreciate it for "relaxed after-hours drinks" (the "piña coladas are the best"); "excellent salads" and other "good" pub grub whet the appetite, while "friendly" service adds further appeal.

Approach Tavern
∇ 22 | 19 | 18 | £4

47 Approach Rd., E2 (Bethnal Green), 020-8980 2321

■ An "old-style East End" pub sporting "modern food and fashion", with staff who look like they're "waiting for Alexander McQueen to hire them", this "always busy" "boozer" in Bethnal Green attracts an "arty" crowd who stop in before or after checking out the gallery upstairs; the tables in the front garden are popular on "sunnier days."

Archduke, The
16 | 15 | 15 | £4

153 Concert Hall Approach, SE1 (Waterloo), 020-7928 9370

■ With a "good view, good nibbles" and "good piano" (and evening jazz Mondays–Saturdays), this Waterloo wine bar is an "old reliable" for "after-work" or "before the theatre" at the South Bank; the staff are "helpful", and bacchic boosters boast it's one of the "best in town."

Archery Tavern
∇ 19 | 16 | 20 | £2

4 Bathurst St., W2 (Lancaster Gate), 020-7402 4916

■ A "real gem of a classic English pub" dating back to 1809, this "proper boozer" on a Bayswater "backstreet" hits the mark "for a pint after a walk in Hyde Park", offering "perhaps the best variety of beer" around (including Badger ale from Dorset) in a "lovely, traditional" setting; "go out of your way to go there" enthusiasts exhort.

Arch635
∇ 21 | 18 | 22 | £3

15-16 Lendal Terr., SW4 (Clapham North), 020-7720 7343;
www.arch635.co.uk

■ When they want to "escape from everyone else", loyalists "love, love, love" this "cool" lounge in Clapham set in a converted railway arch for an evening of "watching football" on a jumbo screen, "playing pool and drinking"; it "gets packed" on weekends, though, when "dancing" breaks out to the "excellent music" spun by DJs.

Argyll Arms
16 | 17 | 15 | £3

18 Argyll St., W1 (Oxford Circus), 020-7734 6117

■ At this "ornate", "historic" (circa 1740) pub near Oxford Circus, "etched glass" and "mirrored walls" "take you back in time" and suggest that it was "once very posh"; now, though, it's used mainly for "shopping breaks" and "serious midday drinking" (it's "great to stand outside in summer") or as a "meeting place before moving somewhere else."

Arizona Bar and Restaurant
15 | 16 | 15 | £6

2 Jamestown Rd., NW1 (Camden Town), 020-7284 4730

☑ It "feels like Phoenix" at this "friendly" Tex-Mex oasis in the very English desert of Camden, where sombreros line the walls and amigos enjoy "slamming tequilas" in a "loud and boisterous" setting; enemigos, though, are unimpressed by the "average" scene and "slow" service.

Artesian Well
11 | 13 | 14 | £3

693 Wandsworth Rd., SW8 (Clapham Common), 020-7627 3353; www.artesianwell.co.uk

☑ A combination of "loud, fierce" "pop cheese and house" music and "laughably OTT decor", including an upstairs glass dance floor ("girls, don't wear a skirt"), pulls in a "lively", "mixed" crowd to this Wandsworth bar and club that's "handy for large groups"; naysayers, though, knock it as "naff" and overly "pricey."

Artillery Arms
21 | 19 | 21 | £2

102 Bunhill Row, EC1 (Old St.), 020-7253 4683

■ This "cosy, friendly" "gem" is a favourite for City workers at lunchtimes and after work, but when the suits head home it morphs back into a "pleasant old-fashioned local" where you can tinkle the ivories of one of London's few remaining open pianos, and it's "handy for the Barbican", too; Fuller's ale and "good value food" also make it "worth a visit."

Ashburnham Arms
▽ 22 | 17 | 25 | £2

25 Ashburnham Grove, SE10 (Greenwich), 020-8692 2007

■ Well off the tourist track in Greenwich, this "backstreet" pub is "everything a local should be", with bar billiards and beer from the renowned Shepherd Neame brewery; it's "small but welcoming" and perfect for "quiet conversation", and in the summer it's "great to sit out front" or on the patio.

Astoria, The ∅
15 | 9 | 11 | £4

157 Charing Cross Rd., WC2 (Tottenham Court Rd.), 020-7434 9592; www.meanfiddler.com

☑ During the week this "sweaty" "rock venue" hosts "great bands", attracting punters undaunted by "dank" digs or "overpriced" beer; on weekends, the "no-frills club" setting gives way to "tacky, hip", "kitschy cool" G.A.Y. nights, when "cute boys" show up to "shake their groove thing."

ATLANTIC BAR & GRILL   17 | 21 | 14 | £7
20 Glasshouse St., W1 (Piccadilly Circus), 020-7734 4888;
www.atlanticbarandgrill.com
☑ "Still glam", this "spacious" Piccadilly perennial with "high ceilings" and a "fab" "1920s" "art deco" look is a "lively haunt" that "hasn't lost its appeal" for many, offering "excellent cocktails" and "great people-watching" in "swanky" surroundings; while cynics sneer it's "way past its sell-by date", citing "overpriced" drinks and a "cheesy" "cattle market" scene, others insist it does the trick for a "drink before a nightclub" or "after the pubs have closed."

Atlantic 66   – | – | – | I
66 Atlantic Rd., SW9 (Brixton), 020-7326 4920;
www.Atlantic66.com
Slap bang on the spot that marked the front line of the infamous Brixton race riots, this new gastro-bar in SW9 appeals mainly to thirtysomethings who have gentrified the area in recent years, offering a somewhat upscale menu, which includes items such as foie gras and "great fish dishes", paired with a global wine list.

Atlas, The   20 | 18 | 18 | £4
16 Seagrave Rd., SW6 (West Brompton), 020-7385 9129;
www.theatlaspub.co.uk
■ Gourmands gush this "super gastro-pub" in Fulham is "dedicated to dining", offering a "varied, original" menu of Italian/Turkish/North African fare, but thirsty boosters are equally beguiled by "reasonably priced drinks" and a constantly changing wine list; a "friendly" ambience, Victorian decor and an outdoor garden add allure.

Attica   18 | 16 | 13 | £8
24 Kingly St., W1 (Oxford Circus), 020-7287 5882
☑ "If Gucci had a bar, this would be it" exclaim enthusiasts who've eyeballed the "models" and "beautiful people" boogying to "funky music" on the "tiny dance floor" at this "decent alternative to Chinawhite" just off Regent Street; the jaded jeer it's "so-o-o two years ago", and are content to leave the "expensive" drinks and "rude" service to the "trust-fund crowd" and assorted "wanna-bes."

Auberge   16 | 17 | 16 | £5
6-8 St. Christopher Pl., W1 (Bond St.), 020-7486 5557
1 Sandell St., SE1 (Waterloo), 020-7633 0610
35 Tooley St., SE1 (London Bridge), 020-7407 5267
56 Mark Ln., EC3 (Bank), 020-7480 6789
www.giardinogroup.co.uk
☑ "Scruffish but appealing", these "after-work" brasserie/bars serving French fare and Belgian beers are strategically

located around commuter hot spots and "can get rather busy in the early evening"; *amis* appreciate the "lively" settings and "reasonably priced" menu, but critics complain it's hard to "to enjoy a beer like it should be enjoyed" in the "overcrowded" rooms.

Audley, The   19 | 18 | 17 | £5

41-43 Mount St., W1 (Bond St.), 020-7499 1843

■ "Even the Queen could love" this "good old-fashioned", "upmarket" Mayfair affair, a "wonderful" spot "for an after-work drink" that's "a bit more posh than your average pub", boasting "beautiful" surroundings and "fabulous decor"; for many, the "quiet, civilised" setting is a "welcome relief" in an "over-fussy" area.

AURA   21 | 18 | 14 | £9

48-49 St James's St., SW1 (Green Park), 020-7499 6655;
www.theaura.com

■ Trendoids tout this St. James's "glamour hangout" where "Justin Timberlake and Matthew Perry were regulars" when in town, and a "fun and sexy" "early 20s" crowd sporting "lots of bare midriffs" comes to "dance all night long" to DJs in a "buzzy" space adorned with a chandelier from the old Claridge's ballroom; while in theory you can pay to join the party, cognoscenti caution "you'd better know someone" if you want to get in.

Australian, The   15 | 12 | 16 | £5

29 Milner St., SW3 (Sloane Sq./Knightsbridge), 020-7589 6027

■ Cricketing memorabilia on the walls of this Knightsbridge pub reminds us that it stands on the site of the pitch where England first played its antipodean cousin; the name notwithstanding, there are almost "no Australians" among the "variety of customers" that frequents this "gentle" "classic", and many are hit for six by the "truly British experience" that awaits.

Avenue   20 | 21 | 18 | £7

7-9 St. James's St., SW1 (Green Park), 020-7321 2111;
www.egami.co.uk

■ "Designed to impress", sporting a "stylish", "minimalist" look and graced with "contemporary art", this converted bank in St. James's is "still popular with the financial and property crowd" and those who just like their bars "very noisy" and "very '90s", offering "very tall" (and "expensive") cocktails in a "comfortable" setting with a "piano player"; while some wags liken the "clean", "modern" decor to a "private hospital ward", others find it "moving."

Babble   18 | 17 | 16 | £6

59 Berkeley Sq., W1 (Green Park), 020-7758 8255;
www.babble-bar.co.uk

◪ For "filling up cheaply" on "post-work happy-hour" cocktails, this Berkeley Square watering hole "does the job", and later on is a "great place to dance your night away"; "you don't have to worry about pretension" from the "fit and flirty bartenders", but critics cringe nonetheless at the "office atmosphere" and the sight of "men in business attire dancing to Kylie."

Babushka   16 | 14 | 14 | £4

41 Tavistock Crescent, W11 (Westbourne Park), 020-7727 9250
354 Kings Rd., SW6 (Fulham Broadway), 020-7352 2828
125 Caledonian Rd., N1 (King's Cross), 020-7837 1924
www.styleinthecity.co.uk
◪ "Lovely lounging" awaits at this "lively", "edgy" trio that attracts a "late 20s to 30s" clientele with house vodkas, "funky furniture" and a "laid-back vibe"; the "retro" decor may "drive you to drink", however, say nyet-niks who also nix the "slow service" and reckon these venues have "seen better days."

Backpacker, The ⊄   10 | 8 | 10 | £3

126 York Way, N1 (King's Cross), 020-7278 8318;
www.thebackpacker.co.uk
◪ A shot chair, a "young", mostly "Aussie" clientele and All U Can Drink Fridays and Saturdays (from 8–10 PM) add up to a "holiday atmosphere" at this King's Cross venue, though it can be too much of a "southern hemisphere rugby meat market" scene for some; pious punters also recommend it for a "post-church drink."

Balham Kitchen and Bar   – | – | – | M

15-19 Bedford Hill, SW12 (Balham), 020-8675 6900
The latest production from the Soho House empire, this "trendy" spot is "just what Balham needed", adding "a bit of glamour" to an up-and-coming neighbourhood; the ambience is "fantastic" for an evening drink and "perfect for a girls' brunch", as well; but wags warn of "pushchairs and screaming kids" during the daytime, when a child-friendly policy goes into effect.

Balls Brothers   13 | 12 | 16 | £4

34 Brook St., W1 (Bond St.), 020-7499 4567
20 St. James's St., SW1 (Green Park/Piccadilly Circus),
020-7321 0882
3-6 Budge Row, EC4 (Bank), 020-7248 7557
52 Lime St., EC3 (Bank/Liverpool St.), 020-7283 0841
22 Mark Ln., EC3 (Monument/Tower Hill), 020-7623 2923
St. Mary-at-Hill, EC3 (Monument), 020-7626 0321
11 Bloomfield St., EC2 (Liverpool St.), 020-7588 4643
6-8 Cheapside, EC2 (St. Paul's), 020-7248 2708
3 Kings Arms Yard, EC2 (Bank/Moorgate), 020-7796 3049
www.ballsbrothers.co.uk
◪ "You know what you're getting" at this "upmarket" City wine bar chain – a "reasonable wine list", "service with a smile", a "great cigar selection" and a "Dickensian" decor –

all of which attracts a solidly "corporate" clientele for "boozy lunches" or "after-work" drinks; while it's "a good place to run into contacts", foes find these "cookie-cutter" venues "atmosphere-less" and "boring."

BALTIC
23 | 24 | 20 | £6

74 Blackfriars Rd., SE1 (Southwark), 020-7928 1111; www.balticrestaurant.co.uk

■ Though it's "slightly out of the way" on the South Bank, this "pricey", "fashionable" vodka venue is "worth the trip" for a "well-stocked bar" serving creative concoctions ("the blueberry martini is yummy!") to a "moneyed" bunch in a "beautiful", "minimalist" space; "amazing East European bar food" and an ambience that's "trendy but not obnoxious" also win props.

BANK
18 | 19 | 17 | £6

1 Kingsway, WC2 (Holborn), 020-7379 9797

☑ "Gordon Gekko would have enjoyed" the "airy", "high-ceilinged" room decked out with mirrors, huge windows and one of the "largest chandeliers in London" at this converted bank in Covent Garden, a "trendy" "after-work" haunt for "legal types" and "yuppies"; while the "flashy" decor and "top-notch" cocktails are right on the money for many, bashers find the "snobby" service and "soulless" setting bankrupt of allure.

Bar Bollywood
_ | _ | _ | E

34 Dover St., W1 (Green Park), 020-7493 0200; www.barbollywood.net

It's "party, party all the way" at this "very chilled lounge bar" in Mayfair located beneath its flash sister Indian restaurant, Yatra; "funky tunes", including live R&B on Fridays, combine with "Bollywood-inspired cocktails" such as the Monsoon Madness to make this a "fun hangout for anyone into Indian music."

Barcelona Tapas Bar
19 | 17 | 16 | £5

481 Lordship Ln., SE22 (East Dulwich/Forest Hill), 020-8693 5111
13 Well Ct., EC4 (Bank), 020-7329 5111
1 Middlesex St., EC3 (Aldgate East/Liverpool St.), 020-7377 5111
1A Bell Ln., E1 (Aldgate East/Liverpool St.), 020-7247 7014
www.barcelona-tapas.com

■ For a bit of "authentic Spain", fans head to this bar/tapas chain that offers a "huge menu" of "excellent traditional" small plates that'll "take you a thousand miles away", paired with a selection of 50 native wines and served in "Moorish" rooms by "friendly" staff; it's all "very Barcelona."

Bar Chocolate
19 | 18 | 15 | £5

26-27 D'Arblay St., W1 (Oxford Circus/Tottenham Court Rd.), 020-7287 2823

■ An arty crowd is sweet on this "relaxed" Soho confection that's a "great place to meet" for daytime coffee or post-work cocktails, as well as a "good spot for first dates", thanks to "friendly" service, subdued music and a dark-red-and-brown-hued decor.

Bar Code 17 | 14 | 16 | £4
3-4 Archer St., W1 (Piccadilly Circus), 020-7734 3342
■ "Lads, skinheads and queens" gravitate to this "raunchy post-work" Piccadilly "boy bar" that beckons with DJs spinning "loud" "commercial" music downstairs, creating a "high energy" vibe and a "delicious, sinister ambience", which conventional sorts find a bit "scary"; "be prepared to be squashed, and often", as it gets "very busy."

Bar des Amis 18 | 14 | 19 | £5
11-14 Hanover Pl., WC2 (Covent Garden), 020-7379 3444;
www.cafedesamis.co.uk
■ A "lovely" "hideaway" "in an alley", this "established" French-style bar/restaurant in Covent Garden offers a Gallic-centric selection of more than 50 wines by the bottle (20 by the glass); "friendly" service helps keep things "relaxed" in the "cosy", "romantic" space.

Bar Gansa 18 | 14 | 14 | £4
2 Inverness St., NW1 (Camden Town), 020-7267 8909
■ This "tiny", "sultry" Camden cantina/restaurant "knows how to let its hair down", offering "excellent tapas" and "great paella" as well as "sangria and the odd impromptu dance display" in a "funky", "welcoming" atmosphere that makes you feel "equally comfortable in a T-shirt or a suit"; flamenco on Monday nights adds allure.

Barley Mow 16 | 10 | 14 | £2
127 Curtain Rd., EC2 (Old St.), 020-7729 3910
■ An "interesting crowd" of modish "slackers" and locals who prefer a pub less "loud and packed" than most head to this corner boozer in Shoreditch to quaff Czech Litovel lager; notwithstanding the DJ booth (where they spin on weekends), this pub remains "small, dark" and "traditional"; N.B. there are also occasional acoustic gigs.

Barley Mow 14 | 12 | 17 | £3
8 Dorset St., W1 (Baker St.), 020-7935 7318
■ "Arrive early to get one of the snugs" made from old pawnbroker's booths that are attached to the bar at this "noisy local" Victorian boozer in Marylebone that caters mainly to "old reptiles" and "advertising" types; even if you don't, you can still "always find a place to sit", which makes it "good for a chat" in a rather dry part of town.

Bar Local ∇ 18 | 16 | 18 | £4
4 Clapham Common, SW4 (Clapham Common), 020-7622 9406;
www.barlocal.co.uk
◪ A "diverse crowd of twenty- and thirtysomethings" enjoy Czech and Belgian beers, paired with a burger-centric menu

that includes a Sunday roast, at this bijou designer bar on Clapham Common south side; claustrophobes clamour over the "small and smoky" space, but to many it's an "appealing" site for "chilling out" on "Saturday and Sunday afternoons."

Bar Lorca   15 13 15 £3
175 Stoke Newington High St., N16 (Stoke Newington/rail), 020-7275 8659

◪ Amigos applaud this "vibrant" Stoke Newington cantina where you can dig into "Spanish newspapers and paella" during the day and dance to Latin music at night (with salsa classes on Mondays and Thursdays); to cynics, it smacks of a "desperate pick-up joint" with a "lecherous clientele."

Barnsbury, The   ▽ 21 21 23 £5
209-11 Liverpool Rd., N1 (Angel), 020-7607 5519; www.thebarnsbury.co.uk

■ Pros proclaim this Islington oasis "away from Upper Street" the "perfect gastro-pub" and some regard it "more a restaurant than a pub", thanks to "great" modern English fare paired with a variety of guest ales; the "attractive" interior of dark wood, open fires and mini-chandeliers is "light and calm", attracting a well-heeled crowd by night and plenty of "mums with buggies" during daylight hours.

Baroque Rooms   — — — M
11a Queensberry Pl., SW7 (South Kensington), 020-7581 4691; www.baroquerooms.co.uk

With decor by the folks who designed Aura, and "sublime cocktails" courtesy of a former Townhouse mixologist, this South Ken neophyte is one of this town's hottest newcomers, attracting a crowd of moneyed young things; chaise lounges, Rubenesque frescos, candelabras and cosy alcoves create a decadent atmosphere befitting the name.

Bar Room Bar   17 15 15 £4
32 Gerrard St., W1 (Piccadilly Circus), 020-7494 1482
111 Kennington Rd., SE11 (Lambeth North), 020-7820 3682
48 Rosslyn Hill, NW3 (Hampstead), 020-7435 0808
www.thespiritgroup.com

◪ DJs, pizzas from a wood-burning oven and sofas for lounging are the hallmarks of this "trendy" chain, though each link has something distinctive to offer – Kennington boasts a terrace overlooking the Imperial War Museum, while in Chinatown, "food alerters" help deal with the crush, and in Hampstead the "outdoor patio" appeals to fresh-air fiends; wiseacres find the decor "stylish, in an Eastern European concrete jungle kind of way."

Bar Rumba   18 14 14 £4
36 Shaftesbury Ave., W1 (Piccadilly Circus), 020-7287 2715; www.barrumba.co.uk

■ "Any day of the week you can always find" "trendy types" and "students" alike shaking their booty to "funky music", from urban and funk to drum & bass, at this "wicked" Soho "sweatbox", which some ravers rate as one of the "best small clubs in London", but hard-core types wait for the weekend, when big-name DJs take over; the atmosphere is "less pretentious" than many other spots, and while it's "too loud to talk", who goes there to chat?

Bar Sia
– | – | – | M

105-109 The Broadway, SW19 (Wimbledon), 020-8540 8339;
www.barsia.com
The designers of this bar set in the listed subterranean Turkish baths under the Wimbledon Theatre, where actors used to relax after performances, have preserved many of the white-tiled steam rooms and converted the sunken tubs into stylish booths; you won't need a towel in this ultracool spot where cocktails are key, though things do warm up on Thursdays with live jazz acts and at the weekend when DJs spin.

Bar Soho
14 | 14 | 14 | £4

23-25 Old Compton St., W1 (Leicester Sq.), 020-7439 0439;
www.BarSoho.co.uk
☑ If you just want to "let your hair down" and "sing the old tunes at the top of your lungs well into the night bus shift", fans tout this "simple" Soho standby where "cheesy retro pop" is the order of the day and there's no shortage of "posing" and "pulling" from a "hilarious crowd"; "frankly skanky" sniff cranky critics who dismiss it as a "boring" "tourist heaven", but for many it has an "excellent feel" to it.

Bar Solo
19 | 17 | 18 | £7

20 Inverness St., NW1 (Camden Town), 020-7482 4611;
www.BarSolo.co.uk
■ Good for a "date" or a "pre-gig drink", when "you don't want a scummy pub", this Camden spot is an "economical" option that's popular with a "young crowd", with noshers giving it high marks for "fab all-day breakfasts"; depending on who you ask, the decor is either "beautifully overstated" or downright "dodgy", and cognoscenti caution it can be "difficult to move" around on weekends.

Bar Sol Ona
14 | 11 | 11 | £4

17 Old Compton St., W1 (Leicester Sq.), 020-7287 9932
■ A "cool bar with cool people", this Soho DJ boogie box (Soho House's sibling) is a "solid late-night option" where you can "dance to Latin music" or munch on tapas with an "interesting crowd"; though it "isn't known to many", the space is "fairly small", so some prefer to "get there early."

Bar 38
13 | 14 | 14 | £4

1-3 Long Acre, WC2 (Leicester Sq.), 020-7836 7794
1 Blacks Rd., W6 (Hammersmith), 020-8748 3951
30-33 The Minories, St. Clare House, EC3 (Aldgate/
Tower Hill), 020-7702 0470

(continued)
Bar 38
91-93 St. John St., EC1 (Farringdon), 020-7253 5896
Unit C, 16 Hertsmere Rd., E14 (Canary Wharf),
020-7515 8361
☑ High street locations add appeal to these "convenient" chain pubs that are "popular" spots for an "after-work" tipple or "Sunday afternoon lounging" in "vibrant" yet "down-to-earth" settings; foes, though, fault their "paint-by-the-numbers" formula and dismiss them as little more than "noisy", "overpriced" "clones" with "zero style."

Bartok   20 | 19 | 17 | £4
78-79 Chalk Farm Rd., NW1 (Chalk Farm), 020-7916 0595;
www.meanfiddler.com
■ A "real one-off", this Chalk Farm spot provides a "civilised respite" in a "busy area", as perhaps the "only live classical music [venue] in London"; jazz and traditional world with a modern spin are performed as well in a "somber" space with lots of "comfy old sofas and chairs", which is an especially "nice environment" for a "Sunday chill-out"; N.B. it's now showing short films on the first Sunday night of every month.

Bar Vinyl   19 | 18 | 17 | £3
6 Inverness St., NW1 (Camden Town), 020-7681 7898;
www.vinyladdiction.co.uk
■ "Indie groovers" gravitate to this "cheeky Camden bar" where you can "buy your vinyl downstairs" while DJs spin tunes upstairs; "tasty" eats complementing a selection of Euro-lagers and cocktails and the "friendly" service make up for the fact that it's usually "too packed" and "way too loud."

BEACH BLANKET BABYLON   19 | 21 | 13 | £6
45 Ledbury Rd., W11 (Notting Hill Gate), 020-7229 2907;
www.beachblanketbabylon.uk.com
☑ While some feel it's "not at the top of the trendy list" anymore, this "charming, bizarre" "paradise" with a "stupendous", "Gaudí-esque" decor is still the "trusty favourite" of many a Notting Hiller and, for savvy shoppers, a "good place to end a day in Portobello"; yet, wet blankets kick sand at the "snooty", downright "appalling" service and "Chelsea wanna-be" clientele.

Bed   19 | 21 | 16 | £5
310 Portobello Rd., W10 (Ladbroke Grove), 020-8969 4500;
www.styleinthecity.co.uk
■ With a "groovy" Moroccan setting boasting lanterns, candelabras and palms, nightly DJs and a live saxophonist on Sundays, this "laid-back" Notting Hill hangout is a real souk-cess with the "Portobello gang"; it can get "crowded on weekends", so those in-the-know recommend the "afternoon or early evening."

Bedford, The
21 | 15 | 17 | £3

77 Bedford Hill, SW12 (Balham), 020-8682 8940;
www.thebedford.co.uk

☑ There are "lots of scenery changes" at this "massive" "old-style" boozer-cum–gastro-pub in Balham, a triple-decker offering a "popular comedy club", live music (including gospel and jazz on Sundays), salsa classes, karaoke, a ballroom and football on a big screen – and, oh yes, food and drink; advocates reckon it's the "best entertainment in the area", but wags warn "prepare to get your bum pinched."

Bedroom Bar
– | – | – | E

62 Rivington St., EC2 (Old St.), 020-7613 5637

With tin buckets hanging from the ceiling, upturned dustbins for seats and a bed tucked away in a private area, this Hoxton bar resembles a set for a Harold Pinter play, with whitewashed brick walls and metallic pillars adding a quirky cool touch; no one is ready for bed, though, when a team of DJs gets things going with an eclectic mix of tunes.

Beduin
– | – | – | VE

57-59 Charterhouse St., EC1 (Farringdon/Barbican),
020-7336 6484; www.beduin-london.co.uk

The decor of this Moroccan-styled bar in Smithfield, replete with throws, hookahs and ornate lights, evokes a traditional souk, and the large, three-floor venue boasts a balcony as well as plenty of alcoves and niches for snuggling; the main attraction, though, is the dance floor, with DJs spinning on Wednesdays–Sundays.

BELGO
18 | 16 | 16 | £4

50 Earlham St., WC2 (Covent Garden), 020-7813 2233
72 Chalk Farm Rd., NW1 (Camden Town/Chalk Farm),
020-7267 0718
www.belgo-restaurants.com

☑ "Euro Disney for beer lovers" is how devotees describe this "monastic-themed" duo that offers a "delightfully overwhelming" selection of more than 60 "habit-forming" Belgian brews served by "habit-wearing waiters", as well as "classic moules frites" and other "dependable" menu items; it's a bit "expensive" to critics, who also warn of a "loud", "crowded", "tourist"-heavy scene at the popular Covent Garden location.

Belle Vue
▽ 18 | 16 | 15 | £3

1 Clapham Common Southside, SW4 (Clapham Common),
020-7498 9473

■ Though this revamped pub on the corner of Clapham Common now has "modern decor", loyalists declare it's still the "cosy, calming" boozer of yore; a young professional crowd gravitates here for "consistent" pub fare and nine types of draught beer served by "friendly" staff.

Belushi's
`13` `13` `15` ∟

9 Russell St., WC2 (Covent Garden), 020-7240 3411
13-15 Shepherd's Bush Green, W12 (Shepherd's Bush),
020-7407 1856
161 Borough High St., SE1 (London Bridge), 020-7939 9700
48-50 Camden High St., NW1 (Mornington Crescent),
020-7388 1012
www.belushis.com

☑ This chain of centrally located "typical American" "dive bars" attracts "tons of students and expats" and "dropouts" who knock back jugs of brightly coloured cocktails in "lively" yet "relaxed" environs; it's "too much like a college party" for curmudgeons, though, who dismiss it as the "McDonald's of London nightlife"; N.B. the Camden and South Bank branches are connected to hostels.

Bierodrome
`17` `15` `15` `£4`

67 Kingsway, WC2 (Charing Cross/Holborn), 020-7242 7469
44 Clapham High St., SW4 (Clapham North), 020-7720 1118
173-174 Upper St., N1 (Highbury & Islington),
020-7226 5835
www.belgo-restaurants.com

☑ "Belgo's younger fashion-conscious" siblings offer an "amazing" selection of "yummy" Belgian beer and "reasonably priced grub" (moules frites feature strongly) to a largely "twentysomething" crowd; the decor is "trendy", with "loads of tables" and "comfy chairs", and the ambience is "relaxed", but it can get "noisy" and "overcrowded."

Bishops Finger, The
`18` `15` `18` `£3`

9-10 W. Smithfield, EC1 (Farringdon), 020-7248 2341;
www.shepherd-neame.co.uk

■ A "landmark establishment", this Smithfield pub appeals to "no-nonsense" "beer drinkers" with a thirst for an "excellent range" of venerable Shepherd Neame brews in a "friendly", "unpretentious" setting without any "trendy or beautiful people or great cocktails"; aficionados advise it "gets a bit crowded" "after work."

Black Cap, The
`16` `14` `18` `£5`

171 Camden High St., NW1 (Camden Town), 020-7428 2721;
www.theblackcap.co.uk

■ One of Camden's rare same-sex spots, this "unpretentious local cabaret" built on the site of a 17th-century witch's house attracts a large and varied clientele with "drag and DJs" as well as "fun acts" that make for "cheesy fun on a Friday"; just "don't expect the glam side of gay bars."

Black Friar, The
`21` `23` `17` `£3`

174 Queen Victoria St., EC4 (Blackfriars), 020-7236 5474

■ An "absolute gem" of a pub by Blackfriars Station, this "triangular shaped" building has an "outrageous" art deco interior (circa 1916), while "gargoyles" and a chuckling

...r give it a curiously "medieval" feel;
...setting is a "good conversation starter"
...ts go down quickly" for boozers varying
from... ...ity suits to university gals" to "locals."

Black Horse, The
∇ 17 | 15 | 19 | £6

168 Mile End Rd., E1 (Stepney Green), 020-7790 1684;
www.theblackhorsebar.com

■ Though it's decidedly "male-dominated", all are welcome
at this late-night (4 AM on weekends) gay-mixed pub
on the Mile End Road that is by turns a clubby venue with
DJs, a "transvestite lounge" and cabaret with "bad drag
and singing acts"; "everybody is very warm" here and the
staff is "attentive."

Black Lion, The
∇ 19 | 14 | 18 | £3

2 S. Black Lion Ln., W6 (Stamford Brook), 020-8748 2639

■ A pleasant stroll down a riverside path takes you to this
venerable Hammersmith boozer that's "nicely tucked away"
from the hordes; the garden is "fantastic" for those "long
summer evenings", while the interior is always "cosy",
though some still pine for the former "skittle alley" that's
been converted into a function room.

blagclub
∇ 16 | 10 | 14 | £6

68 Notting Hill Gate, W11 (Notting Hill Gate),
020-7243 0123
222 Kensal Rd., W10 (Westbourne Park), 020-8960 2732
www.blagclub.com

■ You might expect a "cool, laid-back" vibe at a venue
with a Hindu shrine motif, but this lounge/club (sorry,
microclub) duo also boasts "hot and sweaty dance floors"
that make it a "place to be in the wee morning hours"; a
few find it "aggressively trendy", but devotees describe
the scene as "more arty than chic."

Bleeding Heart Tavern, The
19 | 18 | 18 | £4

19 Greville St., EC1 (Farringdon), 020-7404 0333

■ Nuzzled next to its sibling restaurant, this "fabulously
cosy" pub on the Holburn-Clerkenwell border serves up
"excellent" Adnams ales and what fans deem is some of
the "best pub food in London"; a "romantic", "quaint" setting
and "friendly" service warm the hearts of many who find it
ideal for a drink "after work", with a "date" or a "friend."

Blend
20 | 17 | 18 | £8

1A Shorts Gardens, WC2 (Covent Garden), 020-7240 5959;
www.blend.uk.com

■ A long cocktail list with 17 original house concoctions,
"deep purple decor" and slate floor are all part of the
"stylish" mix at this somewhat "pricey" Covent Garden
establishment; "quiet and peaceful" and "not too trendy",
it's a "hidden gem" in a "great" location in the heart of the
Seven Dials district.

Blind Beggar
13 | 11 | 12 | £3

337 Whitechapel Rd., E1 (Whitechapel), 020-7247 6195

■ The Shoreditch site where gangster Ronnie Kray gunned down a rival is now a "typical East End pub" opposite Whitechapel Hospital with "no references to its unpleasant past" (although the "blood-red lights" remind some of that "famous hit"); while mob mavens "only go for the historical value", traditionalists praise this "unpretentious watering hole" as a "great place to kick back."

Blue Anchor, The
18 | 16 | 17 | £3

13 Lower Mall, W6 (Hammersmith), 020-8748 5774

◪ A popular gathering spot on Boat Race day thanks to its "great location", this "cute" 400-year-old Hammersmith riverside boozer is predictably "heaving as soon as the sun comes out"; it's appeared in films such as *Sliding Doors*, but despite its star status and "popularity with tourists", it's "cosy in winter" and offers a nice respite from the "suits."

BLUE BAR
24 | 24 | 21 | £9

Berkeley Hotel, Wilton Pl., SW1 (Knightsbridge), 020-7235 6000; www.savoy-group.co.uk

■ Located beneath the Berkeley Hotel in Knightsbridge, this "sublimely swanky" "hot spot" is where the "hip go to sip", "redefining hotel bar drinking" with a "glam" interior courtesy of David Collins, 50 varieties of whiskies, "inventive drink concoctions" and "outstanding nibbles"; a natural for those who want to "socialize with the power crowd", it's also "cosy" enough for a "first date" or a "tête-à-tête."

BLUEBIRD
18 | 19 | 16 | £6

350 King's Rd., SW3 (Sloane Sq.), 020-7559 1000; www.conran.com

◪ Packed to the rafters with a "very Chelsea crowd", this "loud and popular" King's Road destination appeals to fans with its "smart" "Conran design", "classy" ambience and "delicious food and wine"; but "basic fare" at "inflated prices" lead contrarians to conclude it's "had its day."

Blue Posts
13 | 10 | 14 | £3

28 Rupert St., W1 (Piccadilly Circus), 020-7437 1415

■ A "traditional old man's pub" is rare so deep into the West End, which makes fans appreciate this "quintessential London" local in Soho with its "lovely, smoky atmosphere" and Hoegaarden and various bitters on tap all the more; it's often "packed after work" with a crowd that sometimes includes a "Carnaby Street" crew and slumming "celebs."

Blues Bistro & Bar
15 | 15 | 16 | £4

42-43 Dean St., W1 (Piccadilly Circus), 020-7494 1966; www.bluesbistro.com

■ "You won't get the blues" at this "relaxed" little spot on Soho's Dean Street that serves as a "quiet place for drinks after work" (with "great food" thrown in) for a slightly older clientele and as a "late-night joint" with DJs on Fridays; it also sports a private room with its own bar that's "useful when you're throwing a party."

Bluu
20 | 17 | 17 | £4

1 Hoxton Sq., N1 (Old St.), 020-7613 2793; www.bluu.co.uk
■ This "casual, relaxed hangout" on the former site of the Blue Note Club still has "a bit of the Hoxton edge" (i.e. "pretentious in a low-key type of way") to go along with a "top shooter menu" with "reasonable" prices and a "gem of a bar counter"; the decor may be "past its sell-by date", but most still find it "comfy and stylish."

Boisdale
22 | 20 | 21 | £6

15 Eccleston St., SW1 (Victoria), 020-7730 6922;
www.boisdale.co.uk
■ Boosters boast there's "still no place better to go have a scotch and a trip to the good life" than this late nighter on the Victoria/Belgravia border that claims to have Europe's best selection of Cuban cigars to go with an "endless" whisky list, "clubby" setting and "noisy but nice" live jazz in the Macdonald Bar; a few frown at the "silly prices" and "fee after 10 PM" for the music, but most agree it's "worth it."

Bonds Restaurant & Bar
22 | 21 | 20 | £9

Threadneedles Hotel, 5 Threadneedles St., EC2 (Bank),
020-7657 8088; www.theetoncollection.com
■ Though it's "overrun by suits" ("hey, it's the City") and somewhat "expensive", this "opulent" converted bank hall attached to Bank's Threadneedle Hotel is the "place to be" for hobnobbing with "beautiful people" over "fantastic" cocktails in a "sophisticated", "attractive" space; it's a "cool place after work" for the local bankers and brokers, but closed on weekends.

Box
19 | 16 | 15 | £5

32-34 Monmouth St., WC2 (Covent Garden), 020-7240 5828;
www.boxbar.com
■ Cognoscenti claim this "mostly gay hangout" in Covent Garden is "where the boys are", and a "relaxing place" (albeit a bit "small") to "grab a beer or a cappuccino and gab with your friends" in an atmosphere that's "lively but mostly attitude-free"; for twisted types, however, it's "best in summer where you can sit outside and watch tourists get mowed down as they attempt to manage the Seven Dials."

Bradley's Spanish Bar
20 | 16 | 16 | £3

42-44 Hanway St., W1 (Tottenham Court Rd.), 020-7636 0359
■ "Hidden" on a backstreet between Oxford Street and Tottenham Court Road, this "tiny" Spanish-themed spot is usually "packed" with a slightly "bohemian" crowd and home to what platter purists call the "best jukebox in London", crammed with an all-vinyl collection of '60s

classics; the "intimate", "charming", slightly "scruffy" quarters can get "noisy" and "smoky."

Bread & Roses 21 18 18 £2
68 Clapham Manor St., SW4 (Clapham North), 020-7498 1779; www.breadandrosespub.com
■ It's "like chilling out at a civilized, friendly grown-up's house" at this "down-to-earth" Clapham "boozer", a "modern local pub" that "caters to all ages and classes" with "excellent" Worker's Ale and other spirits poured in bright, "spacious" digs with a glass-walled conservatory; gastronauts find it "worth dropping by for the food" alone, and suggest Sundays are especially "good for kids", featuring international food and music themes.

Bricklayer's Arms 18 14 17 £2
31 Gresse St., W1 (Goodge St.), 020-7636 5593
■ A "traditional drinking hole" from Sam Smith, this Fitzrovia pub is "perfect" for a "quiet drink and a read of the paper", especially if you can "get a seat by the fire or on a sofa"; it's "one of the few quiet spots around" on weekends, but regulars recommend you get "there early" on weekdays when the "after-work crowd fills it up fast."

Bricklayer's Arms 20 14 16 £3
63 Charlotte Rd., EC2 (Liverpool St.), 020-7739 5245
■ There's "plenty of life" in this "beautiful" "backstreet" pub say fans, and though it's located in trendy Shoreditch, it attracts a mixed bunch of "old working men" and "City airheads" on their way to the local fleshpots; though it gets especially "rammed at the weekends", it still maintains its "spit 'n' sawdust" character and "friendly" spirit.

Brixton Bar & Grill – – – E
15 Atlantic Rd., SW9 (Brixton), 020-7737-6777
Another sign of SW9's gentrification, this Brixton newcomer sports a sleek and trendy design with plenty of wood and leather and a chandelier; on offer is a menu of 'world tapas' bites reflecting the area's multicultural mix, West End–standard cocktails and DJs spinning mellow tunes.

Brixtonian Havana Club ▽ 19 15 16 £5
11 Beehive Pl., SW9 (Brixton), 020-7924 9262; www.brixtonian.co.uk
■ With more than 200 types of rum, Latin music, cigars, Caribbean food and a perpetual "party atmosphere", this Cuban-themed nightspot offers a taste of the "real Brixton"; the interior is "beautiful" and "a bit wacky", and while the cocktails may be "expensive", they're also "lethal."

Browns 17 17 16 £5
4 Great Queen St., WC2 (Holborn), 020-7831 0802
◪ "It's forever 1985" at this "relaxed and stylish" Covent Garden club and bar that's still a "crowd puller" after all

these years, where a "lovely staff makes great martinis" to the strains of tunes spun by DJs; "it's fine for a quick drink after work or in the early evening", but proletarians pass on it later at night when the "footballers, glamour models and other rich twits" roll in.

Buckingham Arms
19 | 17 | 19 | £2

62 Petty France, SW1 (St. James's Park), 020-7222 3386; www.youngs.co.uk

■ A "well-used" Young's venue in St. James's, this "lively", "traditional" "old man's pub" pours "top-notch" ales for "civil servants" and others "who like good beer" after work in a "clean" and "quiet" setting; those in-the-know also recommend the "good home cooked food" at "lunchtime."

Bug Restaurant & Bar
17 | 17 | 14 | £3

The Crypt, St. Matthew's Church, SW2 (Brixton), 020-7738 3366; www.bugbar.co.uk

■ For an "underground feel", it's hard to top this "dingy but relaxed" bar/club in the crypt of St. Matthew's Church at the hub of Brixton, where DJs spin tunes into the wee hours for a trendy but "unpretentious" crowd that "dances madly"; though on "hot weekend nights" the "compact" space can become a "sweatbox", it's still "sweet" to fans.

Builder's Arms
20 | 16 | 16 | £4

13 Britten St., SW3 (Sloane Sq.), 020-7349 9040

■ Flexing an "imaginative menu" of "upscale food" and a "charming interior", this "refurbished" country-style gastro-venue in Chelsea is the "epitome of the modern English pub", according to fans; for "thirtysomethings who want a little more" from their boozers, it does the trick for "dinners", "brunches" or "a break from shopping on the King's Road."

Bull's Head
22 | 16 | 20 | £3

373 Lonsdale Rd., SW13 (Barnes Bridge/rail), 020-8876 5241; www.thebullshead.com

■ Swingers swear some of "the best jazz at the best price in all of London" can be found at this "enduring" "riverside pub" near Barnes Bridge hosting live acts with "none of the Soho spangle"; the "nice" space is big enough for punters to "hide from the awful locals"; N.B. Monday is blues night.

Bull's Head
▽ 17 | 12 | 16 | £3

15 Strand on the Green, W4 (Gunnersbury), 020-8994 1204

■ Housed in a Grade 1 listed building that was Cromwell's headquarters during the Civil War (the crowd is considerably less bullish now), this Thameside pub in the pretty Chiswick on the Green area is blessed with an "inspiring location" where you can "watch the river" from the "cosy upstairs room"; "wonderful Sunday brunches can be had" here, and a wide selection of wines and ales is "just right for summer drinks in the sun."

Bunch of Grapes
16 | 13 | 15 | £4

207 Brompton Rd., SW3 (Knightsbridge), 020-7589 4944
◪ A "good old-fashioned local", this "friendly boozer" in Knightsbridge gets a lift from its proximity to Harrod's as well as its "inexpensive" pours; "fine, but not spectacular" shrug sceptics, who frown at all the "Sloanes" and "tourists", and "avoid it at lunch" when it's "crowded with office workers."

Bünker Bar
– | – | – | M

(fka Freedom Brewing Company)
41 Earlham St., WC2 (Covent Garden), 020-7240 0606;
www.bunkerbar.co.uk
The umlaut over the 'u' in the name hints at the *bierkeller* aspirations of this huge underground Covent Garden hall that spells beer 'bier' and sells draughts in steins as well as pints; despite *die Affektiertheiten,* though, it's changed little from when it was the Freedom, and thankfully kept its best asset – one of the only open microbreweries in town that allows you to see the brewer hard at work.

Bush Bar & Grill
21 | 19 | 17 | £5

45A Goldhawk Rd., W12 (Goldhawk Rd./Shepherd's Bush), 020-8746 2111
■ "The place in the Bush to see and be seen", this "hidden" "gem" in Shepherd's Bush garners a "devoted following" of West Londoners who down "gorgeous" cocktails amid "stylish, beautiful" surroundings; "no-attitude" service "makes an evening here a relaxing event."

Cactus Blue
16 | 16 | 16 | £6

86 Fulham Rd., SW3 (South Kensington), 020-7823 7858
◪ "As close to Texas as you can get in London", this sprawling, "fun and cheap" South Ken Southwestern-theme spot rounds up urban cowboys with "quirky decor", 80 types of tequila, "dangerous cocktails", "nice bar food" and "friendly" staff; "as trendy as fajitas can get" razz renegades who bash the "clichéd, contrived" concept.

Cadogan Arms
14 | 14 | 16 | £5

298 King's Rd., SW3 (Sloane Sq.), 020-7352 1645
■ A "traditional" pub with a "nice neighbourhood feel" and "pleasant" staff on the King's Road in Chelsea, this "comfortable" "hangout" is a popular haunt for pool-playing "teenagers" and "footie fans" who come to watch matches on two giant screens; though it's occasionally crammed with "Sloanies" and "young local wealthy kids", it's still "good for a quick drink" according to regulars.

Café Boheme
18 | 16 | 15 | £5

13-17 Old Compton St., W1 (Leicester Sq.), 020-7734 0623;
www.cafeboheme.co.uk
■ For "something semi-civilised late at night", "artistes", "cool folks" and Soho-cialites "with lots of money" flock to

this "reliable" Old Compton Street "French-style brasserie and bar" that *amis* anoint "one of the most stylish and accessible venues" in the neighbourhood; "mean cocktails" and food that "never disappoints" are served in a "relaxed" setting with a "Parisian" ("without the attitude") vibe.

CAFÉ DE PARIS
16 | 17 | 13 | £8 |

3 Coventry St., W1 (Leicester Sq./Piccadilly Circus), 020-7734 7700; www.cafedeparis.com
☑ "Dress to impress" when you go to this "timeless classic" beneath Leicester Square with a "beautiful space" and nonpareil "people-watching"; and though it's "hard on the wallet" and "about as French as a kiss without tongues", groupies gush it's still a "good place to go crazy during the week" and "not a bad place to end the night" on weekends; only if you like "tourists" and "posers", retort cynics.

Café Lazeez
14 | 15 | 15 | £6 |

21 Dean St., W1 (Tottenham Court Rd.), 020-7434 9393
93-95 Old Brompton Rd., SW7 (South Kensington), 020-7581 9993
88 St. John St., EC1 (Farringdon), 020-7253 2224
www.cafelazeez.com
☑ At its best, this chain of "upscale" bar/restaurants offers "good value" Northern Indian cuisine and "eager-to-please" service to a "trendy crowd" in a "sophisticated" setting with appealing "ambience"; but malcontents mutter the "food can be hit-or-miss", and dismiss it as a last resort "for people who don't know where else to go" after hours.

Café Med
17 | 15 | 17 | £5 |

184A Kensington Park Rd., W11 (Notting Hill Gate), 020-7221 1150
320 Goldhawk Rd., W6 (Stamford Brook), 020-8741 1994
22 Dean St., W1 (Tottenham Court Rd.), 020-7287 9007
21 Loudon Rd., NW8 (St. John's Wood), 020-7625 1222
370 St. John St., EC1 (Angel), 020-7278 1199
149 Kew Rd., Richmond (Richmond), 020-8940 8298
☑ "Basic, but pleasant", these Mediterranean-themed bars are "dependable" "neighbourhood spots" with "wonderful food" and "big sofas" suitable for a "quiet girlie night" or a "chilling out" "Sunday"; but "high prices" and a "boring", "cheesy" scene leave sceptics decidedly underwhel-med.

CAFÉ ROUGE
12 | 12 | 12 | £4 |

2 Lancer Sq., W8 (High St. Kensington), 020-7938 4200
227-229 Chiswick High Rd., W4 (Chiswick Park), 020-8742 7447
15 Frith St., W1 (Tottenham Court Rd.), 020-7437 4307
46-48 James St., W1 (Bond St.), 020-7487 4847
26 High St., SW19 (Wimbledon), 020-8944 5131
40 Abbeville Rd., SW4 (Clapham Common/Clapham South), 020-8673 3399
27-31 Basil St., SW3 (Knightsbridge), 020-7584 2345
Hays Galleria, Tooley St., SE1 (London Bridge), 020-7378 0097

(continued)
CAFÉ ROUGE
38 High St., NW3 (Hampstead), 020-7435 4240
120 St. John's Wood High St., NW8 (St. John's Wood),
020-7722 8366
www.caferouge.co.uk

☑ Francophiles insist these "warm, casual" French-style bistro-bars are "worth a visit" for "dependable" nosh and "good wine" in a "relaxed" "family atmosphere" with a "continental feel", while purists find the "formulaic", "faux" setting and "variable" fare gaul-ling; still, for many this chain remains an "easy, nice" and "cheap" option.

Cafe Sol
– – – E

(fka Bridge & Tunnel)
4 Calvert Ave., E2 (Old St.), 020-7729 6533
No longer the scruffy venue it formerly was, this two-floor bar and club in Shoreditch now has a brighter feel and a bigger emphasis on food; otherwise, it's business as usual, with plenty of Hoxton hairdos nodding away to Brazilian beats pumping through the much-admired sound system until the 2.30 AM closing time (Thursdays–Saturdays).

Cafeteria
– – – VE

124 Ladbroke Grove, W10 (Ladbroke Grove), 020-7792 0801
With retro white plastic chairs and other trendy decorative touches, this "cool" Ladbroke Grove haunt is "wicked fun", offering "great tunes and good drinks" in a "very NY" setting; attached is a restaurant of the same name that early fans insist is one of "London's hippest Sunday brunch places."

Calf, The
20 18 18 £3

87 Rectory Grove, SW4 (Clapham Common), 020-7622 4019
■ For a "quiet Sunday session" "relaxing with the papers" in "comfy leather armchairs", twentysomethings in Clapham hoof it to this "chilled" gastro-pub; surveyors are split over when to go ("best in the summer" vs. "lovely in the winter"), but no matter what season, it's "always overcrowded."

Camden Brewing Co
18 19 16 £4

1 Randolph St., NW1 (Camden Town), 020-7267 9829;
www.camdenbrewing.co.uk
■ This north Camden bolt-hole "attracts a young crowd" with a "trendy" "open-plan" interior featuring white leather sofas and a metallic bar, a stylish garden graced with "fashionable flowers" and a selection of "great beers" (though, despite the moniker, they don't brew their own); four house cats patrol the rooms (pet them at your own risk).

Camden Head
17 15 17 £2

2 Camden Walk, N1 (Angel), 020-7359 0851
☑ The "location is the best thing" about this "Victorian" boozer in Islington, and it takes advantage with an outdoor patio "overlooking the Camden passage antique market"

that's "lovely in summer"; some sniff that it's "run-of-the-mill" otherwise, but a nice selection of "guest ales" and occasional comedy acts add allure; it's also rumoured to be home to a ghost named George.

Candy Bar
19 | 18 | 15 | £5

4 Carlisle St., W1 (Tottenham Court Rd.), 020-7494 4041;
www.thecandybar.co.uk

☑ "Sugar babes" and "gorgeous girlies" flock to Soho's "main lesbian" venue, a three-level bar and club with "cute" decor and a "mellow vibe"; others, however, are "uncomfortable" with a "disappointing" crowd that's "too much of a clique"; P.S. while it is "men-friendly", boys can get in only as guests of girls.

Cantaloupe
21 | 17 | 16 | £4

35-42 Charlotte Rd., EC2 (Old St.), 020-7613 4411;
www.cantaloupe.co.uk

■ The place that "set the trend in Hoxton" in the late '90s, this "funky hangout" is still the "epitome of an offbeat" local watering hole, with a "noisy, arty and incredibly lively" vibe; "it gets the balance just about right" between noshing and quaffing with "yummy" bites and a "well-appointed bar."

Cantina Vinopolis
17 | 16 | 16 | £5

Vinopolis Museum, 1 Bank End, SE1 (London Bridge),
020-7940 8333; www.vinopolis.co.uk

☑ As you'd expect from a bar connected to the "Vinopolis theme park", "you can't beat the wines by the glass" here, with 300-plus varieties to choose from, paired with "good nibbles"; while some find the "atmosphere surprisingly good" in the "chic", "cavernous" space, others deem it "cold" and a bit "touristy."

Captain Kidd
22 | 20 | 20 | £4

108 Wapping High St., E1 (Wapping), 020-7480 5759;
www.captain-kidd.com

■ With "views over the river" and a "fantastic terrace", this "delightful" "traditional pub" in Wapping overlooking Execution Dock, where the pirate-hunter Kidd was hanged in 1701, is "awesome in warm weather"; inside there's lots of "nooks and crannies" that "encourage conversation", a "good vibe" and "excellent" Sam Smith's beer; N.B. The Gallows restaurant is upstairs.

CARGO
23 | 22 | 17 | £4

Kingsland Viaduct, 83 Rivington St., EC2 (Liverpool St.),
020-7739 3440; www.cargo-london.com

■ "Deservedly busy", this "innovative" Shoreditch venue nuzzled beneath railway arches attracts a "mixed" and "friendly" crowd with an "eclectic mix" of music featuring "world sounds and cool beats" from live bands and DJs in a "large", "moody and dark" space with a "jazzy vibe"; with two bars serving "tasty drinks" and a restaurant offering an "interesting", "reasonably priced" menu of Spanish-style bites, it's a "one-stop shop" for many.

Castle   20 | 18 | 18 | £5
100 Holland Park Ave., W11 (Holland Park), 020-7313 9301
■ "Laid-back and stylish", this revamped "old-fashioned" pub in Notting Hill is a "sleek operation" with a "great location", "cosy-cool" vibe and a "large back lounge with comfy couches" that's a "good spot to chat"; "good pub fare" on a daily changing menu is the crowning touch.

Cat & Mutton Pub   – | – | – | M
and Dining Room
76 Broadway Mkt., E8 (London Fields), 020-7254 5599
If this Hackney boozer seems familiar at first glance, it might well be – in its former bog-standard incarnation it purportedly served as the model for the Queen Vic in *EastEnders*; since those days, though, it has undergone a gastro renovation and now it's all mismatched furniture and specials boards, with modern British chow on order and a garden for outdoor dining and drinking.

CC Club   14 | 14 | 14 | £7
13 Coventry St., W1 (Piccadilly Circus), 020-7297 3200; www.cc-club.co.uk
☑ You'll have to book to get on the guest list of this "trendy and impressive" private pleasure palace in Piccadilly, but insiders insist it's a "guaranteed good night" with "great music" and the possibility of "celeb spotting"; only if "you are 20 or less" sneer cynics who snap at the "crowded" scene, "too loud" music and "too much attitude."

Cellar Gascon   22 | 20 | 21 | £5
59 W. Smithfield, EC1 (Farringdon), 020-7796 0600
■ For a "quick trip to Southern France without the Heathrow hassle", this bar attached to the Club Gascon in Clerkenwell offers a "good selection" of wines paired with Gallic-style tapas and "lovely service" amid "beautiful", "atmospheric" surroundings with an ambience that's at once "romantic, fun, casual and elegant"; frugal sorts find it "expensive."

Chandos, The   16 | 13 | 15 | £5
29 St Martin's Ln., WC2 (Charing Cross), 020-7836 1401
☑ Located right by Trafalgar Square, Theatreland and the National Gallery, this "classic pub" is usually "full of smoke" and "overcrowded" with Londoners, playgoers and "tourists" alike thirsty for "exceptionally cheap" Sam Smith's beer; scenesters may find it merely "average", but for most it's "fantastic for meeting groups of friends."

Chapel   17 | 14 | 18 | £4
48 Chapel St., NW1 (Edgware Rd.), 020-7402 9220
■ "Simple, not fussy", this "lounge-type" gastro-pub in Marylebone serves Hoegaarden on tap and a "good range

of wines" paired with modern British and Continental fare in a "relaxed, friendly" setting; the faithful hint it's best weekends when "it's less crowded" with "suits."

Chapel, The
▽ 21 | 19 | 17 | £3

29A Penton St., N1 (Angel), 020-7833 4090;
www.thechapelbar.co.uk

■ Devotees congregate at this "unusual church-themed pub" housed in a converted Islington chapel with stained glass doors and gothic arches and a DJ spinning in the pulpit inside, and a roof terrace for balmy summer nights; the "happy, friendly" staff are one more amen-ity that makes it a "fun start to the evening", even if the crowd occasionally "needs a shove to start dancing."

Charterhouse
20 | 17 | 16 | £3

38 Charterhouse St., EC1 (Barbican/Farringdon), 020-7608 0858;
www.charterhousebar.co.uk

☑ Modelled after NY's Flatiron building, this "stylish" Farringdon bar is a popular "pre-club" hangout where you can "get your groove on" before moving on to the nearby venues; while it's "small enough to have a great ambience" and attracts an "interesting crowd", it can easily get "crowded on weekends", resulting in "slow" service.

Cheers
13 | 12 | 12 | £5

72 Regent St., W1 (Piccadilly Circus), 020-7494 3322;
www.cheersbarlondon.com

☑ "Meet people from around the world" (read: "tourist trap") and "dance to '80s hits" at this "cheap and cheerful" Piccadilly salute to the U.S. sitcom that's "so uncool it's become cool again"; defenders insist it's "not as tacky or expensive as you'd expect" and a "great place to meet people", while the jaded jeer it's best if "no one knows your name" here.

Chelsea Potter
14 | 13 | 14 | £4

119 King's Rd., SW3 (Sloane Sq.), 020-7352 9479

■ A "small peach of a pub" "overlooking the King's Road", this "lively" spot is the perfect place for "watching the trendies and the wanna-bes" walking the Chelsea catwalk; the atmosphere is "vibrant" with strains of the "hippie days", and for shoppers it's a "convenient" "bolt-hole" for a mid-shopping drink.

Chelsea Ram
17 | 15 | 17 | £4

32 Burnaby St., SW10 (Fulham Broadway), 020-7351 4008;
www.youngs.co.uk

■ "Excellent" baa-r food gives this "traditional" Chelsea boozer its gastro credentials, and "comfortable, capable" and "lovely" staff contribute to the "real pub atmosphere"; a mixed clientele flocks here, with "elderly regulars propping up the bar" during the day and a "younger crowd" coming in for the "after-work" shift.

CHINAWHITE 23 22 16 £9
6 Air St., W1 (Piccadilly Circus), 020-7343 0040;
www.chinawhite.com
☑ "What a mission to get in" the door, but "what a scene if
you succeed", this semi-private Piccadilly pleasure palace
is still the haunt of choice for "fashion, film and media"
types, "playboys and socialites" and other members of the
"clubbing elite", boasting "top DJs", "strong drinks" and a
"fabulous" Balinese decor; cynics, however, are "so-o
done" with the "snotty" staff and "pretentious" crowd, and
conclude it's "time to get over" the hype; N.B. members
only Wednesdays, Fridays and Saturdays.

CHURCHILL ARMS 21 18 20 £3
119 Kensington Church St., W8 (High St. Kensington/
Notting Hill Gate), 020-7727 4242
■ Run by a "fantastic publican", this "top-class" Notting
Hill Gate boozer is "what a pub should be", pouring "cheap
pints" in an "eccentric" space with "bric-a-brac" galore,
a "roaring fire in winter" and a "cosy, buzzy" ambience; add
to the "successful mix" staff who "couldn't be friendlier" and
"incredible" Thai food served in the adjoining conservatory;
N.B. it's best to book if you want to dine.

Cicada 20 18 17 £4
132-136 St. John St., EC1 (Farringdon), 020-7608 1550;
www.cicada.nu
■ A "super-cool Clerkenwell crowd" comes out to this
"buzzy" pub-cum-restaurant for cocktails such as "litchi
martinis" and "nice" Asian-Fusion fare served in a "modern"
space dominated by concrete and leather couches with a
"fantastic" basement private room; a few find the ambience
a "bit serious", but for most it's "worth a try."

CINNAMON CLUB 22 23 20 £9
The Old Westminster Library, 30-32 Great Smith St., SW1
(Westminster), 020-7222 2555; www.cinnamonclub.com
■ "India as you have never seen or tasted" awaits at this
"intimate" "hideaway" set in the Old Westminster Library
just a short walk from the Houses of Parliament, where
"delicious, original" fare and "outstanding", "fantastical"
cocktails are served in a "fabulous" space with a "smooth",
"laid-back" feel; for cineasts, "Bollywood" films are shown
on large glass walls in the downstairs bar.

Circus 21 21 19 £6
1 Upper James St., W1 (Piccadilly Circus), 020-7534 4000;
www.egami.co.uk
☑ Wags dub this "sleek", "pricey" Soho subterranean spot
the "Advertisers' Club" for its regular "expense-account"
clientele from nearby Golden Square, though it's alluring to
an assortment of "beautiful rich people" in search of a
"stylish late-night haunt"; foes are unimpressed by the

"sterile" ambience and "snooty" staff, but even they "must admit it does make a decent cocktail."

Cirque at the London Hippodrome   – | – | – | E
(fka Hippodrome, The)
Leicester Sq., WC2 (Leicester Sq.), 020-7437 4311;
www.londonhippodrome.com
Relaunched with a new name after a half-year hiatus and post-*Survey* change in ownership, this new incarnation of the Leicester Square mainstay recalls the legendary venue's history with circus acts, burlesque entertainment and Folie Bergere–style dancers while updating the image with electro-glam disco music; N.B. the new attached restaurant, La Plume, serves East-West fusion fare.

Cittie of Yorke   20 | 20 | 16 | £3
22 High Holborn, WC1 (Chancery Ln.), 020-7242 7670
■ "Vaulted ceilings", "massive vats above the bar" and an "old stove in the middle of the room" take you back to "medieval" times at this "atmospheric" Sam Smith's boozer (circa 1430); legal eagles from Gray's Inn come to quaff "good cheap beers" in "cosy booths" and "nooks and crannies", even if a few back-biters groan that "ye olde benches can cause aches in ye olde butt."

City Barge   ∇ 21 | 19 | 19 | £3
27 Strand on the Green, W4 (Gunnersbury), 020-8994 2148
■ "Marvellous at lunchtime" but also "cosy at night", this 15th-century Chiswick "riverside pub" with "plenty of old-world charm" "gets packed on the terrace as soon as there's a bit of sun"; as it's located at the city's lowest point by Kew Bridge, the rising tides sometimes reach the tables.

City Pride   18 | 14 | 17 | £2
15 Westferry Rd., E14 (Canary Wharf), 020-7987 3516;
www.glendola.co.uk
■ Views of Canary Wharf and the Dome and a "nice outdoor area" are the main sources of pride for this "honest" Docklands drinkery serving Fuller's beverages; otherwise, it's "your typical after-work watering hole" with a "friendly" vibe, which makes up for the fact that it's "a bit rundown."

Clachan   14 | 12 | 14 | £3
34 Kingly St., W1 (Oxford Circus), 020-7494 0834
■ Locals laud this "interesting, darkish" "old-fashioned pub" "tucked away in the backstreets" on the Soho side of Regent Street that attracts the attention of precious "few tourists"; it's a handy stop "after shopping at Liberty."

CLARIDGE'S BAR   25 | 25 | 24 | £9
Claridge's Hotel, 49 Brook St., W1 (Bond St.), 020-7629 8860;
www.savoy-group.com
■ "One of the swankiest bars in all London", this David Collins–designed art deco den in Claridge's Hotel in Mayfair

is "like seeing a movie from the '30s", a "civilised and sublime" setting for patrons to partake of vintages from the Champagne Library and original cocktails such as The Flapper, and there's a fumoir for cigar smokers as well; though some find it a bit "stuffy", for most it's "pure class" and ideal for impressing "that special person."

Clerkenwell House
19 | 16 | 15 | £3

23-27 Hatton Wall, EC1 (Chancery Ln./Farringdon), 020-7404 1113

■ "More like an arty coffeehouse than a bar", this "grungy, laid-back" Clerkenwell hangout has a "cool", "mellow lounge feel"; though it's located on a "seedy-looking side street", it attracts an "'in' crowd" of "early twenties" who enjoy the "pool tables", "good food and drinks."

Click
21 | 17 | 19 | £8

(fka Click Club)

84 Wardour St., W1 (Piccadilly Circus), 020-7734 5447; www.clicksoho.com

◪ "Getting a lot of attention" from "gossip columns" as a hot spot for "international celebs", "models and footballers", this spangly Soho joint appeals to those who "like R&B and overpriced drinks" in a glam setting complete with red carpet entrance and mirrored hallway; cynics snap it's really "patronised by Page 3–reading pikeys" and that the doormen "leave you waiting outside just to give the impression of a packed interior."

Clifton
22 | 19 | 18 | £4

96 Clifton Hill, NW8 (St. John's Wood), 020-7372 3427

■ Legend has it that Edward VII's rendezvous with actress Lillie Langtry took place in this discrete bolt-hole in a swish street in St. John's Wood, but nowadays it's just a "charming local pub" that's "perfect for a quick drink or a long lunch on a Sunday", doling out "homey food and good beer"; though there are usually "no tourists", the "friendly" staff will make "expat Americans" and other "outsiders" "feel at home."

Coach & Horses
18 | 14 | 15 | £4

42 Wellington St., WC2 (Covent Garden), 020-7240 0553

■ The "only outlet in central London for real (i.e. from Dublin) Guinness", this "friendly traditional" Covent Garden Irish pub garners a stout following; in addition to the black stuff it serves 70 types of whisky in a "no-frills" setting with a hint of "yesteryear", and its location, where the odd luvvie has been known to trot by, makes it a handy "meeting point" for the pre-theatre crowd.

Coach & Horses
16 | 13 | 17 | £5

5 Bruton St., W1 (Green Park/Oxford Circus), 020-7629 4123

◪ A "quintessential, adorable Tudor-style British pub", this "relaxing" Mayfair hangout serves up "good ales" and "decent pub fare" in a "low-key" setting; while it can be "too smoky" and "packed during happy hour", and sometimes morphs into "tourist central", devotees insist it's "worth it for the friendly patrons" alone.

Coach & Horses
17 | 12 | 13 | £3

29 Greek St., W1 (Piccadilly Circus), 020-7437 5920

■ "One of the few old man pubs" in the neighbourhood, this "busy, traditional" "public house" attracts "all walks of Soho life" for a "yap over a pint", with the "spirit of Jeffrey Bernard" and the *Private Eye* (and lots of "wanna-be JBs") adding to the "bohemian" atmosphere; while some detect signs that proprietor Norman Balon may be "softening up", many feel he's still "London's rudest landlord."

Coach & Horses
22 | 18 | 19 | £3

27 Barnes High St., SW13 (Hammersmith), 020-8876 2695; www.youngs.co.uk

■ Regulars of this "small, smart" "local" "in the middle of Barnes village" rate it "excellent, especially in the summer", thanks to a "beer garden", while in winter a "log fire is included in the price of a pint"; it's a "friendly, cosy" and "comfortable" hangout for the area's well-heeled denizens.

Coal Hole
13 | 14 | 13 | £3

91 Strand, WC2 (Charing Cross), 020-7379 9883

◪ A "good pub that doesn't try to be anything else", located a few doors from the Savoy, this "scruffy and smoky" venue with an underground wine bar is "always packed" with "Covent Garden tourists" and theatregoers, with lots of "suits during after-office hours"; some find it "uninspiring" no matter how "authentic" it may be, and reckon it must be an "acquired taste."

Coat & Badge
19 | 15 | 17 | £2

8 Lacy Rd., SW15 (Putney Bridge), 020-8788 4900

◪ With a "lovely view over the Thames" to complement "good food and ale", this "spacious" Putney "riverside" boozer has a "great outdoor area" that pulls in plenty of punters in the summer; though it's "always busy", the ambience remains "pleasant", if somewhat "plastic", but locals lament that it's "sadly filling up" with "tourists."

Cock Tavern
16 | 12 | 16 | £3

27 Great Portland St., W1 (Oxford Circus), 020-7631 5002

■ Built on the site of London's biggest cock pit just a short stroll north of Oxford Circus, this "excellent Sam Smith's pub" boasts "fabulous decor" of brown wooden booths and etched glass; cronies crow the "super food" and "cheap" beer are a "surprisingly good value", which is why it's so popular at "lunchtime" and "after work."

Cocomo
– | – | – | M

323 Old St., EC1 (Old St.), 020-7613 0315

"Vintage chaises longues and poufs", a "football table in the middle of the bar" upstairs and other grace notes "add to the character" of this Moroccan-themed Shoreditch spot; a coffee bar by day, it morphs into a "trendy", "very Hoxton" hangout serving "killer strawberry daiquiris" and other libations by night.

COLLECTION, THE 18 19 14 £7
264 Brompton Rd., SW3 (South Kensington), 020-7225 1212;
www.the-collection.co.uk
☑ "Pull on the Manolos" before heading to this "swanky" South Ken "stunner" where a "glass-paved entrance corridor" leads you into a "high-ceilinged" room filled with a collection of "babes", "trustafarians" and "Chelsea suits" "trying to pull"; to fiery fashionistas, however, it's a "has-been" plying "pretentious punters" and "Eurobankers" with "overpriced" drinks" and "too-loud" music.

Comedy Café – – – M
66-68 Rivington St., EC2 (Old St.), 020-7739 5706;
www.comedycafe.co.uk
This purpose-built comedy venue in Shoreditch emblazoned with paintings of characters from *The Beano* on the facade serves Tex-Mex fare and burgers with drinks at tables inside where you sit and take in stand-up routines on stage, by top comics as well as new acts every Wednesday; insiders warn that hecklers will "be shown the door."

Comedy Store 23 11 12 £4
1 Oxendon St., SW1 (Piccadilly Circus), 020-7344 0234;
www.thecomedystore.co.uk
■ Champions chortle you're "guaranteed a good night" of live stand-up at this Piccadilly comedy "cabaret" that's always "good for a laugh" and never short on "atmosphere"; cackling cognoscenti recommend the "late show, when the comics mess about more" and it's often "hard to keep your drink down" from all the guffaws, though some killjoys crack that the "price of a pint is funnier than the jokes."

Compton Arms 19 15 18 £2
4 Compton Ave., N1 (Highbury & Islington), 020-7359 6883
■ A "village pub in the middle of Islington", this "friendly" "hideaway near Highbury Corner" sports a "leafy garden" for quaffing Greene King ales in the summer, while inside the rooms are "small" and "comfortable"; a "good ol' booza", it also serves bangers and mash and "tremendous fat chips" to a "wide age-range of regulars", "mostly locals", although note that it's full of "Arsenal supporters before games" and screens Gunners' matches as well.

Comptons of Soho 17 12 14 £3
53-57 Old Compton St., W1 (Leicester Sq./Tottenham Court Rd.),
020-7479 7961; www.comptons-of-soho.co.uk
■ "If you like your gay bars butch", regulars recommend this "old-style, low-tech" two-floor venue on Old Compton Street that's "hopping most any night" with a crowd that

includes both "skinheads and club kids"; it's "one of the friendlier" joints of its kind around, and it "knows what it is and delivers it in spades"; N.B. DJ nights on Mondays, Fridays and Saturdays.

Coopers Arms
17 | 15 | 17 | £4

87 Flood St., SW3 (Sloane Sq.), 020-7376 3120;
www.thecoopers.co.uk

■ Even in Chelsea, sometimes you just want a "quiet", "unpretentious" boozer with "friendly" service and "not a lot of flash", so fans recommend this "proper drinker's venue" courtesy of Young's; it's "a popular place" to read the "newspapers" on a Sunday, and it also serves "tasty", "reasonably adventurous" nosh.

Cork & Bottle
21 | 16 | 18 | £6

44-46 Cranbourn St., WC2 (Leicester Sq.), 020-7734 7807;
www.donhewitson.com

■ Oenophiles anoint this "cavelike basement" in the unlikely environs of Leicester Square one of the capital's "finest and busiest wine spots" thanks to a "superb" selection of *vinos* and "very good champagnes" paired with perfectly "decent" fare and served in a "great, intimate space"; it's "difficult to get a table when it's busy", but the "staff is always very helpful."

CORNEY & BARROW
14 | 14 | 14 | £4

3 Fleet Pl., EC4 (St. Paul's), 020-7329 3141
16 Royal Exchange, EC3 (Bank), 020-7929 3131
2B Eastcheap, EC3 (Monument), 020-7929 3220
37 Jewry St., EC3 (Aldgate/Tower Hill), 020-7680 8550
1 Leadenhall Pl., EC3 (Bank/Monument), 020-7621 9201
19 Broadgate Circle, EC2 (Liverpool St.), 020-7628 1251
5 Exchange Sq., EC2 (Liverpool St.), 020-7628 4367
12-14 Mason's Ave., EC2 (Bank/Moorgate), 020-7726 6030
111 Old Broad St., EC2 (Liverpool St.), 020-7638 9308
9 Cabot Sq., E14 (Canary Wharf), 020-7512 0397
www.corney-barrow.co.uk

☑ You "can't fault the quality of the wines" at this unique wine bar bunch that work as "after-work drinks meeting places" for "City boys and girls" in need of "unwinding"; but while some favour the "upmarket, bustling" vibe and white-and-wood decor, others find the ambience "clinical" and the quality "inconsistent across the chain."

Couch
∇ 17 | 14 | 12 | £4

97-99 Dean St., W1 (Tottenham Court Rd.), 020-7287 0150;
www.massivepub.co.uk

☑ Sporting an "eclectic mix of wooden tables and old leather sofas", this "great alternative" in the heart of Soho is a "welcoming and cosy" lunch spot before the "punters roll in", and a "cool little place for starting" an evening; when it "gets busy", though, it "can be a nightmare" according to critics who complain that, oddly enough, there are "not enough couches."

Counting House
14 | 16 | 12 | £3

50 Cornhill, EC3 (Bank), 020-7283 7123; www.fullers.co.uk
◪ A "sensational space" with an "impressively high ceiling", this converted City bank is a reliable venue for "Fuller's ales", "pub food" and "good service"; foes find the "cavernous" quarters somewhat "bland", though the ambience becomes rather "boozy" when it "gets busy" with a "noisy, drunken and corporate" crew.

COW
21 | 17 | 16 | £5

89 Westbourne Park Rd., W2 (Westbourne Park), 020-7221 5400
◪ This Bayswater gastro-pub run by Tom (son of Terence) Conran consists of an upstairs dining room serving "great Guinness and oysters" and other "superb" offerings, and a "fun" old-fashioned Irish bar popular with West London trustafarians who are as "cool, trendy and pretty" as the staff; it's "small and always packed", and some report experiencing "difficulty getting service."

Crazy Bear
– | – | – | VE

26-28 Whitfield St., W1 (Goodge St.), 020-7631 0088; www.crazybeargroup.co.uk
A new addition to the thriving Fitzrovia scene, this bar and restaurant is an offshoot from Oxfordshire hotel of the same name, and most of the action takes place in the basement bar that wows punters with red leather walls, ostrich-skin barstools and a bar made from fireplaces; perhaps the most extraordinary touch, though, is the all-mirrored bathrooms that some might find a bit disorienting after a couple of Asian-inspired cocktails.

Cross, The
22 | 22 | 16 | £5

Arches 27-31, York Way, N1 (King's Cross), 020-7837 0828; www.the-cross.co.uk
■ A "little bit of Ibiza" comes to King's Cross at this "cool and crisp" dance venue "for those who take their clubbing seriously", with three "intimate" rooms, "two terrace areas" and six dance floors where the "pumping" music entertains a "good-looking crowd that wants to have a good time"; a few claustrophobes are a bit cross that it "packs too many in"; N.B. Friday Fiction night is gay night.

Cross Keys
18 | 17 | 17 | £3

31 Endell St., WC2 (Covent Garden), 020-7836 5185
■ The King and the Fab Four live on at this "warm and welcomy" Covent Garden spot, proud owner of a napkin autographed by Elvis, assorted Beatles memorabilia and other "bric-a-brac"; a facade festooned with flowers and foliage greets you at what loyalists say is "one of the few remaining proper boozers" in a "tourist-ridden wasteland."

Cross Keys
19 | 19 | 18 | £5

1 Lawrence St., SW3 (Sloane Sq.), 020-7349 9111;
www.thexkeys.co.uk

■ A "good escape" in a "superb location", this Chelsea sibling of the Artesian Well works equally well "for drinking parties", "to dissect a bad date, or a good one, with a glass of wine in front of an eyebrow-searing warm fire", or to dine on "solid" British fare in the glass-ceilinged conservatory; the "airy, spacious" digs boast an "arty" decor highlighted by "Greek statuary" and a "Buddha fireplace."

Crown
17 | 15 | 18 | £3

116 Cloudesley Rd., N1 (Angel), 020-7837 7107;
www.fullers.co.uk

■ Set in a listed building that served as a coaching inn in the 1500s, this "honest, lively" Fuller's in Islington with a "fabulous old circular bar" is "perfect for Sunday afternoon beers" and "decent, if a bit fancy, gastro-pub grub"; it "gets very crowded", but most say it's "worth the trek."

Crown, The
∇ 21 | 18 | 18 | £5

233 Grove Rd., E3 (Bethnal Green), 020-8981 9998;
www.singhboulton.co.uk

■ It's fitting that the furniture is "recycled" at this "relaxed but basic" all-organic boozer, but loyalists insist there's still "no better place to leaf through the Sunday papers or a book"; a "superb" upstairs dining room overlooks "luscious" Victoria Park, where you can dine and sup on the six types of certified organic "amber nectar" and, if you're in the mood, even get married – it's now licensed for weddings.

Crown & Greyhound
∇ 19 | 15 | 11 | £6

73 Dulwich Vlg., SE21 (North Dulwich/rail), 020-8299 4976

■ Set in a former coach house that is now a listed building, this "unspoilt" "Victorian" pub in Dulwich Village is a "traditional English" establishment with a "garden"; radicals rail at the "middle-class" crowd, but for others the family-friendly "environment" and "location" are simply "lovely."

Crown & Sceptre
∇ 18 | 13 | 18 | £3

26 Foley St., W1 (Oxford Circus), 020-7307 9971

☑ Set on a corner in the heart of trendy-once-more Fitzrovia, this "refurbished" old boozer is a "local worth travelling for", pouring pints for punters in an airy space with a high, ornately carved ceiling and a decor that mixes traditional Victorian and modern elements; sceptics shrug it's just "ok."

Cru
∇ 25 | 22 | 22 | £5

2-4 Rufus St., N1 (Old St.), 020-7729 5252; www.cru.uk.com

■ At once "charming and hip", this bar/restaurant/deli boasts a "great kitchen" churning out food that's "much better than the Hoxton location would suggest"; with regular wine tasting evenings and artwork by local types on display (de rigueur in this part of town), it's a "very cool loungey bar" for the "thirtysomething" crew.

Cuba
16 | 14 | 13 | £6

11-13 Kensington High St., W8 (High St. Kensington), 020-7938 4137; www.barcuba.info

☑ Whether you're looking for "civilised tapas" or some "unsophisticated frenzied drinking", regulars recommend this relatively "cheap" Kensington late nighter where you can boogie to "Latin rhythms" from DJs and live acts; while some question how "authentic" it really is, foes grouse it's genuinely "noisy" and "cramped."

Cuba Libre
18 | 17 | 15 | £4

72 Upper St., N1 (Angel), 020-7354 9998

■ "Upper Street's answer to old Havana", this Cuban bar "mixes mean drinks and plays great tunes" for an "unusual" clientele in a "lively atmosphere" that's "fun for groups"; while critics complain there's "not enough room" and it's "always too crowded", bargain hunters are willing to brave the masses for "good happy-hour deals."

Cubana
17 | 17 | 14 | £4

36 Southwick St., W21 (Paddington), 020-7402 7539
48 Lower Marsh, SE1 (Waterloo), 020-7928 8778
www.cubana.co.uk

☑ At these South Bank and Paddington hermanos, amigos assert the "fabulous mojitos", "nice surprises" on the food menu and "DJs spinning salsa" and live bands on weekends are worth wading through the "crowds"; sniff cynics, who also find "you don't mind waiting" for service, the tropical trappings with lots of "Cuban souvenirs" are a bit "clichéd."

Cutty Sark Tavern
17 | 15 | 13 | £3

4-6 Ballast Quay, SE10 (North Greenwich), 020-8858 3146

■ "River views" from "nice benches" outdoors and a "great garden area" put wind in the sails of this venerable vessel "off the Thames path", though it also gets a boost from a "friendly staff"; not surprisingly, it attracts a "full" crew of "tourists", but for many it's nonetheless "worth the train ride to Greenwich."

Davy's
17 | 15 | 16 | £4

17 The Arches, WC2 (Charing Cross/Embankment), 020-7930 7737
Hand Court, 57 High Holborn, WC1 (Holborn), 020-7831 8365
Crown Passage, Pall Mall, SW1 (Green Park/St. James's Park), 020-7839 8831
161 Greenwich High St., SE10 (Greenwich), 020-8858 7204
10 Creed Ln., EC4 (St. Paul's), 020-7236 5317
31 Fisherman's Walk, E14 (Canary Wharf), 020-7363 6633
www.davy.co.uk

☑ "Authentically traditional – down to the sawdust on the floor", this stalwart chain serves up "quality wines" ranging in price from "reasonable" to "very expensive" as well as "good solid food" and "decent beer" to a generally "posh" clientele; the setting gets mixed responses – the jaded find it "cheesy" while others consider it "comically charming."

De Hems 17 | 13 | 15 | £3
11 Macclesfield St., W1 (Piccadilly Circus), 020-7437 2494
■ Located on the fringes of Chinatown, this beer emporium is nonetheless "very Dutch", from the selection of both well-known and rare Netherlands beers down to the oak panelling; "pleasant" and "spacious", it's "handy for pre/post-Chinese drinks" and is definitely "the bar for drinkers" in this neighbourhood, especially when there's a "party" going on, though its proximity to Soho means it's sometimes "full of suits."

Denim 15 | 18 | 12 | £6
4A Upper St. Martin's Ln., WC2 (Leicester Sq.), 020-7497 0376
◩ This Covent Garden triple-decker bar/club is as "trendy" and "stylish" as ever, cronies insist, with its "cool decor" and video screens, "good DJs", "excellent cocktails" and a "good-looking crowd"; foes find it a bit faded, however, and fault the "ridiculously expensive drinks", "tetchy staff" and "posy", "nouveau moolah" clientele.

Destino – | – | – | E
25 Swallow St., W1 (Piccadilly Circus), 020-7437 9895;
www.destinolondon.co.uk
Located in the building that hosted London's first ever Spanish restaurant, this three-floor Latin American bar/restaurant/deli/club offers "tasty" cocktails and beer and bar fare that includes Cuban sandwiches, seviche and selections from a taco bar in a "lively" setting; most punters are impressed, though some caution about the "very odd door policy."

Detroit 19 | 19 | 17 | £5
35 Earlham St., WC2 (Covent Garden), 020-7240 2662;
www.detroit-bar.com
◩ At this "upmarket and classy" cocktail haven in Covent Garden, the "twisty turny" collection of "subterranean rooms" resembles "a cross between the *Flintstones* and *Star Wars*"; "fabbo concoctions" and DJs spinning tunes contribute to a "great vibe", though morbid malcontents liken the experience in the "cavernous" quarters to "being buried alive" and "paying for the privilege."

Dial 17 | 18 | 19 | £8
The Mountbatten, 20 Monmouth St., WC2 (Covent Garden),
020-7836 4300
◩ This "stylish" bar attached to the Mountbatten hotel in the "eye of the storm" of Covent Garden (by the Seven Dials) is handy for a "post-shopping drink" or "meeting a group of friends", especially if you snaffle some "leather chairs" and a "place by the window"; though a few find it

"dull" and "too much like a hotel bar", the "friendly service" makes for an "always pleasurable experience."

Digress   13 | 12 | 14 | £4

1 Ropemaker St., EC2 (Moorgate), 020-7382 1690;
www.digress-city.co.uk

☑ A "friendly, comfortable bar" with three sleekly designed rooms in the office-land of Moorgate is inevitably going to be crammed with a "young crowd", though the dress code (no jeans or trainers) tends to limit it to "trendy City types"; while it's good for "large groups", dissenters dismiss the scene as a "meat market" (there's "no draught beer" at the bar, either, but we digress); N.B. closed at weekends.

Dirty Dick   16 | 14 | 15 | £4

202 Bishopsgate, EC2 (Liverpool St.), 020-7283 5888;
www.youngs.co.uk

☑ A "noisy drinking hole" located right opposite Liverpool Street Station, this "lovely boozer" with "old-world pub decor" (right down to the "sticky wooden floor") and a "pithy attitude" attracts a mix of "gents", "commuters" and "tourists"; it's usually "heaving on weeknights" and "very busy on Fridays", but if you're expecting a glam scene, then you don't know, er, Richard.

Dish Dash   15 | 16 | 17 | £5

11-13 Bedford Hill, SW12 (Balham), 020-8673 5555;
www.dish-dash.com

☑ "Original cocktails" such as the Zamshid (a blend of vodka and passion fruit) and the Persepolitan (a rhubarb-flavoured take on the Cosmo) and Persian cuisine and decor set this Balham bar/restaurant apart from its neighbours, and fans praise the concept as "exciting and lively"; even lukewarm punsters concede that while it's "not really somewhere to dash, it does make a good dish" of kebab.

Dog & Duck   17 | 14 | 15 | £4

18 Bateman St., W1 (Oxford Circus/Tottenham Court Rd.),
020-7494 0697; www.mitchellsandbutlers.co.uk

■ With walls covered in original Victorian tiling from 1897 and a listed interior, this tiny Soho corner boozer is "a very pretty pub" serving "excellent ale"; though a few yelp over its somewhat "grungy" mien, devotees hope it "never changes", for that's just "the way [they] like" their pubs.

Dogstar   15 | 10 | 11 | £3

389 Coldharbour Ln., SW9 (Brixton), 020-7733 7515;
www.thedogstar.com

■ While some feel it may have "lost a bit of its edge" since its apex in the late '90s, this dark, "smoky and tiny" pub/club in the heart of Brixton is still "busy every night", drawing a "decent crowd" with DJs and occasional film screenings on Sundays; whether you're in the mood for "daytime chill or evening dancing", it's "lively fun" according to fans.

$

– | – | – | VE

(aka $ Grills and Martinis)

2 Exmouth Mkt., EC1 (Farringdon), 020-7278 0077

"What kind of a name is this?" ponder perplexed punters over this new, hipper-than-thou Clerkenwell bar and grill where martinis are the name of the game; the answer may lie in the "glam" ("verging on kitsch") decor – oversized black-and-white photos, perpex boxes and leather banquettes – that embodies the essence of bling.

DORCHESTER BAR

23 | 21 | 24 | £9

Dorchester Hotel, 53 Park Ln., W1 (Hyde Park Corner), 020-7629 8888; www.dorchesterhotel.com

■ "Glitzy glam" rules at this "flashy throwback of a bar" in Mayfair's Dorchester Hotel with Liberace's piano in a corner and so much gold you'll "need your sunglasses"; "polite" service and "very private tables" in "comfortably elegant" environs are an "excellent mix for a meaningful date" ("if you can't seal the deal here, forget it"), while "lovely" live jazz adds to an experience that will "make you feel rich – until you see the bill."

DOVE

25 | 18 | 18 | £3

19 Upper Mall, W6 (Hammersmith/Ravenscourt Park), 020-8748 5405

■ "Low beams and riverside views" of the Hammersmith stretch of the Thames, a "wide choice of Belgian beers" and Fuller's ales and "tasty" fare may have been some of the charms that attracted the likes of Ernest Hemingway and Graham Greene to this "olde worlde" pub that is the smallest public bar in the *Guinness Book of Records*; its location makes it "ideal for a summer evening", while the two "real fireplaces" make it "good for winter", too.

Dover Castle

18 | 15 | 18 | £3

43 Weymouth Mews, W1 (Great Portland St.), 020-7580 4412

■ A "great local pub" snuggled in a cobbled mews near Portland Place in Marylebone, this Sam Smith's venue is an unspoiled "cosy" "old man's" boozer with a cheerfully "out-of-date decor" and a TV as the only entertainment; given its location, it's well-placed as an opener to an evening.

Dover Street

17 | 15 | 15 | £5

8-10 Dover St., W1 (Green Park), 020-7629 9813; www.doverst.co.uk

◪ "Lots of champagne", "dancing after dinner" to "great jazz", blues, soul or R&B and "a real Mayfair atmosphere" get this wine bar "hopping", and with a 3 AM closing time it's a "good place to end the evening", while at lunchtime it attracts a "mostly professional" crowd with "fine" French-Med fare; a few dismiss it as a "cheery pick-up joint", while aficionados insist "you'll always have a good time, despite your better instincts" – just "be prepared to spend money."

DRAGON
24 | 18 | 16 | £3

5 Leonard St., EC2 (Old St.), 020-7490 7110

■ Hidden away down a back alley and "behind a blank door", this "grubby, vibrant, loud" bar is a "refreshing change" from the usual Shoreditch fare where you can "jump up to the music and spill your beer", but be "ready to get pushed around", because it can get "wild" when it's "very busy"; still, the crowd is "good-natured", with lots of "media types", and the "battered sofas" and fireplace make it a "fantastic place to chill"; N.B. it's now open until 2 AM at weekend.

DRAPER'S ARMS, THE
23 | 20 | 22 | £5

44 Barnsbury St., N1 (Highbury & Islington), 020-7619 0348

■ A backstreet "haven" for a "lively older crowd" and "well-heeled Islington families", this gastro-pub offers "inventive twists on classic British fare" and a "good wine list" (as well as Belgian and guest ales) in a "nice, airy" space with a "great garden"; though some think of it as "more of a foody" spot, a "pint and a chat" on "lazy leather couches" have made for "many a happy Sunday afternoon."

Drayton Arms
15 | 13 | 16 | £3

153 Old Brompton Rd., SW5 (Earl's Court), 020-7835 2301

■ As good a place as any to "sit and watch the Ferraris go by" at the outdoor tables in summer, this spacious "low-key" local is popular with South Ken Sloanes, offering "good draughts on tap" and 20 mostly New World wines by the glass in recently revamped quarters with a '70s theme; it gets especially "lively" on Saturday nights when a DJ spins.

dreambagsjaguarshoes
18 | 13 | 14 | £4

34-36 Kingsland Rd., E2 (Old St./Liverpool St.), 020-7729 5830; www.dreambagsjaguarshoes.com

☑ Wags wonder if the "mouthful" of a moniker of this "trendy DJ bar" in Shoreditch is "some sort of blood alcohol level test", but it's really the combined names of the two shops that once occupied the site; a "deliberately lo-fi" gaff, it's "busy mid-evening" with an "arty" crowd of "eccentrically dressed cool young things", and critics observe it "can take a long time to get served", which may be the real source of all the "pretentious pouting" that goes on.

Dublin Castle ⇗
17 | 8 | 14 | £2

94 Parkway, NW1 (Camden Town), 020-7485 1773

■ Groupies tout this "beer-soaked" Camden venue as the "birthplace of London indie music" where bands such as Madness and Blur cut their teeth, and it "consistently puts on the best bands" around, with three acts a night, most of them still unknown; "North London wideboys", "students" and others ignore the "run-down" digs and just "go for the gigs."

Duke of Cambridge
20 | 18 | 20 | £4

228 Battersea Bridge Rd., SW11 (Clapham Jct./rail), 020-7223 5662

■ "Great grub", "friendly", "accommodating" service and an outdoor patio make this Battersea boozer a "fine spot on a Sunday afternoon"; fans praise the "tremendous decor" that appeals to somewhat "yuppy" tastes, while aficionados advise that it's "better for a long lunch than a night out."

Duke of Cambridge
21 | 16 | 16 | £4

30 St. Peter's St., N1 (Angel), 020-7359 3066;
www.singhboulton.co.uk

■ While there's "lots of local competition now", this "trendy" trailblazer off the main drag in Islington, purportedly the original certified organic gastro-pub, still "attracts crowds of all ages", and the "service makes up" for the "busy" rush, keeping the "traditional pub atmosphere" pleasantly "chilled"; the "good range" of eats and drinks wins praise, but pundits point out that purity can be "pricey."

Duke of Devonshire
∇ 21 | 20 | 19 | £2

39 Balham High Rd., SW12 (Clapham South), 020-8673 1363;
www.youngs.co.uk

■ With a "spacious" Victorian interior of the wood-and-etched-glass variety, this "traditional", "lovely old boozer" in Balham pours a good selection of Young's ales and 15 wines by the glass; locals laud the "friendly" "good atmosphere", and the "great beer garden" makes it an area favourite for summertime tippling.

Duke of York
17 | 13 | 15 | £5

7 Roger St., WC1 (Holborn/Russell Sq.), 020-7242 7230;
www.dukepub.co.uk

■ A "hidden gem" on the Bloomsbury/Clerkenwell border, this corner pub with a "quirky 1950s feel" is an appealing option for "a quiet pint and a game of darts" in an "intimate and friendly" atmosphere; there's also a separate, very red dining room serving gastro-pub fare.

Duke of York
19 | 18 | 18 | £6

2 St. Anne's Terr., NW8 (St. John's Wood), 020-7722 1933

■ In a "smart location" on a corner in St. John's Wood, this gastro-pub is normally "packed" and "very happening" thanks to a menu of "appealing" French-Moroccan cuisine; gone is the North African decor, replaced by a modern look featuring leather banquettes and pastel colours.

Duke's Head
21 | 15 | 17 | £3

8 Lower Richmond Rd., SW15 (Putney Bridge), 020-8788 2552;
www.youngs.co.uk

■ A "charming riverside pub" in Putney, this Young's establishment shines in summer with an "endless outdoor drinking space" by the Thames, and its "fantastic location" near the start line makes it a favourite on Boat Race day;

"excellent" traditional English fare, a "friendly, comfortable" atmosphere, a "fireplace" and a "lounge bar overlooking the river" make it a contender anytime of year.

DUKES HOTEL BAR
23 | 22 | 25 | £9

Dukes Hotel, 35 St. James's Place, SW1 (Green Park), 020-7491 4840; www.dukeshotel.com

■ "If you like martinis, this is the place to go" crow cronies of this "elegant and classy" St. James's hotel bar where cocktails are "mixed and served with aplomb" at your table by famed mixologist Tony Micelotta; "deep cushioned armchairs" are part of the "dark", "sophisticated", "old-time" setting, and with a selection of rare cognacs and cigars for sale, it's an all-around "class act"; N.B. smart casual attire please (no trainers).

Dusk
– | – | – | M

339 Battersea Park Rd., SW11 (Sloane Sq.), 020-7622 2112; www.duskbar.co.uk

With an "excellent selection of cocktails", "edgy decor" of dark wooden tables and low leather sofas, a swanky outdoor garden bar that opens in summer and "soft lounge music" from DJs, this "comfortable neighbourhood watering hole" in Battersea is lauded by locals as "the best addition" to the south-of-the-river scene in yonks; make sure you arrive early, though, as "it's already becoming too popular."

Dust
18 | 15 | 12 | £4

27 Clerkenwell Rd., EC1 (Farringdon), 020-7490 5120; www.dustbar.co.uk

◩ A "funky", "cool venue for dancing" to "top tunes", this converted Clerkenwell factory is "heaving" on weekends, when it's open till 4 AM; detractors disdain the "dull" scene as one apt for "thirtysomethings" who are more "aging and anxious" than "young and restless", but few find fault with the "fabulous cocktails" or "cute waiters."

Eagle, The
21 | 17 | 17 | £4

159 Farringdon Rd., EC1 (Farringdon), 020-7837 1353

■ The "original gastro-pub" boosters boast, this classic London feeding and watering hole on the Farringdon Road "keeps going and going" because it's "run by people who know what they're doing", serving up "frothy warm beer", a "good selection of wine" (15 by the glass) and "big gutsy food" accompanied by "music played on a rubbish stereo"; though others have copied the style, it's still a "favourite" of many.

Eagle Bar Diner
∇ 18 | 18 | 16 | £6

3-5 Rathbone Pl., W1 (Tottenham Court Rd.), 020-7637 1418; www.eaglebardiner.co.uk

■ It's not everywhere you can enjoy "a funky cocktail and a great hamburger" together, but this "attractive" "NY"-style Fitzrovia venue just north of Oxford Street offers long lists of "innovative" "new wave martinis" and some of the "best burgers in London"; DJs spinning Latin/Brazilian and funk and green high-backed booths help make this a "groovy place to meet with friends" before moving on into Soho.

E&O
23 | 20 | 19 | £7

14 Blenheim Crescent, W11 (Notting Hill Gate), 020-7229 5454;
www.eando.nu

■ A "sleek oasis amid the grunge of Notting Hill", this "spacious" Asian-themed watering hole is prime "people-watching" territory, attracting a "swanky", "celeb"-studded clientele with "yummy cocktails", 100 wines and "super-tasty" dim sum at the bar; it's a "trendy", "buzzy" scene that has all the makings of a "funky night."

East@West
– | – | – | VE

(fka West Street)
13-15 West St., WC2 (Leicester Sq.), 020-7010 8600;
www.egami.co.uk

A new chef and a new name haven't changed the basics at this Covent Garden bar/restaurant "hidden in a dark street" and housed in what was a brothel that catered to Japanese businessmen; while the kitchen now serves an Asian-accented tasting menu, the basement bar is still "cosy", the crowd "eclectic" and the decor of chocolate-coloured banquettes and a backlit bar remains a "cool" backdrop to tipple Eastern-themed cocktails.

Easton, The
– | – | – | E

22 Easton St., WC1 (Farringdon), 020-7278 7608;
www.theeaston.co.uk

As different as it could be from the previous tenants at its Clerkenwell address (a dubious strip joint), this "totally fab" gastro-pub is "well hidden" but becoming better known for its Aussie-influenced British-European fare (both owners are antipodeans); there's lots of polished wood and some spectacular vintage wallpaper in the airy open-plan room.

ECLIPSE
21 | 18 | 16 | £8

186 Kensington Park Rd., W11 (Notting Hill Gate),
020-7792 2063
57 High St., SW19 (Wimbledon), 020-8944 7722
108-110 New King's Rd., SW6 (Parsons Green),
020-7731 2142
158 Old Brompton Rd., SW5 (Gloucester Rd.), 020-7259 2577
113 Walton St., SW3 (South Kensington), 020-7581 0123
www.eclipse-ventures.com

■ Boogie with "Eurotrash", "eye candy" and other assorted "'it' folk" at this "trendy" chain of "cosy and posy" bar/clubs serving "amazing" drinks such as "passion fruit margaritas" in "funky" rooms that are "always bursting at the seams"; critics warn of "obnoxious bouncers" and a "farcical door policy", and note that while it may be "hip", "you pay for it."

Edge, The
16 | 15 | 15 | £4

11 Soho Sq., W1 (Tottenham Court Rd.), 020-7439 1313;
www.edge.uk.com

■ Four floors with a "different atmosphere" in each, from a Euro-style cafe bar to a glitzy dance club, comprise this "busy, friendly" Soho late-nighter that caters to a "good mix" of gay and straight revellers; at the weekend it becomes camper than "pink tents" with "drag queens" leading the "podium dancing", and for many it's "the only place to go" in the neighbourhood after hours.

Edinboro Castle
▽ 16 | 13 | 15 | £3

57 Mornington Terr., NW1 (Camden Town), 020-7255 9651

■ While surveyors are noncommittal about the recent "major refurb" that turned this Camden venue into a "typical gastro-pub" with a maroon, red and black color scheme, the main attraction continues to be the "huge beer garden" where "barbecue" is served in the summer; otherwise, it does the trick for a "quick drink."

1802
▽ 23 | 20 | 19 | £6

1 West India Quay, E14 (West India Quay), 087-0444 3886;
www.searcys.co.uk

■ Set in a Grade-1 listed red brick warehouse (circa 1802) and boasting a "stylish and airy interior", this NY-style bar "stands out" as one of the "best places in Canary Wharf", where a "friendly crowd" gathers for a "quiet drink towards the start of the night"; while some find the scene a tad "formulaic", for others it "does the job."

Elbow Room
18 | 17 | 15 | £4

103 Westbourne Grove, W2 (Bayswater), 020-7221 5211
89-91 Chapel Mkt., N1 (Angel), 020-7278 3244
97-113 Curtain Rd., EC2 (Old Street/Liverpool St.), 020-7613 1316
www.theelbowroom.co.uk

■ A "well-dressed young crowd" hustles to this "trendy" pool-joint trio to work on their breaks if they're not on the "dance floor" or just "chilling out" over drinks and "burgers" and other American-style fare; "purple tables" highlight the "funky" decor, and the scene is "hip" but also "cosy and comfortable", with DJs spinning on weekends.

Electric Ballroom, The ⊅
16 | 10 | 14 | £3

184 Camden High St., NW1 (Camden Town), 020-7485 9007;
www.electricballroom.co.uk

◪ Thirty years young and located in a "massive" three-floor space that's been in use since the '40s, this Camden haunt is still a "must for the alternative crowd" who dance to "weird" music as well as the odd bit of "metal"; while the "old" digs may "need better decor", it's a "great place to see bands" from time to time, and Friday's Full Tilt (which "hasn't changed for 12 years" at least) is "ace" – just be sure to "wear the right clothes."

El Vino

16 | 15 | 17 | £5

47 Fleet St., EC4 (Temple), 020-7353 6786
6 Martin Ln., EC4 (Cannon St.), 020-7626 6876
30 New Bridge St., EC4 (Blackfriars), 020-7236 4534
Alban Gate, 125 London Wall, EC2 (Barbican), 020-7600 6377
www.elvino.co.uk

■ An "institution that should be preserved in claret and cigar smoke", this family-owned chain of "old-fashioned" wine bars boasts one of the "finest lists" you'll find, with 170 *vinos* as well as ports, sherries and Madeiras; a few find the "conservative atmosphere" a bit "stuffy", but for oenophiles who "don't mind lawyers", the "great selection" of pressings is worth it.

Elysium

19 | 19 | 16 | £8

68 Regent St., W1 (Piccadilly Circus), 020-7439 7770;
www.elysiumlounge.co.uk

◪ Located beneath but unrelated to and "nothing like" the staid Cafe Royal hotel, this "glamourous" Regent Street nightclub is like a "lush" "casbah" decorated with "pillows, candles and all things Eastern" and peopled by a "beautiful" crowd; agnostics argue it's "more hype than substance", with "insane prices" but "no real charm", while believers insist whether you "socialise by the bar" or "dance your pants off to pumping music", it's a "blast."

Embassy

17 | 17 | 18 | £8

29 Old Burlington St., W1 (Green Park/Piccadilly Circus),
020-7851 0956; www.embassylondon.com

◪ For "clubbers who don't want to compromise on their taste buds", this Mayfair club and bar serves "excellent" Modern British–Euro fare in an "elegant" upstairs dining room, while the "glamourous" basement with a red glass-topped bar is usually "full of posh totty"; insiders insist it's still "trendy", but less diplomatic detractors deride it as an "Essexland" for "B-list celebs" and "posers" "flashing their cash"; N.B. call to get on the guest list.

End, The

21 | 18 | 15 | £4

18 West Central St., WC1 (Tottenham Court Rd./Holborn),
020-7419 9199; www.endclub.co.uk

■ "For a hard-core night", a "cool", "diverse" crowd seek out this "difficult to find" club just off High Holburn to bop "until dawn" to "dark, pumping" music from a "killer sound system"; "Mondays are saved" thanks to glammy Trash night, when live acts play "punk, goth – the works" and the "dancing is crazy"; N.B. closed Tuesdays and Wednesdays.

ENGINEER, THE

20 | 17 | 17 | £4

65 Gloucester Ave., NW1 (Camden Town/Chalk Farm),
020-7722 0950; www.the-engineer.com

■ "Rich bohemians" and celebrity "Primrose Hillbillies" flock to this well-constructed gastro-pub that claims to be one of the first places to bring "new British cooking" into the area; foodies fawn over the "good quality" fare, while others insist that it's the "gorgeous garden", "perfect for those summer evenings", that "makes it a winner."

Enterprise, The   19 | 18 | 19 | £5
38 Red Lion St., WC1 (Holborn), 020-7269 5901
■ Sitting "on a good route for pub crawls" about the Holborn area, this "conservative" boozer has a "literary" feel (which means "middle-aged" to some); the tiled walls and original gas lighting in the front of the pub give it a "great vibe" and it's "surprisingly friendly" for such a central location; N.B. it's now a Mitchells and Butlers venue.

Equinox   11 | 11 | 11 | £6
5-7 Leicester Sq., WC2 (Leicester Sq.), 020-7437 1446
◪ Enthusiasts exhort "stop whining about the tourists and boogie down" to "commercial" tunes at "one of Leicester Square's most famous nightspots" where "comfy seats", a "big dance floor" and "lots of dark corners for pulling" make it a "fun place for singles to mingle"; a "tacky" "meat market" full of "leery men", with "bad music" to boot, is more like it sniff cynics, who recommend it only if you "can't get in anywhere else."

Evangelist, The   19 | 18 | 17 | £7
33 Blackfriars Ln., EC4 (Blackfriars), 020-7213 0740;
www.massivepub.com
■ "Well-priced cocktails", "good bar snacks" and a "good lunch menu" win over many a convert to this gastro-pub set in a Blackfriars backstreet, and plenty of "seating options" contribute to a "comfortable" experience; though it "can be overwhelmingly noisy" at night, proponents preach it "can't be beaten" for a midday bite and is also "great for after-work drinks."

Exhibit, The   – | – | – | M
12 Balham Station Rd., SW12 (Balham), 020-8772 6556;
www.theexhibit.uk.com
Featured as a venue in a BBC2 dating programme, this Balham bar/restaurant dishes up modern European and British cuisine and sports a "swanky decor" highlighted by a large aquarium, as well as an outdoor garden; the only rub is its location next to a supermarket, and "who wants to look out on a car park?"

FABRIC   22 | 20 | 15 | £5
77A Charterhouse St., EC1 (Farringdon), 020-7336 8898;
www.fabriclondon.com
■ Five bars, three dance floors and "wall-to-wall club kids" is what you'll find at this "industrial"-looking Farringdon super-club where "mind-blowing music" from a "sound system to die for" (the "legendary" woofer will make you "feel like you're being defibrillated") is probably "not for

the over-thirties" crowd, but "serious dancers" up for a "long night" only; regulars note it can get "unbelievably rammed" and the "warren of bars and rooms" is "like a maze" for the uninitiated.

Fenchurch Colony Wine Bar & Brasserie
16 | 16 | 17 | £8

14 New London St., EC3 (Tower Hill), 020-7481 0848; www.thecolonies.co.uk

■ With a "good location for City workers", this wine bar is a "classy" option for "insurance brokers" and other business types in the mood to celebrate (or commiserate), with a "quality" list of more than 50 *vinos* as well as a "good selection" of champagne, plus bar and brasserie menus; sceptics sigh it's "nothing special" and a bit "overpriced."

Fiesta Havana
17 | 15 | 14 | £5

17 Hanover Sq., W1 (Bond St./Oxford Circus), 020-7629 2552
490 Fulham Rd., SW6 (Fulham Broadway), 020-7381 5005
www.fiestahavana.com

■ "Mojitos and salsa – bring it on" shout satisfied señors and señoritas who salute these "little Cubas" as "great places" for a bit of "tequila"-fuelled "merengue"; rebels, though, rant over the "cheesy" scene and "cramped" conditions that turn the dance floor into a "sweat box."

FIFTH FLOOR BAR
18 | 17 | 17 | £7

Harvey Nichols, 109-125 Knightsbridge, SW1 (Knightsbridge), 020-7235 5000; www.harveynichols.co.uk

■ Surveyors are split over this bar above Harvey Nick's department store in Knightsbridge – advocates insist it's "better than its pulling-joint reputation", a "classy" "meeting place" for those times "when you want to impress", where you can "chill out on comfy chairs"; contrarians counter it's a scene reminiscent of "a tube train crush on an evening", full of "divorcees", "overstuffed businessmen" and chaps "old enough to be your father."

Filthy MacNasty's
18 | 15 | 15 | £3

(fka Filthy's Bar & Kitchen)
68 Amwell St., EC1 (Angel), 020-7837 6067; www.filthymacnastys.com

■ Pogues and Popes fans are hopeful they "might see Shane MacGowan" at this "trendy Irish pub" in Islington, where "friendly staff" serve "excellent Guinness", 30 varieties of whiskies and "good pub food" in a "dark, welcoming" space with tatty sofas; "live music and book readings" also help make it popular among the local "intelligentsia."

Fine Line, The
11 | 11 | 13 | £4

77 Kingsway, WC2 (Holborn), 020-7405 5004
31-37 Northcote Rd., SW11 (Clapham Jct./rail), 020-7924 7387
182 Clapham High St., SW4 (Clapham Common), 020-7622 4436

(continued)

Fine Line, The

1 Bow Churchyard, EC4 (Mansion House/St. Paul's),
020-7248 3262
124-127 Minories, EC3 (Tower Hill), 020-7481 8195
1 Monument St., EC3 (Monument), 020-7623 5446
10 Cabot Sq., E14 (Canary Wharf), 020-7513 0255
www.fullers.co.uk

☑ This "dependable" Fuller's chain is a "safe bet for a drink after work", offering a "good selection of wines" and "decent" pub fare in "clean-cut", "upmarket" digs; bashers find them about as "boring", "cold" and "soulless" as a bar full of "suits, suits" and more "suits" could be, but optimists see plenty of "pulling potential" here.

FireHouse

21 | 19 | 16 | £8

3 Cromwell Rd., SW7 (South Kensington), 020-7584 7258;
www.firehousesw7.com

■ Ostensibly members only, this "cool" South Ken spot also admits lucky mortals (provided they're "young" and "beautiful"), who can experience "different atmospheres" on two floors – while upstairs is more of a "bar" with "nude photos" as part of the decor, the downstairs is "clubby", and the only naked things on the walls are "exposed brick"; P.S. it "goes off till very late" (3 AM to be precise).

Fire Station, The

15 | 16 | 13 | £4

150 Waterloo Rd., SE1 (Waterloo), 020-7620 2226;
www.wizardinns.co.uk

☑ Set in a converted fire station, this "brash", "atmospheric" pub is usually "heaving" with "young people" quaffing ales and tucking into "good food", and it's also a "great place to meet" if you are heading for the South Bank and Waterloo; though the space is "huge", alarmists sound off that it can get "overpopulated" and "too-o-o loud."

Firevault

∇ 22 | 24 | 16 | £6

36 Great Titchfield St., W1 (Oxford Circus), 020-7580 5333;
www.cvo.co.uk

☑ A "most unusual place", this "cosy basement cavern" in Fitzrovia doubles by day as a fully functioning fireplace showroom, and by night it attracts a crowd of "advertising and design people" who imbibe "fantastic cocktails" "surrounded by modern fireplaces and furniture"; while some firebrands fume it's "not as hot as it thinks it is", most are cool with the "relaxed and sophisticated" atmosphere; N.B. booking is a must for the evenings.

First Out

∇ 17 | 15 | 17 | £3

52 St. Giles High St., WC2 (Tottenham Court Rd.), 020-7240 8042;
www.firstoutcafebar.com

■ After "many years", this gay and lesbian bar/vegetarian cafe in the West End "still has a refreshingly friendly feel", and its location near Centre Point makes it a "great central meeting place" as well as a "convenient pit stop" for shoppers; the meatless fare is "wholesome" and "nice" with "cocktails", though a few punters plead "please get draught beer"; N.B. no unaccompanied males are admitted on Girl Fridays between 8 PM–11 PM.

Fishmarket (Champagne Bar)   20 | 19 | 17 | £9
Great Eastern Hotel, Liverpool St., EC2 (Liverpool St.), 020-7618 7215; www.fish-market.co.uk
☑ A "class act", this champagne bar housed in Liverpool Street's Great Eastern Hotel is just the place to mark a "special occasion" or share some "bubbly with someone you love", as long as "you can bear the suits" who are legion or the somewhat "dull" interior; still, for many it's "worth a visit just so you can sneak a peek at the amazing hotel."

Fitzroy Tavern   17 | 13 | 14 | £3
16 Charlotte St., W1 (Tottenham Court Rd.), 020-7580 3714
☑ The pub that gave Fitzrovia its name, this Sam Smith's boozer is a local "old faithful", formerly the haunt of literati such as Dylan Thomas and now frequented by a "youngish" crowd from the nearby university and offices; reactionaries rail that it "used to have more atmosphere before it was modernised", but for many it remains a "class customer."

Flask   20 | 16 | 16 | £3
77 Highgate West Hill, N6 (Archway/Highgate), 020-8348 7346; www.theflaskhighgate.co.uk
■ A "favourite" of many, including William Hogarth in his time, this venerable pub (circa 1716) in "peaceful" Highgate becomes "enormously popular" once the sun appears, thanks to a "lovely open-air garden" that's perfect for a "lazy summer's evening"; while many wish it "could be transported to the end of my street", locals worry that it's being "spoilt by tourists."

Flask, The   20 | 17 | 19 | £3
14 Flask Walk, NW3 (Hampstead), 020-7435 4580
■ At this "authentically old pub" "in the heart of old Hampstead village", you can "watch the Six Nations" rugby matches on a large screen TV or just "soak in the traditional atmosphere" over pints of Young's beer; the space is "comfortable", with two fireplaces and "Victorian decor."

Florist, The   – | – | – | M
255 Globe Rd., E2 (Bethnal Green), 020-8981 1100; www.thefloriste2.co.uk
Though it professes to be a bar/lounge with cocktails, "authentic tapas", DJ nights and sofas, insiders regard this "tiny" watering hole "tucked away" in Bethnal Green as "a perfect pub" with "great atmosphere", but "not a great range of lagers"; though it's "often busy", the mood is usually "relaxed."

Fluid   20 | 16 | 17 | £4
40 Charterhouse St., EC1 (Barbican), 020-7253 3444;
www.fluidbar.com
■ A "hip" crew pours into this "quirky" "Japanese-themed"
"pre-club lounge" in Smithfields for Kirin on tap, sake and
sushi snacks as an "excellent" way to "get psyched" for
hitting the Fabric next door; for many, however, it's simply a
"relaxing place to hang with friends", with "funky upfront
music", DJs from Japan on Thursdays and kitschy old-
fashioned "video games."

Forum, The ⊟   ∇ 17 | 12 | 14 | £3
9-17 Highgate Rd., NW5 (Kentish Town), 020-7284 1001;
www.meanfiddler.com
■ Built in the '30s as an art deco cinema, this massive mecca
run by the Mean Fiddler group is a "bastion of good gigs",
including rock, alt and R&B acts, with club nights on
Saturdays; artwork by "unknown artists" adorns the bar
where there are "good Mills and Boon books to read",
though most are here only "for the music."

Founder's Arms   21 | 14 | 18 | £2
52 Hopton St., SE1 (Blackfriars), 020-7928 1899
◪ "Excellent views of the Thames" are the real "raison
d'être" of this Young's venue "near the Tate Modern",
although many appreciate the "yummy" beer, "cheap"
prices and "modern, airy" interior as well; detractors,
though, deride the "dodgy" design and grouse that the
scene becomes "too touristy in the summer."

Fox & Anchor   22 | 19 | 18 | £3
115 Charterhouse St., EC1 (Barbican/Farringdon), 020-7253 5075
■ One of the few places around where you can start the
day (or "end the evening") with a "superb" full English
"breakfast and a pint", this "ornate" Nicholson's pub
opens at 7 AM for workers from the nearby Smithfields
meat market; it closes at 7 or 8 PM and over the weekend.

Fox & Grapes   ∇ 23 | 18 | 19 | £4
9 Camp Rd., SW19 (Wimbledon), 020-8946 5599;
www.massivepub.co.uk
■ "A lot of dogs with their walkers" frequent this "lovely
little pub" "after a long walk" on Wimbledon Common for
"great wine choices" and "brilliant cheapish meals" from
a New Zealand–influenced menu, served in an airy, high-
ceilinged "fire-lit" interior with a "cosy" ambience; there
are also Sunday roasts at lunchtime.

Fox & Hounds   18 | 16 | 18 | £3
29 Passmore St., SW1 (Sloane Sq.), 020-7730 6367;
www.foxandhoundsbelgravia.com
■ The spirits now flow freely at this Young's "backstreet
pub" close to Chelsea's Sloane Square that once was the

remaining ale house (serving beer and wine only) not long ago; "reasonably priced food" is another plus, and while the space is "tiny", there's apparently enough room for locals and Sloanies alike.

Fox Reformed, The ▽ 19 15 17 £3
176 Stoke Newington Church St., N16 (Stoke Newington/rail), 020-7254 5975; www.fox-reformed.co.uk

■ "The village feel of Stoke Newington" is alive at this "excellent little wine bar" set in a Victorian building, where "some serious backgammon is played" and oenophiles can join 'Frills' (Fox Reformed Imbibing and Low-Life Society), a tasting club; though a few find the setting a bit "middle-aged and bohemian", for most it works as a "friendly" "one-off."

Freedom 20 17 17 £5
60-66 Wardour St., W1 (Leicester Sq.), 020-7734 0071

■ While some feel this Soho mainstay "still can't work out whether it's gay or straight", most agree it's a "slick and sexy", "high-energy watering hole for trendies" sporting a "relaxed but exciting" upstairs bar and a "sweaty basement dance floor"; a few feel it once "had more edge", but others note it's also "not as pretentious as it used to be."

Freemasons Arms, The 18 15 17 £3
32 Downshire Hill, NW3 (Hampstead), 020-7433 6811

■ "One of the nicest pubs bordering Hampstead Heath" say fans, this traditional old boozer is a "favourite for Sunday lunch", especially in summer, when the "gorgeous beer garden" comes into play; "good food", "cheap drinks" and 18 varieties of wine make it an attractive option "after (or before) a walk on the heath"; N.B. the basement is home to London's only remaining skittle alley, which is now open for play on Tuesdays and Saturdays.

French House, The 20 16 16 £4
49 Dean St., W1 (Leicester Sq./Piccadilly Circus), 020-7437 2477

■ You're "never short of a conversation" at this Soho "institution" "full of history" (past patrons include Charles de Gaulle and Dylan Thomas) where a "wonderful array" of "boozers and bohemians", "actors and writers and would-be actors and writers" prop up the bar, "mobile phones are banned" and there's "no music"; a few are *non*-plussed by the "ladylike" "half-pints" that are poured, but *amis* aver it's all just part of a "very different drinking experience."

Freud 21 17 16 £4
192 Shaftesbury Ave., WC2 (Tottenham Court Rd.), 020-7240 9933

■ Egoists exclaim "please don't tell anyone else about" this "sexy", "smoky den" in Covent Garden that "oozes character" with a subterranean space that's "like a good secret", attracting an id-iosyncratic bohemian clientele; there's nothing complex about the "lovely" service, and the "incredibly cheap" cocktails are the interpretations of many a drinker's dreams.

Fridge Bar
16 | 12 | 13 | £4

1 Town Hall Parade, Brixton Hill, SW2 (Brixton), 020-7326 5100; www.fridge.co.uk

■ You can boogie to music across the spectrum at this "funky, friendly" and "dancey" Brixton bar located next door to its eponymous sibling club; while it's often "crowded" and you may meet the odd "dodgy" character, pros promise a "grand time" nonetheless.

Frog & Forget-Me-Not
18 | 12 | 16 | £3

60 Selkirk Rd., SW17 (Tooting Broadway), 020-8672 6235
204 Dawes Rd., SW6 (Fulham Broadway), 020-7610 2598
32 The Pavement, SW4 (Clapham Common), 020-7622 5230

■ Fans of this trio find its "randomness" "inviting", from the "comfy" sofas that "make you want to cuddle" to "quiz nights" to "bar billiards" (at the Clapham branch); add to the mix "mean but inexpensive Thai" fare and "friendly service", and you have a "lovely pub" that many find hard to forget.

Fuel
18 | 16 | 16 | £3

Covent Garden, 21 The Market, WC2 (Covent Garden), 020-7836 2137; www.fuelbar.co.uk

■ A "good alternative" in Covent Garden, this spacious triple-decker is a "cool spot for a casual catch-up with friends", with "plenty of atmosphere" in a setting where it's "easy to carry on a conversation"; frugal types fume that it's "expensive", but for many it's "one of the safest bets for a late-night drink" in this area.

Funky Munky
19 | 16 | 19 | £4

25 Camberwell Church St., SE5 (Oval), 020-7277 1806

■ "Cheap drinks" and DJs and dancing until 2 AM at the weekends attract a "lively crowd" with a sizable student quotient to this "cool", clubby Camberwell dive; the space is "cramped" and the decor "could be updated", but the vibe is skater cool and the "happy hour rocks."

Garage, The ⌀
18 | 11 | 13 | £3

20-22 Highbury Corner, N5 (Highbury & Islington), 020-7607 1818; www.meanfiddler.com

■ There's "great live music any night of the week" at this "prototype indie venue" in Islington, a "crowded, hot and stuffy" showcase for rock, hardcore and alt acts, with club nights on weekends; the concrete floor space "would be a perfect setting for watching Motorhead."

Gardening Club, The
15 | 13 | 13 | £4

Covent Garden, 6-7 The Piazza, WC2 (Covent Garden), 020-7497 3154; www.rockgarden.co.uk

☑ "When you want a cheesy night" "partying with tourists" and "American students", regulars recommend this popular club below Covent Garden's Rock Garden restaurant; with "attractive bartenders", "cool decor", "Top 40 music" and an "awesome VIP room", pros puzzle "what's not to like?" – an "overcrowded, stiflingly hot" room, "long queues at the bar" and "dismal DJs" railers respond.

Garlic & Shots
14 | 12 | 13 | £4

14 Frith St., W1 (Leicester Sq./Tottenham Court Rd.), 020-7734 9505; www.garlicandshots.com

✔ "Vampires beware" of this Soho import from Stockholm where garlic shows up in everything, even "flavoured vodka" shots, and the space, decorated with coffins, skulls and spiders, is nearly as "scary" as the "goth" clientele; fans find the drinks and edibles "tasty" and the theme "amusing", but to foes, the whole thing "stinks."

Gate, The
19 | 17 | 16 | £6

87 Notting Hill Gate, W11 (Notting Hill Gate), 020-7727 9007; www.gaterestaurant.co.uk

✔ Some wonder whether this "lovely" Notting Hill venue "is a bar", thanks to the quality of the regularly changing menu of gastro-style fare; though cynics sniff at what they see are its "NYC" pretensions, and find it "not as good" as they'd hoped, it's usually "crowded", especially at weekends, and it's "great fun" for many.

G-A-Y BAR
17 | 14 | 14 | £4

30 Old Compton St., W1 (Leicester Sq.), 020-7494 2756; www.g-a-y.co.uk

■ A "F-U-N" time is in store for the "high NRG" young queer crowd that goes to "see and be seen" at this "out-and-proud" tri-level Soho bar/club with a "good vibe" and flat "TV screens showing music videos"; aficionados of "camp and pop music" affirm that it's "not too cruisy" (albeit decidedly "posy"), though some cynics suggest that it's "showing its age – a cardinal sin in the gay world."

George Bar & Restaurant
20 | 20 | 17 | £5

Great Eastern Hotel, 40 Liverpool St., EC2 (Liverpool St.), 020-7618 7300; www.great-eastern-hotel.co.uk

■ An "eclectic crowd" including "expat U.S. bankers" peoples the wood-paneling-and-glass interior of Sir Terence Conran's "great take on" the traditional bar in the City's Great Eastern Hotel; the historic building boasts "lots of history", and there's a "good but limited pub-grub" menu.

George Inn
23 | 22 | 13 | £3

77 Borough High St., SE1 (Borough/London Bridge), 020-7407 2056; www.georgeinn-southwark.co.uk

■ "A fantastic slice of history", this "lovely pub" in a "cobblestoned [City] courtyard" "near to Borough Market" is "owned by the National Trust" and is one of the "only galleried" "coaching inns left"; "traditional"-ists tout its "mulled wine in winter" and "live folk music" some nights, "but the real draw is the heavy old Tudor building itself", an "ancient" (16th-century) structure with "many small dark rooms" where the "wonderful" "Dickensian" atmosphere "is about as authentic as it gets."

Gipsy Moth
13 | 13 | 15 | £3

60 Greenwich Church St., SE10 (Cutty Sark), 020-8858 0786

☑ "Great for lazy afternoon drinking", this "spacious but busy" Greenwich pub attracts a "wide variety of clientele"; some complain that it's "overcrowded at weekends" "with tourists due to its location" near two famous vessels – its namesake, the Gipsy Moth IV yacht, and the 19th-century clipper The Cutty Sark – but most still say it's "one of the best in Greenwich."

Glasshouse, The
16 | 15 | 14 | £4

The Mermaid Theatre Bldg., Puddle Dock, EC4 (Blackfriars), 020-7248 5444; www.glasshouse-club.com

■ "If you're in that part of town" and fancy something "different", this Blackfriars bar/club and "central meeting spot" in the unlikely venue of the Mermaid Theatre might be just the ticket; each of its three rooms on two floors "has a different theme" and music, plus it offers "good views" over the Thames; N.B. party people appreciate that there's dancing till 5 AM on weekends.

Golden Heart, The
▽ 21 | 18 | 19 | £4

110 Commercial St., E1 (Liverpool St.), 020-7247 2158

■ In a prime position opposite Spitalfields Market, this "lively" spot boasts "lovely people" and "lovely staff", including legendary landlady Sandra Esquilant, who attracts the "arty crowd" that can be seen "propping up the bar"; it "can get pretty noisy" when things get going, but isn't that part of what makes a "good pub"?; P.S. despite reports to the contrary, it's "heart as in internal organ, not hart as in deer."

Good Mixer ⇗
▽ 13 | 9 | 20 | £2

30 Inverness St., NW1 (Camden Town), 020-7916 7929

☑ In the Britpop days of the '90s, this "indie rock heaven" in Camden Town was a home away from home for the likes of Blur and Suede; today, it continues to attract a "good mix of people" with its "easygoing and relaxed" vibe, though some detractors damn it with faint praise, declaring that it's "not bad."

GORDON'S
23 | 20 | 17 | £4

47 Villiers St., WC2 (Charing Cross/Embankment), 020-7930 1408; www.gordonswinebar.com

■ A visit to this "little wine dungeon" near Embankment tube is "like stepping back in time" for those who love its "brick-lined walls" and "candles stuck in old bottles"; the "down-to-earth" staff is "knowledgeable" about the *vinos,* the "huge chunks of cheese" sate appetites and romantics rave that the "quaint" atmosphere makes it an ideal setting for a "smoky rendezvous."

Gossips ⊅
∇ 16 | 11 | 12 | £4

69 Dean St., W1 (Tottenham Court Rd.), 020-7434 4480

◪ This Soho mainstay may be "a hole" with "hideous decor", "vile door staff" and "evil" bartenders providing "awful service", but it's saved from utter ignominy by its "excellent array of alternative nights" where some of London's more unusual characters groove to goth, electro, glam punk, New Romantic revivals and industrial music; besides, at least the punters are always "friendly", which is just as well, as this is a "small" venue.

Grand, The
– | – | – | M |

21-25 St. John's Hill, SW11 (Clapham Jct./rail), 020-7223 6523; www.claphamgrand.com

Enthusiasts "who remember the '80s and '90s" exclaim that "at least once in your life you have to visit" this "cheesy" south London classic sporting wall-to-wall chart hits and a "flashing dance floor"; after a recent revamp, it now also boasts black velvet–clad booths, three new bars and what is purportedly the UK's largest rear projection screen.

Grand Central
17 | 19 | 16 | £3

93 Great Eastern St., E1 (Old St.), 020-7613 4228; www.grandcentral.org.uk

■ Set in a converted bank, this "good Shoreditch choice" attracts "yuppies" and "nice ladies", but architectural aficionados also marvel at its "high ceilings" and "big windows looking out to the square"; as the name suggests, it aspires to an American style, reflected in the 30 bourbons on offer, though cocktails are the tipple of choice; N.B. early (or late) birds note that it opens at 8 AM.

Grand Union Public House
∇ 18 | 16 | 17 | £5

45 Woodfield Rd., W9 (Westbourne Park), 020-7286 1886

■ Most celebrated for its nosh, this gastro-pub is a sibling to next door Woody's and, as you might expect for the Notting Hill location, is designed in a sparse modern style and full of trendy trustafarians and media mafia types; drinkers reckon that it's at its best "in summer on the terrace overlooking the canal", although even enthusiasts can't help noting that "the view of the bus depot decreases the pleasure."

Grapes Public House
23 | 17 | 18 | £4

76 Narrow St., E14 (Limehouse/Westferry), 020-7987 4396

■ Squeezed onto the waterfront and now surrounded by swanky flats, this Limehouse pub circa 1583 was already a veteran when Dickens wrote of it in *Our Mutual Friend*; to this day you can enjoy a "great Sunday lunch by the fire in winter" with a pint of Adnams in its "cosy downstairs" "locals'" boozer, as well as "excellent fish upstairs" at its seafood restaurant with "fantastic river views."

Great Eastern Dining Room/ Below 54

21 | 19 | 16 | £5

54-56 Great Eastern St., EC2 (Old St.), 020-7613 4545; www.greateasterndining.co.uk

■ "A varied mix of people" including lots of "Hoxton types" "unwind and chill" on the "bean bags" and "comfy sofas" at this "cool hangout" in Shoreditch; those with an appetite can nibble on "excellent" Pan-Asian dim sum in the "upmarket" ground-floor bar, while revelers head downstairs for "great music" and dancing.

Green Man, The

15 | 12 | 14 | £3

Putney Heath, SW15 (East Putney/Putney Bridge), 020-8788 8096

◪ Once the watering hole of duellers and highwaymen (Dick Turpin reputedly hid guns upstairs here), this pub now attracts a more sedate clientele, mostly walkers from Putney Heath; there's an impressive beer garden for summer, and a recent Young's refurb has improved both the interior and the traditional menu.

Greenwich Union, The

– | – | – | M

56 Royal Hill, SE10 (Greenwich), 020-8692 6258

The one-and-only outlet for the "excellent beers from the Meantime Brewery", this Greenwicher with modern yellow-and-orange decor and "comfy armchairs" is mostly known for its brews, though "great tapas" in the evenings and live music on Mondays, Thursdays and Saturdays are also attractions; in summer, its beer garden and conservatory get crowded with both adults and children.

GRENADIER, THE

24 | 21 | 18 | £4

18 Wilton Row, SW1 (Hyde Park Corner), 020-7235 3074

■ Set "in a perfect mews street" in Belgravia, this "ancient and atmospheric" pub revels in "exceptional Englishness" and specialises in "fantastic Bloody Marys"; some sigh that it's "the worst-kept secret in town", as it's always "overcrowded", but those with rumbling tummies say that the "good restaurant" makes up for it.

Griffin

▽ 17 | 9 | 13 | £3

93 Leonard St., EC2 (Old St.), 020-7739 6719

■ This good old-style pub is an honest boozer with "a bit of edge to it", as well as what some music-lovers label the "best jukebox in Hoxton"; though it may be a "competitor in the grunge stakes", it's an option for a pint "away from the Shoreditch circuit", and fans reckon that it's "splendid for a few sharpeners before heading into town."

Ground Floor Bar

19 | 18 | 16 | £5

186 Portobello Rd., W11 (Ladbroke Grove/Notting Hill Gate), 020-7243 8701; www.firstfloorportobello.co.uk

■ One of the first in the area to gentrify, this "Notting Hill classic" is famed for its "comfy couches" and is handy for a post-Portobello pint as well as some good old-fashioned nosh; ground hogs say it's still "the only place to drink" in the area, so it's no wonder it attracts an "eclectic crowd."

Grouse & Claret, The   ▽ 16 | 15 | 17 | £3
14-15 Little Chester St., SW1 (Hyde Park Corner/Victoria), 020-7235 3438
■ Boosters of this "good backstreet pub" owned by the Hall & Woodhouse brewery (makers of Badger beer) say there's "nothing to grouse about when you've got a good ol' reliable hangout like this"; "tucked away" "in Belgravia", the "pleasant" premises are "nicely" kept, but they're also "small", meaning they're "usually busy."

Guinea   21 | 16 | 20 | £4
30 Bruton Pl., W1 (Bond St./Green Park), 020-7409 1728
■ With its "charming", "no-pretence" atmosphere, "nice" Young's beer and "great steak"-and-kidney pies, this "classic neighbourhood boozer" "hidden away" in a Mayfair mews near Berkeley Square appeals to locals and American tourists alike; though its restaurant is actually bigger than its "small bar", it's still "everything a pub should be", leading champions to cheer "long may this survive."

Ha!Ha! Bar & Canteen   16 | 14 | 15 | £4
6 Villiers St., WC2 (Charing Cross/Embankment), 020-7930 1263
43-51 Great Titchfield St., W1 (Oxford Circus), 020-7580 7252
390 Muswell Hill Broadway, N10 (Highgate), 020-8444 4722
www.hahaonline.co.uk
◪ "Always packed out", these chain triplets attract a core of young office types who swear that they're "fun"; some, though, complain that they're "soulless" and "nothing special", adding that they're "appropriate for after-work drinks" but "not the sort of place you'd spend all night in."

Halfmoon   18 | 15 | 18 | £3
93 Lower Richmond Rd., SW15 (Putney Bridge), 020-8780 9383; www.halfmoon.co.uk
■ Since 1963, this Putney mainstay has been a "great place to catch" "live music south of the river", and has seen performances from the likes of Bo Diddley, the Rolling Stones and Van Morrison; the bar itself is a large, light, traditional affair with wooden floors, and the beer comes from Young's.

Hamilton Hall   12 | 16 | 14 | £2
Liverpool St. Station, concourse, EC2 (Liverpool St.), 020-7247 3579; www.jdwetherspoon.co.uk
◪ The "extravagant decor" of this "vast Wetherspoon's" pub in Liverpool Street Station originally adorned the ballroom of the Great Eastern Hotel, and the chandeliers are still among its best assets; the location ensures that it's always "full of suits" and "far too busy" at commuter times, and the sheer size means it's "like having a drink in an aircraft hanger", but it nevertheless "does the job" for most.

Hand in Hand
19 | 16 | 17 | £3

6 Crooked Billet, SW19 (Wimbledon), 020-8946 5720
■ A "great summer boozer", this "country-style" Young's pub is particularly packed when the tennis tournament is on thanks to its prime location "just off Wimbledon Common"; commoners confide that it also does a "good Sunday lunch" and has "excellent burgers" to go with the bitters, leading lauders to label it a "fine" "favorite."

Hanover Grand ⊅
14 | 13 | 11 | £5

6 Hanover St., W1 (Oxford Circus), 020-7499 7977; www.hanovergrand.com
☑ Known for its "Friday night School Disco" (uniforms mandatory), this Mayfair club tends to be "full of hen-night" revelers and "drunk lads" downing "vodka and Red Bull"; some insist that the whole thing is "still good fun" "for a dance-and-drink night", but others find "nothing grand here", dismissing it as an "enormous pick-up joint" that's too "yesterday" and best suited to those who "have a desperate need to be 21 again."

Hare & Billet
17 | 13 | 15 | £2

1A Hare & Billet Rd., SE3 (Blackheath/rail), 020-8852 2352
☑ With views over Blackheath, this "old-style pub" was a staging post on the road out of London in days gone by, and it now lubricates locals with "good" brews accompanied by a "limited menu" that includes popular Sunday roasts; some are so attached they reckon it's a "shame to publicise it too heavily", though others lament the "lack of choice" resulting from a "much-clipped range of beers" lately.

Harlem
– | – | – | E

78 Westbourne Grove, W2 (Bayswater/Queensway), 020-7985 0900; www.harlemsoulfood.com
From the stable of DJ-producer Arthur Baker, this "way-cool Notting Hill" bar/diner/restaurant/club is praised for its "fantastic decor", "fun hip-hop", "great" soul food and "good drinks" such as its famous "fresh passion-fruit martinis"; "be prepared to queue", though, as it tends to get "ridiculously busy", and be warned that some "staff are not attentive" enough to suit all surveyors.

Hartley Bar & Dining Rooms, The
– | – | – | M

64 Tower Bridge Rd., SE1 (Borough/London Bridge), 020-7394 7023; www.thehartley.com
Taking its name from a now-defunct jam factory nearby, this smart new gastro-pub in Borough caters to the bright young things who moved in when the manufacturer moved on, serving hearty modern Euro fare paired with a robust wine list in an extremely red dining room; on Tuesdays it serves up jams of a different sort, with live classical guitar and jazz alternating each week.

...ern ☞
20-760...
...W14 (Hammersmith/Shepherd's Bush),

21 | 16 | 17 | £4

■ Offering "great" gastro-style food amid funkily sparse surroundings, this "truly outstanding local" in Shepherd's Bush is peopled with "plenty of beautiful (and well-to-do)" folks and "friendly" staffers that make for a "laid-back atmosphere"; though its popularity means it can get "too crowded", the only real downside is its cash-only policy.

Head of Steam
1 Eversholt St., NW1 (Euston), 020-7383 3359

19 | 16 | 21 | £2

■ Even if you don't have "time to spare at Euston", it's "worth taking a train anywhere as an excuse" to stop at this "train-spotter's paradise" that enthusiasts call "London's best station pub"; as befits the "handy location", "railway memorabilia" "adorns the walls", and a "wide selection" of "superb beers" (plus "real cider") "served by friendly staff" makes it "ideal for a pre- or post-journey drink."

HEAVEN
Villiers St., under the Arches, WC2 (Charing Cross), 020-7930 2020; www.heaven-london.com

20 | 16 | 14 | £5

■ A "mixed hetero"-and-queer crowd of "trendy young" things who are "up for a laugh and not taking themselves too seriously" pack out this "spacious" Soho venue, especially on the near-legendary Saturday nights; it's a "funny, informal" place that remains "exciting after all these years", and even though some reckon it's "oh-so-'80s" it's still the case that "hot boys go to heaven" for "the definitive gay London experience."

Hen & Chickens Theatre Bar
109 St. Paul's Rd., N1 (Highbury & Islington), 020-7704 7621; www.henandchickens.com

17 | 15 | 16 | £2

◪ Roosting below an "upstairs theatre" that's well known as a comedy venue, this "drinking hole" on Upper Street is "usually busy" and so has a "lively atmosphere"; some say it's "a bit grungy" and "smoky", but more are pleased by its "unpretentious", "facade-less" vibe, chirping that it's egg-sactly what they want.

Henry J Bean's
195-197 King's Rd., SW3 (Sloane Sq.), 020-7352 9255
273-275 Camden High St., NW1 (Camden Town), 020-7482 0767
www.henryjbeans.com

13 | 12 | 13 | £4

◪ With "reasonably priced" "bar food" "to accompany the drinks", these "loud and simple American-style places" attract a "lively, young and friendly crowd" of locals and "tourists"; they work as a "standby" for some, although sophisticates sneer that they're "tacky", "typical chain" outposts with "nothing unique about" them; P.S. the Chelsea branch has a "fantastic" "oasis" of a beer garden.

HERBAL
23 | 19 | 19 | £3

10-14 Kingsland Rd., E2 (Old St.), 020-7613 4462;
www.herbaluk.com

■ The "queues are getting longer" at this "fresh and innovative" Shoreditch club set in a high-ceilinged, high-windowed old warehouse made of exposed brick and oak beams; with big-name DJs and a "laid-back feel" that attracts a "chillin'" crowd (including the likes of Kate Moss and Jarvis Cocker), "there tend to be too many people", but that doesn't stop groupies from gushing that it's the place for "urban chic."

Highgate, The
– | – | – | E

53-79 Highgate Rd., NW5 (Kentish Town), 020-7485 8442
Set in an old warehouse near Parliament Hill in Kentish Town, this "excellent bar/pub" impresses punters with its "comfy seats" and "large space" done up in exposed-beam, post-industrial chic; it doles out "good drinks" and has a "superb" restaurant downstairs, making it a "nice place for a quiet drink" and a plate of fashionable fusion-y food.

Hill, The
18 | 16 | 17 | £6

94 Haverstock Hill, NW3 (Chalk Farm), 020-7267 0033
◪ Original Victorian stained glass and chandeliers create a "cool atmosphere" in which to sample the "good food" and other delights of this "brash, noisy, trendy and popular" gastro-pub in Chalk Farm; most agree that there's a "great feel" to the operation, though a minority moan that it's "pricey"; N.B. there's a beer garden for summer days.

hog's head
13 | 13 | 15 | £3

23 Wellington St., WC2 (Covent Garden), 020-7379 1807
11-16 Dering St., W1 (Bond St./Oxford Circus), 020-7629 0531
25-27 Wimbledon Hill Rd., SW19 (Wimbledon), 020-8947 9391
55 Parkway, NW1 (Camden Town), 020-7284 1675
77-78 Upper St., N1 (Angel), 020-7359 8052 ⇱
5-11 Fetter Lane, EC4 (Chancery Ln.), 020-7353 1387
12 Ludgate Circus, EC4 (Blackfriars), 020-7329 8517
1 America Sq., EC3 (Tower Hill), 020-7702 2381
Cowcross Place, EC1 (Farringdon), 020-7251 3813
171-176 Aldersgate St., EC1 (Barbican), 020-7600 5852
www.laurelpubco.com
◪ A "young professional crowd" of converts claims this "upmarket" group of "fun" taprooms impresses with "spacious" venues and "good atmosphere"; even those who find them to be "rather anonymous" and "only slightly better than the average chain pub" report that they're "usually redeemed by the quality of the beer."

HOLLY BUSH, THE
25 | 22 | 19 | £3

22 Holly Mount, NW3 (Hampstead), 020-7435 2892
■ "A Hampstead gem", this "historic", "quirky" pub started life as a 17th-century stable and reportedly hosted literary

luminaries including Johnson and Keats; with bare-plank floors, "homey, wood-panelled" decor, hand pumps for the beer and a coal "fire in winter", it has "real character", and the "upstairs has great dining, too", leading boozers to bless it as "everything a pub should be."

Holy Drinker
21 | 17 | 17 | £3

59 Northcote Rd., SW11 (Clapham Jct./rail), 020-7801 0544; www.holydrinker.co.uk

■ "One of the coolest" in the area, this "Clerkenwell-style lounge/bar in the heart of Battersea" offers a "nice change from chain pubs" with its "great [bottled] beers", "wicked cocktails" and a selection of 25 wines; the "cosy" vibe is abetted by "fireplaces to snuggle 'round in winter", though worshippers warn you'll have to "get there straight after work to get a table."

Home
18 | 18 | 15 | £4

100 Leonard St., EC2 (Old St.), 020-7684 8618; www.homebar.co.uk

■ Swanky leather sofas and loungey lighting add to the "dark and charming" vibe at this "grown-up" Shoreditch spot where a "glam crowd" dances to "groovy music" and foodies can partake of a "chilled weekend lunch" in the attached restaurant; its "trendy" rep notwithstanding, homies note that on many weeknights it's "suits a-go-go."

Hoop & Grapes, The
∇ 17 | 15 | 15 | £2

47 Aldgate High St., EC3 (Aldgate), 020-7265 5171

■ Customers have been walking through the wonky timber front door of this Shoreditch stalwart since 1598 – it's the only pub that survived the Great Fire of 1666 – and today it's an "unassuming" boozer "run by a good landlord" who serves "real ales" and cigars; regulars report they've "always had an enjoyable evening here."

Hope & Anchor
16 | 12 | 17 | £3

207 Upper St., N1 (Highbury & Islington), 020-7354 1312

■ "Where punk began" declare devotees about this classic Islington venue where the Sex Pistols met the Ramones, still attracting a "great" (seemingly "psychotic") crowd with "excellent" live music (followed by a DJ) in the basement nightly; though it looks a bit "shabby" after all these years, it's still "special."

House, The
– | – | – | E

63-69 Canonbury Rd., N1 (Highbury & Islington), 020-7704 7410; www.inthehouse.biz

As advertised, this laid-back "modern boozer" in Islington is "literally a house with a cosy fireplace and couches", where a "lively young crowd" and an "older but still groovy bunch" make themselves at home over "sensational" gastro-style fare in the restaurant; there's outdoor seating offering what sardonic surveyors call "spectacular views of a huge council estate and a busy road."

Hoxton Square Bar & Kitchen   23 18 16 £4
2-4 Hoxton Sq., N1 (Old St.), 020-7613 0709

☑ A "favourite on the arty scene", this "trendy" Hoxton hangout is "great for people-watching", attracting a "groovy crowd" with "squashy sofas", "excellent beer" and a "cool vibe" in a "fashionable", minimalist concrete-walled space; the "service doesn't keep up" with the rest of the place, however, perhaps because the staff seem to "think they're too hip to serve you."

HUSH   20 20 17 £8
8 Lancashire Ct., W1 (Bond St.), 020-7659 1500; www.hush.co.uk

■ A "beautiful bar" located somewhat aptly "behind Bond Street" (it's part-owned by Roger Moore's son Geoffrey), this "chic", yet "cosy" Mayfair affair is the "perfect dating spot" for a "posh and polished" clientele, with "cocktails on par with the best of London", "intimate nooks" that are "great for nuzzling" and a courtyard that's "absolutely divine" in "nice weather"; the hoi polloi, however, are shaken, not stirred, by how "expensive" it is.

ICA Bar & Cafe   19 14 14 £3
Institute of Contemporary Arts, The Mall, SW1 (Charing Cross/ Piccadilly Circus), 020-7930 3647; www.ica.org.uk

■ "Well worth" a day membership to the ICA near Trafalgar Square according to fans, this "hip venue" is a "funky" "alternative to more mainstream places" for "black-clad arty types with oblong glasses" ("piercings advised") where "something always seems to happen", including "great club nights" (though some of the music can be "downright weird") while it's "a bit expensive", the "convenient" locale and "late licence" to 1 AM make it a "favourite" during the week.

Ifield   19 18 18 £4
59 Ifield Rd., SW10 (Earl's Court), 020-7351 4900

■ A "funky mix of locals and hipsters" "hangs out" at this "smart and stylish" pub off the Fulham Road that boasts a "nice wine list" and "friendly staff"; "heads turn when you walk through the door" as people-watchers "look to see what celeb walked in", while less star-struck punters are content to come here for "a pint with the mates after a football game."

Imperial, The   15 12 14 £3
577 King's Rd., SW6 (Fulham Broadway), 020-7736 8549

■ "They keep the blue flag flying high" at this King's Road boozer that gets "very busy" on match days with a "football crowd" in the "mostly 20–35" age group that probably doesn't notice the curious nautical decor, complete with "mermaid montages"; even when it's "packed", though, it's "gloriously friendly" – as long as "you're wearing your Chelsea kit", boosters add with a wink.

Infernos
▽ 15 | 8 | 8 | £5

146 Clapham High St., SW4 (Clapham Common), 020-7720 7633;
www.infernos.co.uk

☑ For "no-frills boozing and flirting", this Clapham "meat market" is "fast becoming a favourite" for "twentysomething singles" "hankering after their student nightclub days", with music that's as "cheesy" as the pizzas on the menu and three "crowded", "sweaty" dance floors; for some, though, it's a "great place" only if you're "already drunk" and "can't remember making a conscious decision to go there."

Inigo
▽ 16 | 11 | 14 | £4

642 Wandsworth Rd., SW8 (Clapham Common), 020-7622 4884;
www.inigobar.com

■ "No excuses for an early night" at this Battersea "dive" that's "open later than most bars" "throughout the week"; it's a "dark and sweaty" scene with a largely "under-25", "Aussie and South African" crowd "getting down" to some "interesting" music, and "too lively to relax on the sofas"; P.S. insiders warn of "long queues after 11 PM."

Iniquity
– | – | – | M

8-10 Northcote Rd., SW11 (Clapham Jct./rail), 020-7924 6699;
www.iniquitybar.com

Yet another bar on the main Clapham drag of Northcote Road, this newcomer strives for an elegant, louche effect with a minimalist, modern interior with red walls and black leather seating that's unusual for the area; creative cocktails and a DJ get the crowd boogying by the end of the night.

Intrepid Fox ⌿
14 | 13 | 12 | £3

99 Wardour St., W1 (Oxford Circus/Tottenham Court Rd.),
020-7494 0827

■ "Goths, rockers", "heavy metal kids" and "old punks" gather at this "legendary" Soho pub that's also "popular with tourists" who come to gawk at the "scary-looking" clientele to "hardcore" music in the dark, "cramped" space; some find the staff, "covered in leather and piercings", "difficult to approach", but others find them "friendly."

Island Queen
▽ 15 | 18 | 15 | £3

87 Noel Rd., N1 (Angel/Old St.), 020-7704 7631

☑ Time waits for no one, not even this Islington boozer that once counted the Rolling Stones among its patrons in the '70s; still, while pessimists paint a black picture of a "weary local" that's "gone downhill", pros see a "lively" mariner-themed room that's "always packed" with punters who flock here for "real ale", pool and tunes from a "loud jukebox."

Isola
19 | 22 | 17 | £7

145 Knightsbridge, SW1 (Knightsbridge), 020-7838 1044

■ Maintaining a "balance of sophistication and relaxed cool", this "trendy", "atmospheric" Knightsbridge spot is a popular venue for "a cocktail after work" or sampling from a "fab wine list", including a "huge range of Italians", and "good nibbles" before dining in the restaurant downstairs; "spacious" quarters and a "sleek" decor add to the "nice feeling of decadence."

Jamaica Wine House
20 | 17 | 18 | £3

12 St. Michael's Alley, EC3 (Bank), 020-7929 6972; www.massivepub.com

■ A "cracking little City bolt-hole" "hidden down an alley", the "'Jampot'" (circa 1652) was the first of the famous London coffeehouses in the 17th century and fans say entering the "great building" is still "like going back in time" despite a recent renovation; serving a menu of luxurious sandwiches and "well-kept" beers, it's the "favourite" of many workers, who suspect that "more business gets done here than at the office."

Jamies
14 | 13 | 15 | £4

119-121 The Minories, EC3 (Tower Hill), 020-7709 9900
13 Philpot Ln., EC3 (Monument), 020-7621 9577
34 Ludgate Hill, EC4 (St. Paul's/Blackfriars), 020-7489 1938
50-54 Kingsway, WC2 (Holborn), 020-7405 9749
54 Gresham St., EC2 (Bank), 020-7606 1755
58-59 Poland St., W1 (Oxford Circus), 020-7287 7500
74 Charlotte St., W1 (Goodge St.), 020-7636 7556
www.jamiesbars.co.uk

◪ "One of the less unpleasant chains", this "dependable" wine bar group appeals to a "lively crowd" of "city bods" and "suits" thanks to "service with a smile", a list that includes 58 selections by the glass and "above-average" fare; "completely unremarkable" sniff cynics who remark anyway on the "overpriced" offerings and "dull" ambience.

Jazz After Dark
▽ 17 | 11 | 18 | £4

9 Greek St., W1 (Leicester Sq./Tottenham Court Rd.), 020-7734 0545; www.jazzafterdark.co.uk

■ A "cheap and cheerful" alternative to nearby Ronnie Scott's, this "relaxed" Soho spot showcases live jazz and blues acts six nights a week in a "tiny, intimate" space where you can order a full meal or tapas along with libations (including 30 varieties of cocktails); a few find the digs a bit "seedy", but those in tune with the "lively" vibe say it's "worth it for the music."

JAZZ CAFE
23 | 15 | 16 | £4

5 Parkway, NW1 (Camden Town), 020-7916 6060; www.jazzcafe.co.uk

■ "Chill and experience some real talent" at this "excellent" live venue in Camden for some of "the best jazz in London" according to aficionados, as well as blues, hip-hop and other acts; while the "crammed" setting and "uninspired decor" strike a few cracked notes, the layout "offers many choices for drinking, eating and enjoying the music", and those with itchy brothel creepers will be "dying to dance"; N.B. Fridays and Saturdays are club nights.

JD Wetherspoons
10 | 11 | 15 | £4

Victoria Station, Unit 5, Victoria Island, SW1 (Victoria), 020-7931 0445

☑ "You can't knock the prices" at this "safe bet" in Victoria Station for "a quick one on the way home"; while critics find the "crowded, noisy and smoky" scene "appalling", pragmatists pronounce it a "good value" and an "acceptable fallback" when "nothing else is available."

Jerusalem
19 | 17 | 14 | £4

33-34 Rathbone Pl., W1 (Tottenham Court Rd.), 020-7255 1120; www.thebreakfastgroup.co.uk

■ While some say it's "no longer the talk of the town", this large candlelit basement bar in Fitzrovia with "long wooden benches and mirrors" and "brilliant music" spun by DJs is still "great fun with a big group" and a "splendid place to avoid the fizzy drinkers"; "well-located" "in the heart of medialand", it sucks in a crowd of "hipsters" (including the occasional "C-list celeb") and "suits."

JERUSALEM TAVERN
25 | 23 | 20 | £3

55 Britton St., EC1 (Farringdon), 020-7490 4281; www.stpetersbrewery.co.uk

■ Representing the "diametric opposite of chic", this "snug and rustic" "gem" "feels like it's been there forever", and fans tout it as "one of the most atmospheric pubs" around; as the "only outlet in London" for the whole range of the St. Peter's brewery's "excellent" and "unusual" ales, it "makes Clerkenwell bearable" for many beer drinkers, but since it's open weekdays only, it "gets crowded" "once workers start spilling out of their offices."

Jewel
21 | 22 | 18 | £6

4-6 Glasshouse St., W1 (Piccadilly Circus), 020-7439 4990; www.jewel-bar.co.uk

■ A "beautiful place for beautiful people", this "huge hideaway behind Piccadilly circus" boasts a "glitzy look" featuring "velvety chairs, chandeliers", a "disco ball" and a "lounge feel"; live music, DJs and signature cocktails named after jewels all contribute to the "girls' night out" vibe, and revellers reveal it can get "crazy on a Saturday night."

Jim Thompson's
– | – | – | M

617 King's Rd., SW6 (Fulham Broadway), 020-7731 0999

A revamped menu of Thai fare and a refurbished space are attracting locals and tourists alike to this Chelsea gastro-pub on King's Road; for many, though, the main attraction is the spectacular array of bric-a-brac from Thailand decorating the room, including paper lanterns, Buddhas, puppets and other paraphernalia – which are all for sale.

John Snow
▽ 17 | 15 | 20 | £5

39 Broadwick St., W1 (Oxford Circus), 020-7437 1344
■ Regulars recommend this Sam Smith's boozer as "one of the hidden treasures of Soho", where you can "almost always get a seat, even on a Friday" and a "pint for under two quid"; the atmosphere is "cheerful" in the "cosy" space that still has some of its "original features" dating from 1850.

Jolly Gardeners
– | – | – | M

61-63 Lacy Rd., SW15 (Putney Bridge), 020-8780 8921
Until recently the preserve of old gents sipping pints, this Putney pub is the latest boozer in the area to undergo a makeover, with carpet and dartboards giving way to exposed wood and brickwork; it offers a good range of beers, including Old Speckled Hen and Hoegaarden, paired with a menu of modern European grub.

Jongleurs/Bar Risa
17 | 13 | 13 | £4

49 Lavender Gardens, SW11 (Clapham Jct./rail), 020-7564 2500
Middle Yard, Chalk Farm Road, NW1 (Camden Town), 020-7428 5929
Bow Wharf, 221 Grove Rd., E3 (Mile End), 020-8980 7874
www.jongleurs.com
☑ "Great comics" are what keep this "rowdy" but "grown-up" chain of comedy bars "always packed" according to fans – it's surely not the "cramped" digs, "nonexistent" service or "inedible" food, wags weigh in; P.S. the "very drunk" punters you may encounter in the audience are not part of the official "entertainment."

Jorene Celeste
▽ 17 | 17 | 19 | £3

255 Kentish Town Rd., NW5 (Kentish Town), 020-7485 3521
153 Upper St., N1 (Angel/ Highbury Islington), 020-7226 0808
■ Some hold up these Islington and Kentish Town siblings as "epitomes of a high-class English pub" with their "dimmed lights and funky artwork", while others see them as "back-to-basics" boozers "great for a quiet drink"; most all agree on the "pleasant" service and "good selection of mezze."

Julie's
22 | 20 | 19 | £5

135 Portland Rd., W11 (Holland Park), 020-7727 7985;
www.juliesrestaurant.com
■ "A gorgeous place to conduct the business of romance", this Holland Park/Notting Hill wine bar is one of "the most romantic spots in London" say surveyors smitten by the "elegant" atmosphere; it's also "one of the best places to relax" over "chatty drinks with friends", though it's "expensive" enough to make some wallet-watchers wince.

Junction Tavern, The
– | – | – | M

101 Fortress Rd., NW5 (Tufnell Park), 020-7485 9400
At this Kentish town gastro-pub, "fantastic" food is prepared in an open kitchen and served by "friendly, helpful" staff in a

space that boasts leather sofas and a fireplace as well as a conservatory for warm weather – in sum, a "great local."

JUST ORIENTAL
23 | 24 | 19 | £7

19 King St., SW1 (Green Park), 020-7930 9292;
www.juststjames.com

■ Fans feel justified in proclaiming this "inviting" St. James's bar the "grooviest after-work joint in the area", a "terrific venue" in a "beautiful setting" "to meet up for cocktails" and a "light bite" of Asian cuisine; the staff are "helpful" and "obliging", and the only quibble is that "it should stay open later."

Kabaret
20 | 14 | 13 | £6

16 Beak St., W1 (Oxford Circus/Piccadilly Circus), 020-7287 8140;
www.kabaret-london.co.uk

■ A "trendy" Soho staple that's "off the beaten track", this "tiny" spot attracts a crowd of "hipsters", including "some interesting celebs", wont to "dance bizarrely" to live rock or jazz acts when they're not chuckling at stand-up comics; while some find it "strange" (and "even stranger to get into") and in "desperate need of an interior refit", for many it's still a "nice, intimate venue" with "great atmosphere"; N.B. you have to be on the guest list to enter.

Kazbar
∇ 19 | 15 | 13 | £4

50 Clapham High St., SW4 (Clapham North), 020-7622 0070;
www.kudosgroup.com

■ The theme nights and daily happy hours (all day on Mondays) continue at this Clapham mixed bar, though it's no longer the camp heaven it once was; punters report that it's now a "lively, bustling music" venue bristling with video screens that makes for a "good pre-club" warm-up, and warn that it gets "really popular on Saturdays."

KEMIA BAR
24 | 24 | 18 | £7

25 Heddon St., W1 (Oxford Circus/Piccadilly Circus),
020-7434 4040

■ When you relax into the "Moroccan boudoir-style" cushions and take "a few puffs at the hookah, it's almost possible to feel you're in North Africa" at this "dark and sexy", "cavelike" Piccadilly member's club that caters to a "glitzy clientele"; the atmosphere is "amazing", but the "cavern" of a club is "immensely hard to get in" (it's open to nonmembers Mondays and Tuesdays only, and only when a live act is performing).

Kettner's
17 | 16 | 16 | £5

29 Romilly St., W1 (Leicester Sq.), 020-7734 6112;
www.Kettners.com

■ Aficionados aver "there's nowhere better for discrete liaisons" than this "civilised" Soho champagne bar that was originally set up by Napoleon III's chef in 1867 and later became a "haunt of Oscar Wilde"; with a "huge" selection of bubbly to choose from and "comfy sofas" highlighting the slightly "worn but superb" decor, this is "style in an old-fashioned way."

Kick
22 | 15 | 18 | £3

43 Exmouth Mkt., EC1 (Farringdon), 020-7837 8077
127 Shoreditch High St., E1 (Liverpool St./Old St.), 020-7739 8700;
www.cafekick.co.uk

■ European beer and "table football rule" at this kicking duo, an "entertaining change" where the theme is far more Beautiful Game than lager lout; "promotions early in the evening" get the ball rolling and it pours beers from footballing nations around the world; the Clerkenwell branch has a "very continental" feel, and you can enter monthly competitions at the Shoreditch sibling, which also hosts film nights every week.

Kingly Club
– | – | – | E

4 Kingly Ct., W1 (Oxford Circus), 020-7287 9300;
www.kinglyclub.co.uk

This Soho private members' club is located on the former site of the legendary Pinstripe Club, where Profumo met Christine Keeler and Oliver Reed and Peter O'Toole slaked their thirsts, but it's uncertain what they would make of this postmodern production with its video installations, glass bar, underlit white leather sofas and retractable roof; celebs are still on the menu, attracted as much by the cocktails (some 40 unique concoctions) as the spectacular interior.

King's Arms
∇ 21 | 20 | 20 | £3

25 Roupell St., SE1 (Waterloo), 020-7207 0784

■ If your "pub crawl" takes you to Waterloo East, regulars recommend stopping in to this 300-year-old "backstreet" boozer for "great beers and service" and no small amount of "charm"; three fireplaces keep things cosy in the winter and there's a conservatory for summer, as well as a courtyard for private parties.

King's Head Theatre ⊄
20 | 18 | 18 | £3

115 Upper St., N1 (Angel/Highbury & Islington), 020-7226 0364;
www.kingsheadtheatre.org

■ "Good ale" and "decent" live music create "a wealth of atmosphere" at this late-night Upper Street option preferred by a "varied" clientele of "luvvies" and "bohemians" for an "after-theatre pint"; it's retained its original Victorian pub trappings – lots of velvet and mahogany, working gas lamps and an "antique till" (they still charge in pounds, shillings and pence).

King William IV
20 | 18 | 18 | £3

77 Hampstead High St., NW3 (Hampstead), 020-7435 5747;
www.KW4.co.uk

■ A painting above the bar called 'Friends of Dorothy' depicts 60 years in the history of the Willie, a "large, attractive" Hampstead pub just a stone's throw from the Heath that claims to be London's oldest gay venue; it's a "relaxed, friendly" scene in comfortable surroundings with a beer garden, enlivened by cabaret shows and theme nights, and though there are always "lots of boys" at the bar, anyone is welcome.

Knights Templar ∇ 16 21 18 £3
95 Chancery Ln., WC2 (Chancery Ln./Holborn), 020-7831 2660;
www.jdwetherspoon.co.uk
■ You can "schmooze with barristers" at this Wetherspoon's boozer housed in a "cavernous" former bank "adjacent to the Royal Courts of Justice" that's "well worth a visit" for the "stunning", "wonderfully decorated" interior; "good value food and drinks" are served in the "light and airy" environs, though sometimes it can get so packed, there's "rarely enough staff to meet the demand."

Kosmopol 19 16 19 £8
138 Fulham Rd., SW10 (South Kensington), 020-7373 6368;
www.kosmopol.co.uk
■ A "trendy, funky bar" for "civilised people" on Fulham Road, this "small", "laid-back" spot run by a "personable" Swedish owner wins praise for "excellent cocktails" and a "good selection of flavoured vodkas" poured in sleek, "stylish" surroundings; there's a DJ on Thursday nights, and a bongo player on Fridays and Saturdays.

Ku Bar ⊅ 14 15 17 £4
75 Charing Cross Rd., WC2 (Leicester Sq.), 020-7437 4303;
www.ku-bar.co.uk
■ With a marathon happy hour that lasts from noon to 9 PM, this largely gay bar on Charing Cross Road gets "very busy", especially on weekends, with a "young and trendy" crowd, who throw back "great cocktails" under the watchful eyes of gay icons whose photos adorn the walls; cohorts coo it's "quite a ku for the neighbourhood."

Ku De Ta 14 18 17 £9
9 Glass House St., W1 (Piccadilly Circus), 020-7439 7771;
www.elysiumlounge.co.uk
■ Cronies crow that this cocktail bar perched above the Elysium Lounge off Regent Street works equally well as an opener before "heading downstairs for a boogie", a "big night out" by itself or simply for "after-work" libations; a "chilled-out" ambience and futuristic decor highlight the "great space."

Kudos 15 14 14 £4
10 Adelaide St., WC2 (Charing Cross), 020-7379 4573;
www.kudosgroup.com
■ "The name says it all" about this "cute, friendly" Covent Garden gay/lesbian spot (a sibling of Escape and Kazbar) according to partysans full of praise for Camp Cowboy

Karaoke on Mondays, speed dating and other theme nights, as well as endless cheap drinks deals and "helpful" staff; live jazz and a downstairs video dance bar also add to the "fun."

Lab
21 | 18 | 21 | £7

12 Old Compton St., W1 (Leicester Sq./Tottenham Court Rd.), 020-7437 7820; www.lab-bar.com
■ Devotees of this Soho cocktail crucible would "live there if [they] could" and "work [their] way through the best drink list in town", created by "attentive, helpful" and "entertaining" "professors" in a "funky" "retro" "basement bar"; though it can get "very busy", the "trendy, buzzing" ambience makes up for it; N.B. to guarantee entry on the weekend, call to get on the free guest list.

Ladbroke Arms
20 | 17 | 19 | £4

54 Ladbroke Rd., W11 (Notting Hill Gate), 020-7727 6648; www.capitalpubcompany.co.uk
■ "Quaint and busy" with a mostly regular, "attractive 30s and 40s crowd", this "unpretentious" "country pub in Notting Hill" is a "favourite" of many for its "beguiling" grub, solid wine list and selection of spirits that includes 58 whiskies and 20 brands of cognac; its "relatively quiet location" and outdoor terrace make it an "excellent" choice "in summer."

La Finca
16 | 13 | 15 | £4

185 Kennington Ln., SE11 (Kennington/Vauxhall), 020-7735 1061
96-98 Pentonville Rd., N1 (Angel/King's Cross), 020-7837 5387
■ "Good vibes" and a "real Spanish atmosphere" fill these twins in Kennington and Islington that amigos appraise as "some of the best salsa places in town", offering "dance lessons" as well as a tapas menu and happy-hour specials; the decor has recently received a boost, and many find the "cosmopolitan" scene inviting.

La Grande Marque
▽ 17 | 15 | 17 | £6

47 Ludgate Hill, EC4 (Blackfriars/St. Paul's), 020-7329 6709; www.lagrandemarque.com
■ "Definitely a City bar", this swish converted bank on Ludgate Hill offers a "good choice of champagnes" and some 100 wines, a lunch menu and bar snacks in the evening and occasional evening tastings; though the clientele is made up largely of suits, regulars report a scene that can get "rowdy and fun."

La Mancha
▽ 18 | 16 | 14 | £4

32 Putney High St., SW15 (Putney Bridge), 020-8780 1022; www.lamancha.co.uk
■ Surveyors report "wonderful experiences" at this "fab" Spanish tapastry in Putney serving "authentic sangria" and "good" small plates at the bar or at tables amid "comfortable" surroundings with a "lively atmosphere";

cineastes also find it an ideal option "for a snack before or after the movies" at the nearby cinema.

LAMB, THE
23 | 23 | 18 | £4

94 Lambs Conduit St., WC1 (Russell Sq.), 020-7405 0713; www.youngs.co.uk

■ This "old-style Victorian" watering hole in Bloomsbury "gets everything spot on" – the "superb", "beautiful" original decor (including cut-glass snob screens) that's still "in good repair", "nice food" and "good Young's ales", and a "charming", "chatty" atmosphere; "deservedly popular", especially with the "artistic" set, it's quite "possibly the perfect pub."

Lamb & Flag, The
21 | 18 | 16 | £3

33 Rose St., WC2 (Covent Garden/Leicester Sq.), 020-7497 9504

■ "Was that Charles Dickens who just walked in?" crack cronies of this "ancient" "traditional pub in the heart of Covent Garden" that's always "crowded" with a "diverse crowd", from "accountants" to "tourists", who quaff "excellent ales" and "delish bitters" in "small", "smoky" quarters with "plenty of nooks" and a "real old English feel"; it's "expensive" but "friendly", and many agree the "old 'Bucket of Blood'" (so nicknamed when it was a bare-knuckle boxing venue) has "never looked better."

Lamb Tavern
21 | 18 | 20 | £3

10-12 Leadenhall Mkt., EC3 (Bank/Monument), 020-7626 2454; www.youngs.co.uk

■ Housed in a listed building in the middle of Leadenhall Market, this "lively" Young's boozer is a great "lunchtime" or "after-work" option for those who work nearby, and "well worth a visit" for its "lovely", "traditional" setting and "good selection of bottled beers"; on a summer's evening, you'll find drinkers "spilling out into the market", though not later than 9:30 PM, when it usually closes.

Langley, The
20 | 19 | 16 | £5

5 Langley St., downstairs, WC2 (Covent Garden), 020-7836 5005; www.thelangley.co.uk

■ For many, a "perfect finish to a shopping day in Covent Garden" would be "margaritas and champagne cocktails" at this underground '70s theme bar; later it becomes a "groovy" "after-work" hang, and the "crowds arrive quickly" for one of the "best happy hours in town"; "cool music, cool booths" and a "friendly vibe" "appeal to the masses" as well as the "young, rich and beautiful", though a few haughty types huff over the "scrum of secretaries on the pull."

Lansdowne, The
21 | 17 | 17 | £5

90 Gloucester Ave., NW1 (Chalk Farm), 020-7483 0409

■ In ever-fashionable Primrose Hill, this "excellent" venue "with loads of class" was one of the original gastro-pubs, and 12 years on the "big tables" are still heaving with "tasty"

Modern British and Eclectic fare and "delicious homemade bread" and bottles from a "great wine selection"; the Sunday lunches are "fantastic" (it serves what some call the "best Bloody Mary in London"), and the "atmosphere" is "family"-friendly.

La Perla Bar & Grill   20 | 17 | 18 | £4

28 Maiden Ln., WC2 (Charing Cross/Covent Garden), 020-7240 7400
11 Charlotte St., W1 (Tottenham Court Rd.), 020-7436 1744
803 Fulham Rd., SW6 (Parsons Green), 020-7471 4895
www.cafepacifico-laperla.com
☑ Enthusiasts endorse this "low-key" veteran Tijuana trio for a "good dose of Mexican" fare ("amazing salsas", "quality enchiladas") and an "excellent choice of drinks", including "mean margaritas that'll have you falling over"; the decor may be a bit "cheesy", but the atmosphere is "festive" and the people are "friendly."

Latitude   18 | 17 | 15 | £7

163-165 Draycott Ave., SW3 (South Kensington), 020-7589 8464; www.latitudebar.com
■ "Better-than-average" libations, "dim lighting and plush furniture" and "friendly service" add up to a "winning combination" for a "date" at this "smart cocktail bar" in South Kensington that manages to create a "hip" setting with a "cosy" feel; insiders also recommend it as a "decent place for an after-work drink."

Lavender, The   20 | 15 | 17 | £4

171 Lavender Hill, SW11 (Clapham Jct./rail), 020-7978 5242
24 Clapham Rd., SW9 (Oval), 020-7793 0770
112 Vauxhall Walk, SE11 (Vauxhall), 020-7735 4440
■ The fare at this trio of brasserie/bars located around South London is "always of a super standard" and paired with a "nice wine selection", which is why some regard them as "more of a restaurant than a bar"; they're equally inviting, however, to punters looking for a "relaxed" "local place to hang out" and knock back a few "draught beers."

Leadenhall Wine & Tapas Bar   ▽ 13 | 11 | 14 | £4

27 Leadenhall Mkt., EC3 (Bank/Monument), 020-7623 1818
■ Many agree that there are few locations in the City better than "lovely" Leadenhall Market, where this "relaxed" Spanish-themed enoteca is ensconced; with its tapas menu and selection of wines, sherries and ports, it's "good at lunchtime", though like most establishments in the area, it gets "quiet in the evening."

Legion, The   – | – | – | M

348 Old St., EC1 (Old St.), 020-7729 4441
This trendified Old Street boozer is a "hit" with a loyal legion of Hoxton-ites thanks to "big picnic-style tables" that are "good for groups" and some "excellent food"; the

"great atmosphere" gets a boost from DJs and what partisans proclaim is "the best jukebox in the city."

LIBRARY, THE
26 | 25 | 25 | £10

The Lanesborough, 1 Lanesborough Pl., SW1 (Hyde Park Corner), 020-7259 5599

■ The "perfect backdrop for a leisurely drink", the "hugely civilised" bar of the Lanesborough hotel at Hyde Park Corner is "like a gentlemen's club, but with women", where "posh" patrons sup cocktails in a "sumptuous spread of rooms with book-lined walls and a fireplace" that's "especially good on a cold winter's day"; a "piano player" and "great barmen" who provide nearly "perfect" service add to the "refined, relaxed" atmosphere, and though it's only been around since 1992, it feels like a "classic."

Lifthouse, The
17 | 17 | 17 | £6

85 Charterhouse St., EC1 (Farringdon/Chancery Ln.), 020-7251 8787; www.lifthouse.co.uk

■ This "small bar with basic decor" by Smithfield Market is perhaps quieter than some of its neighbours, if not altogether "unremarkable", but fans report that it "manages to be quite cool" and "pleasant", serving "excellent" mezze and cocktails; it really rises to the occasion in the "summer", when the "French windows" open up.

Light, The
19 | 20 | 16 | £4

233 Shoreditch High St., E1 (Liverpool St.), 020-7247 8989; www.thelightE1.com

■ A "cool, cavernous feel" fills this converted Shoreditch power station, with "exposed brickwork" and lots of chrome to give it an "industrial" look, and while some find it "a little frigid", the "friendly staff" help warm things up; given its location, it can be overrun with "suits" in the week, while at weekends a more "chilled-out, trendy crowd" shows up, but even then the scene can still be like "a zoo."

Light Bar
22 | 22 | 18 | £7

St. Martins Lane Hotel, 45 St. Martin's Ln., WC2 (Leicester Sq.), 020-7300 5599; www.ianschragerhotels.com

◪ At the "über-cool" bar of the St. Martins Lane Hotel near Trafalgar Square, the "amazing" decor by Philippe Starck "makes you feel you're in a computer simulation", while the "great-looking waitresses in black Armani" (are they "moonlighting models"?) and "fabulous drink concoctions" do little to bring you down to earth; the "trendiest of the trendy" gravitate here, resulting in a predictably "posey" scene, and many find the "highly selective" door policy "outrageous" and "silly."

Lime
▽ 12 | 16 | 14 | £3

1 Curtain Rd., EC2 (Liverpool St.), 020-7422 0958; www.limeuk.com

■ The decor is the main pull of this club near Liverpool Street station, with zebrano-veneered walls, mini-screens displaying the menu and nightly specials and other unusual features; an extensive cocktail list and a menu of British and Mediterranean fare add allure, and while it can be "quiet during the week" when it's patronised mainly by City types, the DJ-driven club nights are "gaining a reputation."

Lincoln Lounge, The   ▽ 23 | 19 | 20 | £7

52 York Way, N1 (King's Cross), 020-7837 9339

■ "Battered leather sofas, a set of decks and a long bar" set the tone for this "friendly" King's Cross oddity that attracts "a nice crowd of unpretentious people" with DJs, art exhibitions and the occasional "live act"; regulars recommend it as a good place to "chill" before dealing with "that bastard at the door of your favourite night club."

LING LING@HAKKASAN   25 | 28 | 19 | £9

8 Hanway Pl., W1 (Tottenham Court Rd.), 020-7907 1888

■ Voted No. 1 for Decor in this *Survey*, this "beautiful" Bloomsbury bar "oozes class", with "dark-wood panelling and flattering lighting" and a "dark, mysterious" yet "funky" atmosphere; the "cocktails are wonderful", but "bring some bling" because they're "ouch-inducingly expensive", but if the "high prices seem to put off the hoi polloi", the "expats, tourists and hip Londoners" who frequent this "high-class venue" feel the "chic sophistication" is worth the price.

Living   ▽ 24 | 20 | 17 | £3

443 Coldharbour Ln., SW9 (Brixton), 020-7326 4040; www.livingbar.co.uk

■ "Flirt your socks off" and boogie to some "fun tunes" of the cheesy chart and funky house variety at the weekend at this Brixton mainstay on Coldharbour Lane; it's a "cool venue" with an undeniably "friendly atmosphere" fueled by cheapo cocktails and a 4 AM closing time on Fridays and Saturdays (2 AM the rest of the week), though it "gets hot upstairs when it's busy", which it usually is.

Lobby Bar   ▽ 24 | 26 | 21 | £8

One Aldwych, 1 Aldwych, WC2 (Covent Garden), 020-7300 1070; www.onealdwych.com

■ With a "lovely space", "wonderful drinks" and "very attentive staff", this venue in Covent Garden's One Aldwych hotel is "numero uno" in the eyes of fans; the setting is "classy" with "lots of energy", and while "tables can be in short supply", if you can get one "you feel like a celeb"; P.S. for "after-hours" drinking, you must be a staying guest.

Lomo   19 | 13 | 16 | £5

222 Fulham Rd., SW10 (Earl's Court/Fulham Broadway), 020-7349 8848; www.lomo.co.uk

■ Amigos advise "you'll want to "eat tapas to soak up all the wine" or "good sangria" at this Fulham bar, and that's no bad thing, since the food is "flawless" and "reasonably priced"; it's a "fun environment" for feeding and watering –

especially in summer when the windows open onto the street – though some gripe that "too often the tables are full" in the "tiny" space.

LONG BAR AT THE SANDERSON   22 | 24 | 17 | £8
Sanderson Hotel, 50 Berners St., W1 (Oxford Circus), 020-7300 1400; www.ianschragerhotels.com

◪ The decor by Philippe Starck is "just amazing" and the garden is "fantastic" at this "posh and elegant" bar in Ian Schrager's Sanderson Hotel in Fitzrovia, where a "jet-setting crowd" gather to "see and be seen" over a "wide range" of "yummy", "very expensive" cocktails ("take your mortgage advisor"); it can be "difficult to get a drink" ("that's 'Long' as in wait"), however, and cynics unmoved by the "hype and glamour" see it simply as a "pretentious" "pulling venue" for scenesters "attracted by wealth."

LONSDALE HOUSE   22 | 22 | 17 | £8
48 Lonsdale Rd., W11 (Notting Hill Gate), 020-7727 4080; www.lonsdale.co.uk

◼ Be careful not to "trip over the designer handbags" at this undeniably "girlie" but "achingly hip" bar frequented by a "typical" "well-heeled" "Notting Hill crowd" and a sprinkling of "poseurs"; it's an "outstanding lounge" and the "super swank, super style and super sophistication" will get you in touch with your "sexiest self"; P.S. some whisper that it's getting "hard to get in."

Loop, The   14 | 11 | 11 | £4
19 Dering St., W1 (Bond St.), 020-7493 1003; www.theloopbar.co.uk

◼ "*The* cheesy club in central London", this Mayfair late-nighter is a "big, noisy" venue where there's no shortage of "dancing"; it's "lively" during the week and even more so at the weekends (until 3 AM) when the "cavernous space" becomes a real "meat market", leading those in the loop to laud it as a "good pulling joint."

Lord Moon of the Mall   14 | 15 | 16 | £3
16-18 Whitehall, SW1 (Charing Cross), 020-7839 7701; www.jdwetherspoon.co.uk

◪ A "big, busy" "bargain of a pub" in a converted bank "right next to Trafalgar Square", this Wetherspoon's is a popular haunt for "Whitehall suits drinking on the cheap"; though the "basic" setting has about "as much atmosphere as the moon" according to critics, "good service", "plenty of guest ales" and lots of "space" make it a "decent" spot for locals "doing the tourist run with overseas visitors."

Lord Palmerston, The   ▽ 19 | 13 | 15 | £4
33 Dartmouth Park Hill, NW5 (Tufnell Park), 020-7485 1578

◼ An "excellent" gastro-pub with bare decor and light flooding in through huge windows, this Tufnell Park/ Archway venue serves "fantastic", "brilliantly cooked" dishes paired with selections from a "superb wine list"; the only gripe is that it gets "very, very busy", making it "hard to get a table."

Lord's Tavern Bar & Brasserie ━ | ━ | ━ | I
Lord's Cricket Ground, St. John's Wood Rd., NW8 (St. John's Wood/Warwick Ave.), 020-7266 5980; www.frontpagepubs.com
Following an extensive refurb by the Front Page group, this once exclusive bar at the Lord's cricket ground in St. John's Wood now appeals to a wider public, while keeping the old cricketing one; white walls and varnished wood create a bright, airy atmosphere and there's a greater emphasis on food, with a menu of Traditional British fare on offer.

Lounge ━ | ━ | ━ | M
56 Atlantic Rd., SW9 (Brixton), 020-7733 5229
Although this cosy, tile-fronted cafe/bar is located a stone's throw from what was the front line of the Brixton riots, it's arguably one of the most chilled bars in the area, attracting a mixed and thoroughly laid-back crowd for beers, coffees and snacks, plus live jazz on Wednesdays and DJs on Sundays; a late licence Thursdays–Saturdays also makes this a good addition to the weekend pre-clubbing scene.

Loungelover ▽ 25 | 29 | 19 | £8
1 Whitby St., E1 (Liverpool St.), 020-7012 1234
■ An "English country house on acid" is how dazzled fans describe the "fantastical" interior of this Shoreditch "destination" boasting such "surreal touches" as "six-ft. wine glasses with roses" and a "giant studio light by the gents'"; though some find the "cool" crowd a "little smug" and the menu "too pricey", fans "can't get enough of the cocktails" mixed by barmen who "make Tom Cruise look amateur"; P.S. cognoscenti caution "no booking, no seat" at the weekend.

Lowlander 17 | 17 | 19 | £7
36 Drury Ln., WC2 (Covent Garden/Holborn), 020-7379 7446; www.lowlander.com
◪ A "superb" selection of more than 50 draught and bottled beers, including Lowland treats such as geuze and Trappist ales, is the main attraction of this "authentic Belgian/Dutch cafe bar" in Covent Garden; the "wonderfully relaxed atmosphere", "table service" and authentic food ("good frites") add allure, though some gripe the "prices match the high ceilings", and at times it can get "smoky and loud."

Low Life ▽ 19 | 19 | 15 | £9
34A Paddington St., W1 (Baker St.), 020-7935 1272
■ Loyalists swear this little underground bar is "the best spot in Paddington", where you can down house cocktails in a space decked out with Persian carpets; mainly a music venue with lots of live bands and an open decks night on

when you can spin your own tunes, it's popular as both an "after-work" and pre-club option.

Lupo
16 | 14 | 13 | £4

50 Dean St., W1 (Leicester Sq./Piccadilly Circus), 020-7434 3399; www.lvpo.co.uk

■ A "cross between a pub and a wine bar", this Soho staple is a "nice low-key place to hang out", with a "relaxed, friendly crowd" and a "good, intimate atmosphere" created by many small rooms; early evening drink offers make for a "comparatively cheap after-work tipple"; N.B. it has a 3 AM late licence on Fridays and Saturdays.

Lyceum Tavern
19 | 15 | 20 | £3

354 The Strand, WC2 (Charing Cross/Covent Garden), 020-7836 7155

■ "Conveniently located" on the Strand, this "busy" Sam Smith's venue is perfect for Theatreland and Covent Garden, and it's also within striking distance of Fleet Street; "cheap" beer and home-cooked English fare are on offer and there are "two floors to choose from", with dining upstairs and a downstairs bar highlighted by cosy booths and stage memorabilia on the walls.

Madame JoJo's
20 | 14 | 14 | £4

8-10 Brewer St., W1 (Leicester Sq./Piccadilly Circus), 020-7734 3040; www.madamejojos.com

■ "Twisted old drag queens", "good cabaret" and buckets of "kitsch" await at this Soho classic that's "fabulous even if you're not gay"; all kinds of "beautiful, funky people" "groove right down to the floor" to "outrageous soul, funk and R&B" in the "intimate", slightly "shabby" space; N.B. the £37 cover includes food and entry to the Sound Republic club.

Magdala, The
∇ 18 | 15 | 17 | £3

2A South Hill Park, NW3 (Belsize Park/Hampstead Heath), 020-7435 2503

■ This "friendly" pub "tucked out of the way up a hill" opposite Hampstead Heath railway station is perhaps best known as the spot where Ruth Ellis, the last woman hanged in Britain, shot her lover dead in 1955; nowadays it dishes up "good food of the gastro-pub variety" from an upstairs restaurant, while the downstairs is divided into a traditional bar and a cafe-style room.

MANDARIN BAR
23 | 23 | 21 | £10

Mandarin Oriental Hyde Park, 66 Knightsbridge, SW1 (Knightsbridge), 020-7235 2000; www.mandarinoriental.com

■ By day a "playground for ladies who lunch" and by night a "singles hot spot" for "nouveau riche types" and the "see-and-be-seen crowd", this "very swanky" bar in the Mandarin Oriental in Knightsbridge is "worthy of splashing the cash" for "fun, whimsical cocktails", "yummy Chinese bites" and the experience of "being waited on hand and foot" in an "atmosphere of luxury"; in a word – "chic, darling"; N.B. there's a £5 cover charge after 11 PM.

Maple Leaf, The
14 | 13 | 13 | £4

41 Maiden Ln., WC2 (Charing Cross/Covent Garden), 020-7240 2843

■ Loyalists laud this Covent Garden spot as "London's premier Canadian bar", where "expats" and Yukonnoisseurs quaff Labatts and Molson, and "hockey junkies" are hooked by games on big screens in a "country tavern" setting; it's also "great on Canada Day" (July 1st).

Market Bar
▽ 18 | 17 | 15 | £5

240A Portobello Rd., W11 (Ladbroke Grove), 020-7229 6472

■ A chandelier, red walls and bare floors are part of the "unpretentious" environment at this Notting Hill bar that's popular among local "musicians and artists"; there's a DJ on Saturdays and a late licence on weekends, but aficionados advise it's best for "live jazz on a sunny Sunday afternoon."

Market Place
17 | 14 | 14 | £5

11-13 Market Pl., W1 (Oxford Circus), 020-7079 2020

■ "A great, relaxed place in the centre of town" from the owners of Cantaloupe and Cargo, this little DJ bar just north of Oxford Street in Fitzrovia "r-r-rocks" with "great music" and "buff babes"; the atmosphere is "appealing" in the small downstairs bar that's "decorated like a sauna" with bare wood walls, while the "outside spill-over area" is especially "nice on sunny summer days."

Market Porter, The
22 | 16 | 19 | £2

9 Stoney St., SE1 (London Bridge), 020-7407 2495

■ A "real ale festival in a pub" offering an "inspiring range" of 25 to 35 beers each week, this little "gem" of an old boozer "well-situated by Borough Market" is always "crowded"; with a 6 AM opening, it's "handy for breakfast" for traders and others who want to start the day with "a pint – or five."

Marquess of Anglesey
16 | 15 | 16 | £3

39 Bow St., WC2 (Covent Garden), 020-7240 3216; www.youngs.co.uk

■ Conveniently located, with "a great outlook on Covent Garden", this Young's pub is one of the "best options in the area" for a pre-opera tipple or other occasions; although some find the atmosphere downright "charmless" when it gets "very busy" with "tourists", "wooden panelling" and "friendly service" give it "loads of character", and for many punters, "reasonable beer makes up for" any glitches.

Marquis of Granby
17 | 14 | 15 | £3

51-52 Chandos Pl., WC2 (Charing Cross/Leicester Sq.), 020-7836 7657

■ "Refreshingly ordinary" amid all the "Covent Garden pretense", this "basic backstreet boozer" is for those who "prefer quieter venues", and though it's just a stone's throw from Trafalgar Square, it's "relatively tourist-free"; the "narrow" corner space is often "smoky and crowded", but it's "worth the squeeze" for "good pints, great nosh" and an "old-fashioned" ambience.

Marylebone Bar & Kitchen   20 | 16 | 19 | £6
74-76 York St., W1 (Marylebone), 020-7262 1513

■ "Lots of beautiful people" flock to this "cute" corner bar in Marylebone for a "good range of drinks" and a seafood-centric menu, served in "eccentric-looking" surroundings decorated with a '70s theme; "pleasant at lunch time", it can get "noisy and smoky" later in the evenings.

Mash   16 | 17 | 14 | £5
19-21 Great Portland St., W1 (Oxford Circus), 020-7637 5555

◪ This "large", "lively" bar/restaurant just north of Oxford Circus attracts "trendy suits" and "beer lovers" alike with "fantastic" cocktails and "quality" microbrews; open from early morning until 1 AM (with "no entrance fee"), it gets "buzzing" later in the evening, and the "lovely couches" in the "gorgeous lounge" and "funky music" motivate many to "stay until kick-out time", though critics complain that it takes on the aspect of a "huge, heaving pick-up joint."

Mason's Arms, The   ▽ 13 | 12 | 15 | £4
169 Battersea Park Rd., SW8 (Battersea Park/rail), 020-7622 2007

■ Located "on a main road" next to the Battersea Park overground station, this gastro-pub stalwart offers Modern European fare prepared in an open kitchen and served by "friendly" staff in a wood-floor space with "artwork displayed on the walls"; a "nice outdoor drinking area" adds allure when the weather is agreeable.

Matchbar   19 | 17 | 18 | £5
37-38 Margaret St., W1 (Oxford Circus), 020-7499 3443; www.matchbar.com

■ "Dependable" and "very cool", this Fitzrovia scion matches its similarly named Clerkenwell sibling with the same extensive and original list of "well-made cocktails" and food menu; you can "get a seat even at peak times" in the "stylish" space with "moody lighting", and the place really comes into its own in the summer "when they open the big windows."

Match ec1   19 | 19 | 18 | £5
45-47 Clerkenwell Rd., EC1 (Farringdon), 020-7250 4002; www.matchbar.com

■ With its late-'90s "vibe" and "NY feel", the Clerkenwell flagship of the Matchbar group is "still the best" in the eyes of many fans; "unbeatable" drinks by cocktail king Dale DeGroff, "surprisingly tasty" fare, a "pleasant" space with "plenty of seating" and "DJs not obsessed with volume" are all why it remains a "rare find."

Mean Fiddler 🚫   17 | 12 | 15 | £4

165 Charing Cross Rd., WC2 (Tottenham Court Rd.), 020-7434 9592;
www.meanfiddler.com

■ The original member of the Mean Fiddler group, this Soho classic is, for some, still "the best gig venue around", often showcasing smaller-name acts in the "cosy" space where it's "easy to see the stage" from all angles; retro-holics also recommend Saturday Atomic night, a "cheesy" '70s/'80s homage that's always "good value."

Medcalf   – | – | – | M

40 Exmouth Mkt., EC1R (Angel), 020-7833-3533;
www.medcalfbar.co.uk

Meat figures prominently on the menu of this spare and modern-looking Clerkenwell gastro-pub set in a converted turn-of-the-century butcher's shop, with fleshly delights such as black pudding and terrines on offer, along with a solid wine list and selection of beers, including one from the Meantime Brewery in Greenwich; the scene gets lively at weekend when a DJ starts spinning; N.B. no bookings.

Medicine   17 | 16 | 14 | £4

181 Upper St., N1 (Highbury & Islington), 020-7704 9536
89 Great Eastern St., EC2 (Old St.), 020-7739 5173;
www.medicinebar.net

☑ A "young", "easygoing" crowd, "solid DJs" spinning everything from "'80s pop to gangsta rap" and a no-suits policy make for a "good night out" at this bar/club duo; while some feel the newer, bigger Shoreditch location is "better than the Old Street" original, which looks a bit "well-used", defenders of the latter insist it's "still a winner", though the door policy is a bitter pill for critics (it becomes a "member's club when it suits them") who condemn them as "'kewl' in the worst way."

MET BAR, THE   21 | 19 | 17 | £8

Metropolitan Hotel, 19 Old Park Ln., W1 (Hyde Park Corner),
020-7447 5757; www.metropolitan.co.uk

☑ It may have "lost its magic" since its late '90s heyday when celebs came here to "brawl and interbreed", but the "oh-so-exclusive" bar of Mayfair's Metropolitan Hotel "still has snob appeal" and the feeling that a "lot of mischief might happen" (fueled no doubt by "top-notch cocktails") in the "cool, minimalist" setting; while some sigh that "no one goes there anymore" aside from "investment bankers" and "Z-listers", others feel that the lower star wattage "makes it nice again" – that is, "if you can get in."

Metro Club 🚫   ▽ 16 | 12 | 18 | £3

19 Oxford St., W1 (Tottenham Court Rd.), 020-7437 0964;
www.blowupmetro.com

■ "Smoky, dark" and slightly "scuzzy", this old warhorse of a Soho rock club, which once hosted the likes of Black

Sabbath, now showcases more contemporary bands such as the White Stripes and the Kills in its "small", "dingy" basement; the nightly acts range from Nu Metal to punk, and though the music is "exciting", the crowd can be "odd."

MILK AND HONEY   24 21 23 £8
61 Poland St., W1 (Oxford Circus), 020-7292 9949 ;
www.mlkhny.com
■ In Soho, the "area of trend-conscious but personality-free watering holes", this "oasis" is a "haunt for the refined" where you "don't have to shout to be heard"; the recipe is simple – "beautiful" cocktails that are arguably "the best this side of the Atlantic", a "serious wine list" and "classy" candlelit surroundings that are perfect for a "clandestine meeting"; N.B. non-members may book until 11 PM, but must be accompanied by a member anytime thereafter.

Millbank Lounge   – – – VE
30 John Islip St., SW1 (Pimlico/Westminster), 020-7932 4700;
www.millbanklounge.com
It may resemble a departure lounge, but this Pimlico newcomer is flying high, with the likes of the Black Eyed Peas and Radiohead spotted at the bar; its location, close to the Tate Britain and Millbank, means a curiously mixed crowd of arty folk and Labour Party apparatchiks, who gather over business class—pricey cocktails and snacks in funky, modern (and very rouge) surroundings.

Ministry of Sound   18 17 14 £5
103 Gaunt St., SE1 (Elephant & Castle), 020-7378 6528;
www.ministryofsound.com
◪ "Still the one" in the eyes of many, this "South Bank dance mecca" is a "landmark" on the London club scene that remains at the "cutting edge" with some of the "hottest DJs" around, three rooms and a "fab" VIP section; purists pan it as "way too commercial" and pooh-pooh the "meat market crowd", but for many it will always be a "classic end-of-night" destination.

Mint Leaf   ▽ 20 27 23 £8
Suffolk Place, SW1 (Piccadilly Circus), 020-7930 9020;
www.mintleafrestaurant.com
■ "Divine and original cocktails" in "beautiful surroundings" are the order of the day at this "swanky" Piccadilly addition that's "off the beaten track"; tipplers tout the "great staff" who know their sours from their slings ("they even know how to do a Peruvian Pisco Sour"), as well as the kitchen that dishes out "refined Indian cuisine."

Mistress P's   – – – I
29 North St., SW4 (Clapham Common), 020-7622 5342
Kitschy decor and all-year "Christmas lights" help create a "warm and cosy" atmosphere at this "welcoming" Clapham "hideaway"; karaoke nights, a weekly pub quiz and live

musical acts of various genres add to the attraction of this somewhat "eccentric" but altogether "proper pub."

Monkey Chews ▽ 23 21 19 £3

2 Queen's Crescent, NW5 (Chalk Farm), 020-7267 6406; www.monkeychews.com

■ "Who'd have thought Chalk Farm contained a little gem like this?" ponder punters who go ape for this unassuming den (the name derives from an old expression for being pissed) that's quite "possibly the darkest pub in London" with its subdued red lighting; hungry monkeys can chew on "good food" in the form of seafood and spit-roasted chicken from the open-plan kitchen; N.B. the top floor can be hired for parties.

Mook 14 14 14 £7

90 Notting Hill Gate, W11 (Notting Hill Gate), 020-7229 5396

◪ This "hip" bar near Notting Hill Gate tube station is "always packed" with a strange mixture of "beautiful people", Portobello Market shoppers and "tourists" who come for "drinks and relaxing, cool music"; foes find it about as exciting as a "bank branch" and popular only because it's the "first bar you see coming out of the tube", while advocates applaud it as a "great place for starting a night out on the Hill."

Moonlighting Nightclub ▽ 8 9 10 £3

17 Greek St., W1 (Leicester Sq./Tottenham Court Rd.), 020-7437 5782; www.moonlightingnightclub.co.uk

◪ Depending on your point of view, this long-running Soho nightclub is either "very tacky", "a bad '70s throwback" or simply "a hole with dirt cheap drinks"; despite this, though, it has its fans, especially on Wednesday's Cheapskates night, and the live soul events also attract a good following; N.B. no trainers permitted.

Morpeth Arms, The 19 17 19 £3

58 Millbank, SW1 (Pimlico), 020-7834 6442

■ Housed in a listed building (circa 1854) slap bang opposite the MI6 building and minutes from the Tate Britain, this "reasonable drinking hole" in Pimlico attracts a sundry crowd of artists and locals (and one 19th-century ghost); Young's beer, "quality pub food", an "excellent atmosphere" and patio seating are all part of its allure.

Mulligans of Mayfair ▽ 18 15 20 £4

13-14 Cork St., W1 (Green Park/Piccadilly Circus), 020-7409 1370; www.ballsbrothers.co.uk

■ A "good approximation of an oysters-and-porter Dublin bar", this Balls Brothers–owned Mayfair establishment serves up "fantastic Guinness" as well as modern Irish dishes from the downstairs restaurant in a "relaxed" setting; given the ownership, it's no surprise that many recommend going on "Beaujolais nouveau day."

Museum Tavern

17 | 17 | 15 | £4

49 Great Russell St., WC1 (Holborn/Tottenham Court Rd.), 020-7242 8987

■ A "great location" opposite the British Museum ensures that this "small" traditional Bloomsbury boozer is always "full of tourists" and "scholarly folk" "throwing one back" after assessing the antiquities; "decorated like something from an old movie about London" (think "mirrors and etched glass", carved wooden fittings) it has "lots of history" in its own right, having opened as the Dog & Duck 30 years before its august neighbour was founded in 1753.

mybar

∇ 15 | 15 | 17 | £6

myhotel, 11-13 Bayley St., WC1 (Goodge St./Tottenham Court Rd.), 020-7667 6000
myhotel, 35 Ixworth Pl, SW3 (South Kensington), 020-7225 7500
www.myhotels.com

◪ In keeping with the boutique hotels where they are housed, these "small, quaint" bars in Bloomsbury and Chelsea are designed and decorated according to feng shui principles; grounded groupies are gratified by the "classy quiet" settings where "you can sit down" and find your centre with a freshly mixed cocktail, while sceptics feel stifled in these places with "no atmosphere."

Nag's Head ⌿

18 | 17 | 18 | £3

53 Kinnerton St., SW1 (Hyde Park Corner/Knightsbridge), 020-7235 1135

◪ Though a TV is nowhere to be found and mobile phones are a no-no, the "famous" clientele quaffing "beautiful pints of Adnams" is "entertainment" enough for many at this Belgravia "oasis" where even the "grumpy owner" fits the "proper pub" profile; "good, reasonable food" and "'40s music add to a lovely Sunday afternoon" that in winter wanes into a "perfect eve by the fire."

Nam Long Le Shaker

17 | 13 | 16 | £9

159 Old Brompton Rd., SW5 (Gloucester Rd.), 020-7373 1926

◪ The "young, posh and loaded" "eye each other up" by the lights of their "fluorescent" cocktails at this "brokers'-night-out spot" attached to a Vietnamese restaurant in Earl's Court; the prices are "steep" and so are the "attitudes", but the "lethal" drinks "are bound to ensure a good night with your date"; just don't expect to get to know each other better until you exit – it's "far too crowded around the bar to have a conversation."

Narrow Boat

– | – | – | ┛

119 St. Peter's St., N1 (Angel), 020-7288 9821

A proper old man's pub, complete with strange "boat-themed decor", this Islington boozer is just the thing after a summer's stroll down the Regent's Canal; drinkers can sup their beers and take in the "great view" either from the "balcony" or from the towpath below and soak up the "super-cool vibe."

Narrow Street Pub
▽ 21 | 19 | 19 | £3

44 Narrow St., E14 (Limehouse), 020-7265 8931
■ Some of the food at this curious half-moon-shaped pub near Tower Bridge is so "good", it "needs to be tasted", particularly during the "great summer BBQs" at weekend on the "pleasant" patio; just beware the occasional "flooding" from the rising tides at this Thames-side locale.

Navajo Joe's
16 | 15 | 15 | £4

34 King St., WC2 (Covent Garden/Leicester Sq.), 020-7240 4008; www.navajojoe.co.uk
☑ After loading up on any of 214 tequilas, you'll need those "tasty munchies" to soak up the sauce at this "lively" Southwestern U.S.–themed watering hole in Covent Garden; the underlit marble bar is "great" for a margarita-fuelled "get together", but quiet birds prefer to catch the agave worm in the "upstairs" nest with an aerial view of the waiters "showing off their bottle juggling skills" for "hen parties" and "throngs of American students."

Na Zdrowie
22 | 13 | 22 | £4

11 Little Turnstile, WC1 (Holborn), 020-7831 9679
■ In the spirit of the "little" bar's moniker, "adventurous drinkers" say "cheers to this Polish place" while tipping back "rare imports" from "an unbeatable vodka list"; behind Holburn tube, it remains "relatively undiscovered" by "tourists", and if its "spare decor leaves a lot to be desired", "there are a few functional chairs and tables set up outside" for sipping and snacking on Eastern European bites (the "dumplings make ideal bar food").

New Foundry ⇱
– | – | – | I

86 Great Eastern St., EC2 (Old St.), 020-7739 6900; www.foundry.tv
Maggot racing, (maybe) masterpieces on the walls, "people arguing about historical materialism" and "Joni Mitchell on the stereo" give this Shoreditch one-off a "deliberately down-at-heel, bohemian" feel; it's "a complete dump in the best possible way" say fans of the converted bank that trades in "organic beer"; punters into punishment brave various "art happenings" and Sunday open-mike poetry.

19:20
▽ 18 | 21 | 18 | £5

19-20 Great Sutton St., EC1 (Barbican/Farringdon), 020-7253 1920; www.19-20.co.uk
■ More than just a "pool hall with a downstairs bar", this Clerkenwell spot gets a "bit packed" with a "pre-club" crowd stopping in for "sounds and drinks" as well as billiards in a sleek, bi-level space; romantics report that the "dark corners and interesting sofas" of the underground lounge make it an ideal rendezvous "to meet your date."

93 FEET EAST
22 | 19 | 16 | £4

150 Brick Ln., E1 (Aldgate East/Liverpool St.), 020-7247 3293; www.93feeteast.com

■ At the epicentre of "hip East London", this Shoreditch club/bar in the old Truman Brewery is the site of a "lively, trendy, young scene", with a "quirky" "up-for-it party crowd" grooving to DJ-spun "funky beats" and "cool tunes" on a "huge dance floor"; hard-core types hiss at "mindless" revellers nursing "alcopops", but if "dancing on the tables" is your thing, "this place hops"; P.S. for cineasts there are now "movie events" on Friday nights.

noble rot.
19 | 19 | 16 | £8

3-5 Mill St., W1 (Oxford Circus), 020-7629 8877; www.noblerot.com

☑ For "dancing and drinking" in "dark, dim" digs, punters plug this "boudoir-style" Moroccan-themed bar/club in Mayfair that attracts a "glitzy crowd" of "singles" "raging" on the "cool dance floor" or "making out" in "exclusive, comfy" "alcoves"; while some nobly insist that it's "still incredibly trendy and desirable", rotters rail about the abundance of "suited boys trying to be cool."

No. 5
▽ 22 | 26 | 23 | £7

No. 5, 5 Cavendish Sq., W1 (Oxford Circus), 020-7079 5000; www.no5ltd.com

■ The "very swanky" "scene of many celeb parties", this "fabulous" Fitzrovia venue in the former Spanish embassy is now a hotel with a restaurant, a nightclub, a roof terrace and three bars, including one for cigars; offering "great food, decor, music and cocktails all in one place", it's "expensive", but "worth it" for "plenty of room" to party "without losing cosiness", particularly if you book a suite and rave overnight.

North Pole
20 | 20 | 18 | £3

131 Greenwich High Rd., SE10 (Greenwich), 020-8853 3020; www.northpolegreenwich.com

■ A bipolar place with a sumptuous, ground-floor bar and a minimalist chill-out room called South Pole downstairs, this "great" "boozer" lures cool trekkers to an "out-of-the-way location" in the wilds of Greenwich; a "fun" DJ sets the range from UK garage and R&B, and there's "a restaurant as well", with live piano for a bit of balance.

North Star, The
– | – | – | M

188-190 New North Rd., N1 (Highbury & Islington), 020-7354 5400

Like an "old pub that has been Ikea'd", this Hoxton house has "lots of blonde wood" along its bar, in time-honoured gastro-style; it offers DJs, foosball and (surprise, surprise) "good food from a varied menu", including a hangover fry-up complete with Bloody Mary; sit outside on the terrace and search the night sky for its namesake.

Number 3 Bar

– | – | – | E

*3 New Burlington St., W1 (Oxford Circus), 020-7287 1991;
www.number3bar.co.uk*

Leather sofas, handcrafted wooden tables and candlelight do nothing to keep this "nice" Mayfair casbah relaxed during happy hour when it's so "crowded" with parched after-work drinkers that it's "hard to get served"; come weekends for smooth DJ sounds, or simply escape in your mind while sipping your number one, two or three drink.

Nylon

15 | 14 | 14 | £7

*1 Addle St., EC2 (Moorgate), 020-7600 7771;
www.styleinthecity.co.uk*

☑ "Suits for the boys and anything revealing for the girls is the dress code" at the "mother of all pre-clubbing pick-up joints", a "fabulously cheesy" paean to the '70s where "braying" "bankers eye up bits of fluff" after a hard week of money-counting; the "pretentious" joint is more than "verging on a cattle market", but "City types" are content to "co-mingle" and never mind the bullocks.

NYT

– | – | – | E

*Whitcomb Ct., WC2 (Piccadilly Circus), 020-7581 1158;
www.club-nyt.com*

Visits from the likes of Damon Dash, Jay-Z and 50 Cent have given this club just off Leicester Square a certain cachet that keeps it a cut above the surrounding tourist pits; it's "a proper club" that aims for NY style with a "good sound system, good DJs" and live MC-ing.

O Bar

13 | 11 | 14 | £4

83 Wardour St., W1 (Piccadilly Circus), 020-7437 3490

☑ If you're "looking for cheap beer and a younger crowd", this Soho spot is the place "to get messy in", where you can "dance, do shots and meet all types of characters"; it "feels like you can stay here forever", and you almost can, as it's open into the "wee hours" – in fact, you might have trouble wriggling out if you're "squished up against the wall" in the "American-style frat party" downstairs.

Oblivion

∇ 16 | 16 | 14 | £3

7-8 Cavendish Parade, SW4 (Clapham South), 020-8772-0303

☑ "Banish all reminders of the impending working week" at this Clapham club where "a fun crowd" "get hot 'n' sweaty on a Sunday afternoon to down 'n' dirty tracks"; "go early to get seats", and don't bring anyone with "claustrophobia", as the "funky bar with funky tunes" has gotten "too busy" lately.

O'Conor Don

18 | 16 | 22 | £4

*88 Marylebone Ln., W1 (Bond St.), 020-7935 9311;
www.oconordon.com*

■ "Wonderful Guinness" is the main call of this Marylebone bit o' Erin that's "more Irish and less theme than most", with a polished granite bar, lots of memorabilia and Gaelic grub that's "excellent" enough to "defy the oxymoronic jokes"; all this means it's "the place to be for St Patrick's Day", unless the holiday falls on a weekend when the "well-managed" place is reserved for private parties.

Office   14 | 10 | 13 | £3
3-5 Rathbone Pl., W1 (Tottenham Court Rd.), 020-7636 1598; www.officebar.co.uk
☑ The name's a no-brainer at this Fitzrovian sporting a "certain appeal if you've been drinking with work mates all day"; its cocktails "are not too exciting, but it can be fun when you're hankering" to pogo with a "student" to "a bit of '80s music" until 3 AM; P.S. the mice flee the "cheesy" joint when the cats take over on bank holiday Mondays for the lesbian party '100% Babe.'

O'Hanlon's   21 | 16 | 20 | £2
8 Tysoe St., EC1 (Angel/Farringdon), 020-7278 7630
■ The "best stout brewed in London" just might be at this "cosy", "old Irish pub" in Clerkenwell, "the real thing" for "live Celtic music", "good, homemade pub grub" and "pours from the O'Hanlon brewery"; "it's been traded up" by its namesake owner, "but the beers are still up to scratch", which means it's "very crowded seven days a week."

Oh! Bar   – | – | – | M
111 Camden High St., NW1 (Camden Town), 020-7383 0330
This Camden canteen adds a bit of welcome colour – notably a garish purple – to the sometimes drab NW1 scene; if it's "not very comfy", you can suffer some aches and pains for a 2 AM weekend cocktail; in the summer, reggae, drum 'n' bass and Brazilian beats from the DJs bounce out onto the street through the open front windows.

Old Bank of England   20 | 22 | 17 | £3
194 Fleet St., EC4 (Temple), 020-7430 2255
■ "Beer-swilling" "bankers" and "barristers" believe "somehow the beer tastes better knowing what the building was before" (the Law Courts branch of the Bank of England); transformed by Fuller's into a "superb" "flagship" with a "spacious" interior, it's "a stunning place to have a pint", and though it's "part of a chain" and "very after-work", it's "buzzing" with "character" and "lively individuality."

Old Bell Tavern   ▽ 19 | 19 | 21 | £3
95 Fleet St., EC4 (Blackfriars/St. Paul's), 020-7583 0216
■ "Not every pub has Christopher Wren as its principal architect" like this Fleet Street landmark, built after the 1666 Great Fire to slake the thirsts of labourers working on St. Brides Church; today it's a "good old-fashioned" with cask ale, a wavy wooden floor and "traditional" atmosphere that make it popular with local legal eagles and tourists.

Old Coffee House
▽ 20 | 18 | 19 | £3

49 Beak St., W1 (Oxford Circus/Piccadilly Circus), 020-7437 2197
◼ This "smoky" Soho staple has remained "unchanged" for as long as anyone can remember, with signed photos of (minor) celebrities and stuffed animals staring at your pint; despite the moniker, it's been a temple to booze rather than beans for some time now, and it's the beer (no cocktails) that pulls in advertising types "after work."

Old Red Lion
18 | 14 | 18 | £3

418 St. John St., EC1 (Angel), 020-7837 7816;
www.oldredliontheatre.co.uk
◼ There's been a pub on this Islington spot since the 15th century, and the current venue is attached to a theatre that produces "excellent", slightly offbeat shows, "especially comedians"; for fans it maintains a "certain sleazy charm", in spite of efforts to "tart it up."

Old Ship
20 | 18 | 19 | £3

3 King St., Richmond (Richmond), 020-8940 3461;
www.youngs.co.uk
◼ "A true alehouse" bang in the centre of Richmond, this "worn, warm old" Young's outpost "welcomes you with the feel of a pub of years gone by" (excluding the jumbo screen TV) and a "friendly environment"; a "mix of young and old" quaff "quality beers" and tuck into "good Sunday lunches" in a space with a maritime motif.

Old Ship
19 | 13 | 15 | £3

25 Upper Mall, W6 (Hammersmith), 020-8748 2593;
www.oldshipw6.co.uk
◼ A "wonderful traditional pub on the river", with parts of its 16th-century original building still intact, this Hammersmith stalwart is the place to "meet rowing types", especially on Boat Race day, over "good beer and food"; it gets "jam-packed" at any sign of the "elusive English sunshine", and if you can snaffle a "balcony" pew, it's the "perfect place" to be; P.S. it's also "fantastic in the winter next to the fire."

Old Thameside Inn
▽ 15 | 15 | 15 | £3

Pickfords Wharf, 1 Clink St., SE1 (London Bridge), 020-7403 4243
◼ Located next to the replica of Sir Francis Drake's Golden Hinde and backing on the Clink prison, this converted "old warehouse" commands "great views" over the river and St. Paul's; unsurprisingly, it can be a bit of a tourist trap, but local wage slaves also reckon that it's worth popping in for a pint "at lunchtime or after work."

On Anon
15 | 16 | 13 | £4

1 Shaftesbury Ave., W1 (Piccadilly Circus), 020-7287 8008;
www.onanon.co.uk
◾ Divided into separate "themed floors" (lodge, loft, lounge, booth, study and club), this "multiple-level" Piccadilly

"singles playground" "caters to many different tastes" or those who want "all kinds of music" in one night; opponents aren't likely to return anon to this "tourist central", due to a "meat-markety" vibe and "atrocious service", but defenders insist it's "the place to go with a crowd"; N.B. no trainers or sportswear allowed.

115 @ Hodgsons   ▽ 20 17 16 £9

115 Chancery Ln., WC2 (Chancery Ln.), 020-7242 2836; www.115.uk.com

■ "Barristers" and other legal eagles in search of a glass of wine or port from a "good selection of bottles" convene at this Chancery Lane bar/restaurant set in a 19th-century book auction house; "super-friendly staff" will "treat you like royalty" in "cool surroundings" that include a mezzanine lounge, sofas and a projection TV with an eight-ft. screen.

100 Club   21 14 17 £4

100 Oxford St., W1 (Oxford Circus/Tottenham Court Rd.), 020-7636 0933; www.the100club.co.uk

■ "Not much has changed" at this legendary "cool, secret club" on Oxford Street since it opened in 1943, attracting the likes of The Sex Pistols, White Stripes and Muddy Waters over the decades; it's "dark, dingy and smoky – in a good way", and you can take in the "heady scent of a bygone era" when "jazz-savvy OAPs" put on their "jitterbugging shoes" for live swing jams.

O'Neill's   13 12 14 £3

40 Great Queen St., WC2 (Holborn), 020-7242 5560
14 New Row, WC2 (Covent Garden), 020-7557 9831
2 Goldhawk Rd., W12 (Goldhawk Rd./Shepherd's Bush), 020-8746 1288
66 The Broadway, SW19 (Wimbledon), 020-8545 9931
326 Earl's Court Rd., SW5 (Earl's Court), 020-7244 5921
73-77 Euston Rd., NW1 (Euston/King's Cross), 020-7255 9861
87 Muswell Hill Broadway, N10 (Highgate), 020-8883 7382
65 Cannon St., EC4 (Cannon St./Mansion House), 020-7653 9951
31 Houndsditch, EC3 (Liverpool St.), 020-7397 9841
64 London Wall, EC2 (Liverpool St./Moorgate), 020-7786 9231

◪ "You know what you're going to get" at this "pervasive" chain of "faux-Irish" drinking holes – namely a crowd of "after-work drinkers" downing "cheap beer" and "hangover snacks" in a "homely" setting; bashers boo these "bog-standard" boozers lacking in "class or ambience" but full of "loud and drunk people" and, yet, "oddly", puzzled punters "keep coming back."

1 Lombard Street   19 19 17 £6

1 Lombard St., EC3 (Bank), 020-7929 6611; www.1lombardstreet.com

◪ A "smooth" "buzz" and a converted bank space with a "high ceiling" and glass dome are some of the assets of this "local hot spot" where you can mingle with "power lawyers, brokers and bankers from the City"; aggrieved auditors, however, find the scene surprisingly "loud" and "posy" for such an "old and refined" clientele.

190 Queensgate
20 | 19 | 17 | £7

Gore Hotel, 190 Queensgate, SW7 (Gloucester Rd./ South Kensington), 020-7581 5666; www.gorehotel.co.uk
■ "Trendy" tipplers tout this "hidden gem" in the Gore Hotel near Albert Hall as one of the "best stocked bars in London", offering "incredible" cocktails and "excellent house wines" in a "comfy and homely" setting replete with "polished wood" and "beaten leather sofas"; the "friendly staff keep the crowd real", but because it's "often crowded", regulars recommend "getting there early."

Opal
– | – | – | VE

L'Etranger Restaurant, 36 Gloucester Rd., SW7 (Gloucester Rd.), 020-7584 9719; www.etranger.co.uk
"If the *Flintstones* opened up a lounge", it would look like this basement bar located under Knightsbridge's L'Etranger restaurant, with its "rock walls" and "cavelike" feel; the "utterly charming" staff mix "mean cocktails full of fresh fruit" that promote a little bit of "hip-swaying" after 10 PM, when a DJ comes on, spinning a different genre each night; the whole experience is "entertaining", albeit "expensive."

Opera Tavern
▽ 16 | 14 | 15 | £3

23 Catherine St., WC2 (Covent Garden), 020-7379 9832
■ A "great location" in the heart of Covent Garden's luvvieland helps keep this "small" old theatre bar that dates back to 1879 "busy" with "lots of actors" seeking to refresh those thirsty vocal chords and groundlings in the mood for a pre- or après-curtain tipple; whether you're a player or not, it's a "fun option" "if you're around the piazza."

Opium
21 | 22 | 15 | £8

1A Dean St., W1 (Tottenham Court Rd.), 020-7287 9608; www.opium-bar-restaurant.com
■ A dark, "decadent lounge" where "gorgeous girls", Eastern-accented drinks and "stunning decor" rule, this Soho Vietnamese-style bar/restaurant is "usually packed and usually an experience"; for addicts, "great cocktails" and "delicious food" (albeit at "superstar prices") make it a "wonderful place to spend the night", while those who've kicked the habit see a "pretentious" scene with "often terrible" DJs, "not-so-great" service and posers in dire need of a "reality check."

Orange Brewery
19 | 14 | 17 | £3

37-39 Pimlico Rd., SW1 (Sloane Sq.), 020-7730 5984
■ Not long ago this pub on the Pimlico/Chelsea border was one of the few places in London to brew its own brands of beer, but since the brewery closed down, the "smart set

has moved on", and it's become more of an "old man's" local; it still sports a "lovely interior", and boosters tout it as "the best traditional boozer in this part of town."

Oratory, The
18 | 16 | 18 | £6

232 Brompton Rd., SW3 (South Kensington), 020-7584 3493; www.brinkleys.com

■ With an "upmarket" vibe and a "cheap" yet "lovely wine list", this "calm and not too crowded" Kensington bar/restaurant is a "quirky", "friendly" kind of place with "great food" that works equally well as a watering hole "after a day in the museums" or a "post-work" tipple, or as a "bistro" for a "romantic dinner."

Oscar
▽ 24 | 20 | 21 | £9

Charlotte Street Hotel, 15 Charlotte St., W1 (Goodge St.), 020-7806 2000; www.charlottestreethotel.com

■ Spectacular murals of contemporary British life are part of the "sophisticated surroundings" at the bar of the Charlotte Street Hotel in Fitzrovia; although it "can become crowded pre-dinner" with local media-crities taking a "quick after-work drink", the staff are "experienced" and the "fantastic cocktails" are "worth the wait", making this a "great place to gather", especially in summer when the crowd spills into the street; N.B. there are film screenings on Sundays.

Otto Dining Lounge
18 | 19 | 16 | £6

215 Sutherland Ave., W9 (Maida Vale/Warwick Ave.), 020-7266 3131; www.ottodininglounge.com

■ With its black leather banquettes, neon-green roof lighting and backlit bar, this "cool hangout" is "much needed" in Maida Vale according to locals; though the "service could be better" and some find the vibe a tad "pretentious", expertly mixed cocktails and DJs spinning until 1 AM Thursdays–Saturdays make it a "nice" option for the area.

Oxo Tower
22 | 21 | 17 | £6

Oxo Tower Wharf, Barge House St., SE1 (Blackfriars/Waterloo), 020-7803 3888; www.harveynichols.com

■ "Boy, oh boy, what a view!" exclaim enthusiasts of this "extravagant" South Bank tower where "fabulous cocktails" are mixed by "some of the best bartenders in the capital"; it mainly attracts a crowd of the "young" and "hip" and "suits", though the "romantic" ambience is "great for a date", and the vistas are perfect for "impressing parents" or "visitors"; for many, however, it's just "too expensive for a night out."

Oxygen
17 | 15 | 15 | £5

17-18 Irving St., WC2 (Leicester Sq.), 020-7930 0907; www.oxygenbar.co.uk

■ A "fad bar that's survived", this Leicester Square spot serves up shots of O2 with its drinks, in theory to get you drunk faster (one which sceptics find "ridiculous"); drinkers warn that if the "expensive" libations don't leave you gasping, the "smoky", "crammed-in" atmosphere "at the weekend" just might, but the service at least is "like a breath of fresh air."

Pacific Oriental
15 | 16 | 17 | £4

1 Bishopsgate, EC2 (Bank), 020-7621 9988; www.pacificoriental.co.uk

◪ Unusual for the City, this spacious Bishopsgate bar/brasserie serves "home-brewed" beers from an in-house microbrewery along with Pacific Rim cuisine in a stylish space divided into three rooms (with a restaurant upstairs), including a "cigar room" and a domed room; foes find it "hellishly expensive" for a place that's "nothing more than ok", but at least "it's easy to get served."

Paparazzi Cafe
17 | 15 | 15 | £6

58 Fulham Rd., SW3 (South Kensington), 020-7589 0876; www.paparazzigroup.com

◪ This "buzzy" South Kensington eating and drinking hole clicks with a "chic" "international crowd", thanks to "excellent drinks", "respectable" Italian fare and "live soul" and R&B (Friday–Sunday); negative types find it "too expensive for what it is" and wonder "why people go", while others have had some "unforgettable dates" here.

Paradise by Way of Kensal Green
21 | 16 | 17 | £3

19 Kilburn Ln., W10 (Kensal Green), 020-8969 0098

◼ One of the original gastro-pubs, this Notting Hill staple is a somewhat eccentric "refuge" housed in a circa-1800 building with a "cosy" bohemian atmosphere enhanced by fairy lights and unusual statuary; with such a "good" menu of seafood-centric fare, homebodies find it a "shame it's off the beaten track."

Pasha
20 | 24 | 21 | £8

1 Gloucester Rd., SW7 (Gloucester Rd.), 020-7589 7969; www.pasha-restaurant.co.uk

◼ "Harem cubicles on the ground floor", original Moorish doors and spice boxes create a "nice Arabic atmosphere" at this "impressive" and "beautifully different" Knightsbridge bar and eatery; "friendly" service makes it an "ideal" stop for some "cocktails and mezze" "with friends", while the niches and nooks and crannies are just the thing for a "snuggle."

Paxton's Head
13 | 14 | 15 | £4

153 Knightsbridge, SW1 (Knightsbridge), 020-7589 6627

◼ "Comfortable sofas" and a dark wooden bar help create the "atmosphere of a local" boozer at this three-floored Knightsbridge establishment, a favourite for "visitors who want to go native"; if you don't mind "tourists", "excellent value" Thai fare from the top-floor restaurant and "helpful" service make it a "perfect Sunday afternoon spot" for a "nibble and a pint."

Peasant
19 | 17 | 19 | £3

240 St. John St., EC1 (Angel/Farringdon), 020-7336 7726;
www.thepeasant.co.uk

■ Spectacular wine and beer lists and "fabulous" Modern Euro fare awaits at this "urbane" Clerkenwell gastro-pub with an upstairs restaurant; the atmosphere is "warm", especially in winter when the "roaring fire" gets going, but the most notable feature may be the "beautiful tiled floor" with a mosaic of St. George slaying the dragon.

Perseverance, The
∇ 20 | 19 | 18 | £4

63 Lambs Conduit St., WC1 (Holborn/Russell Sq.),
020-7405 8278

■ A "young version of a gastro-pub with a mixed crowd" of professionals and local students in the Bloomsbury area, this "atmospheric" boozer has managed to preserve its Victorian feel, right down to the wallpaper; regulars recommend it for Modern British eats and "a pint or two" in a "comfy, friendly" and quiet environment in which "conversations are possible."

Phene Arms
16 | 10 | 13 | £4

9 Phene St., SW3 (Sloane Sq./South Kensington), 020-7352 3294;
www.phenearms.com

◪ A recent revamp and the installation of Swedish chef Andre Wessman to the upstairs dining room, Alimente, means that this "excellent Chelsea local" has gone gastro, offering a 'cosmopolitan tapas' menu in the bar; while it still has a "fun atmosphere" and a "nice garden", some punters pale at the "uncosy interior" done in "pastel shades more suitable to a hospital ward", and wail "what the hell happened to this place?"

Pillars of Hercules
16 | 13 | 15 | £3

7 Greek St., W1 (Leicester Sq./Tottenham Court Rd.),
020-7437 1179

■ "Real cask ales", "decent bitters" and Belgian brews, but "no fancy beers" are served at this "cosy" "traditional pub" in the heart of Soho that has been around since the 1700s and earned a mention in *A Tale of Two Cities*; a favourite for literati in the '70s, it's no longer so bookish but "often packed" nonetheless and "friendly to all."

Pitcher & Piano
13 | 13 | 13 | £4

42 Kingsway, WC2 (Holborn), 020-7404 8510
18 Chiswick High Rd., W4 (Stamford Brook), 020-8742 7731
69 Dean St., W1 (Tottenham Court Rd.), 020-7434 3585
11 Bellevue Rd., SW17 (Clapham South), 020-8767 6982
871 Fulham Rd., SW6 (Parsons Green), 020-7736 3910
68 Upper St., N1 (Angel), 020-7704 9974
The Arches, 9 Crutched Friars, EC3 (Tower Hill),
020-7480 6818
28 Cornhill, EC3 (Bank), 020-7929 3989

(continued)
Pitcher & Piano
200 Bishopsgate, EC2 (Liverpool St.), 020-7929 5914
11 Bridge St., Richmond (Richmond), 020-8332 2524
www.pitcherandpiano.com
☑ "You know what you're getting" at this nearly ubiquitous chain of "reliable", "safe but sterile" High Street hangouts, though it's subject to differing interpretations: to fans, they are "roomy" spaces with "nice couches" and a "lively", "friendly" atmosphere – "just what a town pub should be"; detractors see a "noisy", "dreary" "meat-market" scene full of "horny secretaries" and "pissed and stupid" "suits" that "should be called 'Pick Up and Piano'" instead.

PJ's Bar & Grill
18 | 16 | 17 | £6
52 Fulham Rd., SW3 (South Kensington), 020-7581 0025
■ "Anyone who's anyone brunches here" boast boosters of this "upmarket" bolt-hole just "a few minutes walk from South Kensington Station" that attracts a "fun crowd" with "fantastic drinks" and "well-served" American fare; the atmosphere is "lively" but "civilised", and "good service" helps keep things "so-o-o relaxing."

PLAN B
26 | 23 | 24 | £4
418 Brixton Rd., SW9 (Brixton), 020-7733 0926;
www.plan-brixton.co.uk
■ This "awesome" "den" on the main drag in Brixton is "where the party is at" for a "very multicultural crowd" of pre-clubbers dancing to "amazing DJs" spinning hip-hop, house and more, fueled by a healthy selection of cocktails and spirits; fans "can't keep away" from what they call "da best" dance venue "south of the river."

Play
– | – | – | E
58 Old St., EC1 (Old St.), 020-7737 7090; www.playbar.co.uk
With its retro-chic decor of wood and leather and a '70s-inspired club area, this Clerkenwell venue draws a "young crowd" who come out to play on weekends until 4 AM; the "fun DJs" get things going with "good ol' house music" as well as cheesy '80s pop, and though it can be "really crowded" at times, it's usually "great for group parties."

Player, The
22 | 21 | 21 | £6
8 Broadwick St., W1 (Oxford Circus/Tottenham Court Rd.),
020-7494 9125
■ There's "something sexy about this place", a Soho members club from the Match Bar Group (Matchbar, Milk and Honey) in a "secluded basement" that's open to all until 11 PM, with "funky retro surroundings" (think "'70s airport lounge"); playas portray it as a "den of civility" that's "always busy, friendly and lively" and while it can be something of a "trendy-boy paradise", it's nonetheless "refreshingly free of attitude."

Plumbers Arms
▽ 16 | 13 | 17 | £4

14 Lower Belgrave St., SW1 (Victoria), 020-7730 4067

◪ Infamous as the pub where in 1974 Lord Lucan's wife rushed in to announce that he had just murdered their nanny, this "small local" nowadays is a popular stop for commuters and the "after-work" crowd; though it's "quiet" and "friendly", the jaded find it "uninteresting" but for the Lucan connection and sniff "you would expect more from a Belgravia pub."

Point 101
15 | 14 | 14 | £3

101 New Oxford St., WC1 (Tottenham Court Rd.), 020-7379 3112; www.meanfiddler.com

◪ With three glass walls, this "relatively fashionable", offbeat Soho bar "looks like a fish tank" and sits at the bottom of the Centre Point Building, catering to a clientele that's either "a little sleazy" or "down-to-earth", depending on who you ask; while the service can be "indifferent", the DJs spin "good music", but at the *fin du jour*, the "lack of cover charge and late licence are the main appeals."

Po Na Na
16 | 17 | 14 | £5

230-242 Shepherd's Bush Rd., W6 (Hammersmith), 020-7341 5300
82 The Broadway, SW19 (Wimbledon), 020-8540 1616
316 Kings Rd., SW3 (Sloane Sq.), 020-7352 7127
www.ponana.co.uk

◪ These "Moroccan-style" bar/clubs are "very cool places to see and be seen" for "uni types", "pretty teenagers and trustafarians", from the low-ceilinged Chelsea original to the Hammersmith venue that's as big as a "park" to the Wimbledon location with a Bedouin tent VIP room; souk-ceptics find them "overrated" and "way too sweaty", but there's never a shortage of "happy, smiling punters" dancing to "good music."

Pool, The
15 | 14 | 14 | £3

104-108 Curtain Rd., EC2 (Liverpool St./Old St.), 020-7739 9608; www.thepool.uk.com

■ Cue-nnoisseurs hustle to this "cool Old Street venue" for "a leisurely afternoon game" on the three American pool tables upstairs (you have to book in the evening); meanwhile, "the funky downstairs is always bumpin'" with DJs and a dance floor, and "beautiful people enjoying awesome cocktails"; N.B. it's got a late licence.

Pop
18 | 18 | 12 | £5

14 Soho St., W1 (Tottenham Court Rd.), 020-7734 4004; www.thebreakfastgroup.co.uk

■ A "big and colourful" basement bar and club that keeps the "great vibes" going until the early hours (3 AM in the week, 5 on Saturdays), this "retro, small, friendly and glam" Soho nightspot is full of "beautiful people", with the odd "celebrity spotting"; "by the end of the night the whole club turns into a dance floor", and though some hard-core types find the music "a little unoriginal and safe", the atmosphere is "fantastic."

Porterhouse
20 | 19 | 16 | £3

21-22 Maiden Ln., WC2 (Covent Garden/Embankment), 020-7379 7917
201A Castlenau, SW13 (Hammersmith), 020-8748 4486
www.porterhousebrewco.com
◪ A "Dublin bar fantasy for those who've never been there", these outposts of an Irish brewpub offer a "pleasant change from the competition", pouring "stunningly good" house brews that include "some of the best stout and porter in central London"; there are "lots of nooks and crannies" in the "massive", older Covent Garden branch, which may be why "you could grow a full beard waiting to get served" according to some whiskered wags.

Porters Bar
14 | 12 | 14 | £4

16 Henrietta St., WC2 (Charing Cross/Covent Garden), 020-7836 6466
21-22 Poland St., W1 (Oxford Circus), 020-7287 1817
www.porters-bar.com
◪ "Good beer, sensible prices and a pleasant atmosphere" win cheers for this "refreshingly unpretentious" duo owned by the Earl of Bradford, and pros prescribe a "seat at the bar" for the "funny bartenders who make the time fly"; while detractors deride them as "noisy", "tasteless" "money spinners for tourists", cronies consider them "safe bets."

Portobello Gold
19 | 17 | 17 | £4

95-97 Portobello Rd., W11 (Notting Hill Gate), 020-7460 4900;
www.portobellogold.com
■ "More upscale (and uphill) than many in Portobello", this "quirky little" Notting Hill boozer where Bill Clinton once downed a pint shines with "fabulous food" and "friendly service" in a "very hip" setting; a conservatory with a sliding glass roof adds to its lustre as a "summer venue."

Portobello Star ⊄
∇ 16 | 12 | 18 | £4

171 Portobello Rd., W11 (Ladbroke Grove/Notting Hill Gate), 020-7229 8016
■ Now under new ownership, this Notting Hillbilly close to the market is still "small, compact and bijou", with a "nice vibe" and a "good choice of beer"; the jukebox is still there, but it's been joined by a 42-inch plasma screen TV and a spiffed-up bar, part of a face-lift that may outdate the above Decor score.

Positively 4th Street
∇ 23 | 22 | 16 | £4

119 Hampstead Rd., NW1 (Warren St.), 020-7388 5380;
www.positively4thstreet.co.uk
■ A cross between a Prohibition-era "NY saloon" and a "Japanese kitchen", with "Sino-deco" design thrown in

for good measure, this Camden sibling of Monkey Chews is "enough to baffle anyone"; still, "it pulls it off" with a "friendly, intimate" bar and a "sweaty pit of a dance floor downstairs", which make it "a find" in an "unappealing part of town."

Potemkin
18 | 18 | 21 | £5

144 Clerkenwell Rd., EC1 (Chancery Ln./Farringdon), 020-7278 6661; www.potemkin.co.uk

■ Attached to a "great modern Russian restaurant", this light and airy tsar in the Clerkenwell firmament serves up an amazing selection of more than 130 "vodkas to knock your socks off"; the "unusual" bar food includes such authentic delicacies as pickles and stuffed dumplings, and while it's unlikely to herald a revolution, it's certainly "a revelation" to many.

Pride of Spitalfields ⊟
21 | 15 | 20 | £2

3 Heneage St., E1 (Aldgate East/Old St.), 020-7247 8933

■ A "little side street surprise" just off Brick Lane, this "traditional East End pub" drums up "lots of local trade" with its "good range of beers" and "interesting decor"; "artists" and others also find the "wooden-floor" setting "welcoming", adding to the eclectic "mix of people" who frequent this "great place."

Prince Bonaparte
21 | 16 | 16 | £4

80 Chepstow Rd., W2 (Royal Oak/Westbourne Park), 020-7313 9491; www.mitchellsandbutlers.co.uk

■ "Lively without being hectic", this "happening joint" in Notting Hill is a hit for those who want a "low-key" "midweek catch-up" over a "nicely drawn pint" and "good-quality" gastro-grub; come the weekend, though, the character changes and the open-plan space gets "loud and busy" with a "hip crowd" of "pre-clubbing power drinkers" and assorted "trendies."

Prince of Wales
∇ 16 | 16 | 17 | £3

38 Old Town, SW4 (Clapham Common), 020-7622 3530

■ The "unique interior" of this old-style Clapham boozer, stacked to the rafters with sundry bric-a-brac, adds to the "smoky", "classic pub atmosphere", and distracts from the "loud", "commercial" ("boring" to some) music in the background; regulars recommend it for the "afternoon", "after work or long into the night."

Princess Louise
20 | 23 | 17 | £2

208 High Holborn, WC1 (Holborn), 020-7405 8816

■ "One of the best examples of a Victorian pub in London", this "slightly out-of-the-way" Bloomsbury landmark is "worth a detour" for its "superior interior" of dark wood and etched glass and especially the "listed gents'"; it also wins praise for its "cheapish beer", courtesy of Sam Smith's, so it's no surprise that it's frequently "packed."

Princess of Wales ▽ 21 18 20 £3
1A Montpelier Row, SE3 (Lewisham/rail), 020-8297 5911;
www.mitchellsandbutlers.co.uk
■ "A nice boozer where you can chill with your mates" is
how stalwarts describe this "great neighbourhood place"
in Blackheath; punters praise the "ales that are in perfect
condition", and while it's "good in summer to sit outside", it
can get "crazy" due to its "proximity to the Common."

Prism 18 20 18 £6
147 Leadenhall St., EC3 (Bank/Monument), 020-7256 3888;
www.harveynichols.com
■ "After work" this "trendy" City bar gets "loud and busy"
as the "beautiful people flock" here for somewhat pricey
cocktails; located beneath its sister restaurant in the former
Bank of New York building, it sports an "amazing", "elegant"
interior accentuated with white leather seating, though
some quibble about the "acoustics."

Prospect of Whitby 21 19 17 £3
57 Wapping Wall, E1 (Wapping), 020-7481 1095
■ In business since 1522, this "fab riverside pub" in Wapping
has seen Henry VII, Captain Cook and Pepys, among
others, tipple under its roof, and you can still find "plenty
of characters at the bar" made from old ships' masts; it's a
"hidden gem" with a garden "overlooking the Thames",
though regulars rue that it's "firmly on the tourist trail."

Punch & Judy 14 11 12 £4
40 The Market, WC2 (Covent Garden/Embankment),
020-7379 0923; www.thespiritgroup.co.uk
☑ "Not the place for a quiet pint", this "busy, buzzy" Covent
Garden pub is a "great place to watch the world go by from
the balcony", which is why it's always "chock-a-block
with young tourists"; critics cavil that it's "overcrowded",
"overpriced" and the beer's "not very good", but "given
the location", it's a "must-go" for many – "but only once."

Punch Tavern ▽ 18 19 19 £3
99 Fleet St., EC4 (Blackfriars/St. Paul's), 020-7353 6658
■ "You can imagine the booze-soaked lunches of former
Fleet Street hacks" while quaffing a pint of "real ale" at the
aged City boozer that gave *Punch* magazine its name; while
it's still a "blast from the area's past" when it "was the media
capital", a recent renovation has given it a bit more spruce,
and now it's mostly local legal eagles who lunch here.

PURPLE BAR 24 27 20 £10
AT THE SANDERSON
Sanderson Hotel, 50 Berners St., W1 (Tottenham Court Rd.),
020-7300 1444; www.ianschragerhotels.com
■ "Opulence and excess swathe every inch" of this "very
intimate", "deliciously extravagant" bar in the lobby of the

Sanderson in Fitzrovia, arguably "the most glamourous place in town to enjoy a martini" (think "purple leather ceiling, couches and silk wall coverings"); "it's famously hard to get in", but if you do get past the "clipboard and big man who says 'No'", you feel "smug enough not to notice the dent in your wallet" that comes from ordering a "divine" but "frightfully" "pricey" cocktail.

Purple Night Club
18 | 12 | 12 | £5

Chelsea Village, Stamford Bridge, SW6 (Fulham Broadway), 020-7565 1445; www.purplenightclub.com

A "young Chelsea crowd" and a smattering of "celebs" (well, "footballers") "parties" at what some fans say is the "best nightclub in Fulham" (though admittedly "it has little competition"); while wet blankets wail over the "cheesy" decor and a scene so "tacky" you'll want to "drink yourself into oblivion", it nonetheless is always "very busy."

Purple Turtle ⇥
16 | 15 | 16 | £3

61-65 Crowndale Rd., NW1 (Mornington Crescent), 020-7383 4976; www.purpleturtlebar.com

"It's all purple!" cry perceptive punters who groove to this "fresh, funky" Camden bar that gets really "hot and crowded on Friday and Saturday" with an "interesting" crew of "students", "goths" and "cyber-punks"; cynics snort it's "not to be taken seriously" and a bit "painful to look at", but many go for the "excellent" alt music.

Putney Bridge
20 | 21 | 19 | £6

1 Embankment Lower Richmond Rd., SW15 (Putney Bridge), 020-8780 1811; www.putneybridgerestaurant.com

Overlooking the start point of the Oxford and Cambridge boat race, this Putney establishment is unsurprisingly "very popular" on a certain day of the year, though the "great river view" is not its only charm; "funky" and "chic", with decor more "elegant" than most Thameside watering holes, it's "one of the coolest places around", though a "local" and somewhat "snobby" clientele burns a few bridges.

Q Bar
18 | 18 | 18 | £6

12 New Burlington St., W1 (Oxford Circus), 020-7434 3949

Attached to an Italian eatery, this "cool little spot" attracts "a consistent Soho crowd" ranging from "a good mix of people" to an "almost all male" clientele, depending on the night; boosters bravo that it's "impressive" thanks to a wide range of music, two floors of bar space and a "dance floor downstairs" and upstairs.

Quaglino's
19 | 21 | 18 | £9

16 Bury St., SW1 (Green Park/Piccadilly Circus), 020-7930 6767; www.conran.com

"If you like Conran restaurants", then this "cavernous" St. James's restaurant/bar is "the pinnacle", with its white-and-gold "power '80s" interior and the perfect "sweeping staircase" "to make that entrance"; although for some it "stopped being cool a long time ago", it still pulls in a crowd of "well-dressed bankers and gorgeous girls", even if it's now diluted by some "passé" elements.

Queen Mary   ▽ 18 | 13 | 14 | £5

Waterloo Pier, Victoria Embankment, WC2 (Embankment/Temple), 020-7240 9404; www.queenmary.co.uk

■ Moored by the Waterloo Bridge on Embankment side, this "often-crowded" '30s ship with unique views of Old Man Thames and the South Bank is a "good setting" for "group gatherings" and "after-work drinking" in the summer; revellers are also "impressed that it has a late license" (2 AM on weekends), and queue-beaters can now ring up for a spot on the guest list, with guaranteed entrance between 8 and 9 PM.

Queen's Head ⊭   18 | 17 | 19 | £4

8 Flamborough St., E14 (Limehouse), 020-7791 2504; www.youngs.co.uk

■ "Tourists looking for olde England" and Londoners alike laud this "wonderful traditional pub" in Limehouse as a "perfect place for a Sunday lunch in winter", but it's probably "best in the summer, when you can sit outside" in the "good beer garden"; oh, and that pic of the Queen Mum pulling a pint that you see in the Young's pubs? – it was taken here.

Queen's Larder   – | – | – | I

1 Queen Sq., WC1 (Holborn/Russell Sq.), 020-7837 5627

The eccentric name came about because Queen Charlotte commandeered the basement of this Bloomsbury boozer as a larder for the King's food while he was treated nearby for one of his funny turns; nowadays, though, there's no hint of madness here – it's simply a "small" spot that's best "for a drink in the summer", when you can sip while taking a throne on the "outdoor seating overlooking Queen's Square."

Quinns   – | – | – | I

65 Kentish Town Rd., NW1 (Camden Town), 020-7267 8240

With perhaps the "brightest exterior in Camden", this "great pub" behind a blue-and-yellow facade makes hopsheads happy with a "great choice of Belgian" bottled beers, a similar number of German ales and draughts in the double digits; an additional bonus is that it's "open late", with "extended hours on the weekend" that keep things rolling until 2 AM.

Racing Page   ▽ 17 | 15 | 19 | £3

2 Duke St., TW9 (Richmond), 020-8940 4067; www.frontpagepubs.com

■ If you want "a friendly place to watch sport" and sink "a pint in often-lively surroundings", gallop to this "low-key" "locals' retreat" in Richmond, an outpost of the Front Page Pubs chain; "the collection of horse racing memorabilia is impressive", and there's also "good" Thai food that's "perfect to soak up the drink."

Rapscallion
▽ 21 | 19 | 21 | £4

75 Venn St., SW4 (Clapham Common), 020-7787 6555; www.therapscalliononline.com

☒ Located opposite the Clapham Picture house just off the Common, this venue is popular with a pre-cinema crowd and fashionable locals; most come for "excellent-value" Thai food, leading some to say it's "a better restaurant than bar", while others are put off by the "cramped" space "with people standing over you as they drink."

Red
– | – | – | M

(fka Bar Red & Restaurant)

5 Kingly St., W1 (Oxford Circus/Piccadilly Circus), 020-7434 3417; www.redsoho.com

English rococo meets urban Hoxton at this cocktail bar at the Carnaby Street end of Soho, but with low lighting, plush red couches and French-Vietnamese food, this is far nearer the Far East than the East End; the plush surroundings attract a crowd of well-do-do types from the local advertising and media factories who enjoy the unusual drinks (some of which are stirred for precisely six and a half minutes) until the welcome late closing time (1 AM).

Red Bar
▽ 20 | 19 | 20 | £6

Le Méridien Grosvenor House Hotel, Park Ln., W1 (Marble Arch), 020-7499 6363

■ A glass of "champagne or a Kir Royale is the drink of choice" at this "great" "hotel bar" tucked into Le Méridien Grosvenor House, where the "upscale" cocktails are delivered with "French flair"; being so "stylish", though, it's also "very expensive", and interlopers should note that only guests of the hotel are allowed after 11 PM.

Red Lion
21 | 18 | 16 | £7

2 Duke of York St., SW1 (Green Park/Piccadilly Circus), 020-7321 0782

■ "An unfooled-around-with English pub" of the "small, smoky and crowded" variety, this is "one of the few great locals left in the area"; the traditional decor and "good selection of beers" pulls in a mixed crowd of "residents", "labourers" and other "local workers", and it's so "popular" that "on nice days the crowd blocks the street."

Red Lion
▽ 22 | 18 | 17 | £7

48 Parliament St., SW1 (Westminster), 020-7930 5826; www.redlion-london.co.uk

■ "Don't be surprised if you bump into the odd" MP at this classic "politicos pub" right by Parliament Square and opposite the Treasury; built in 1900, it occupies a site that's hosted various public houses since 1435, and an earlier incarnation "inspired Dickens", as commemorated by his

bust gracing the facade; those in-th...
"upstairs is better than down", alth...

Red Lion
1 Waverton St., W1 (Green Park), 020-
■ A "cute little hideaway" in Mayfai... ...ming,
traditional" watering hole "tucked away... a quiet street"
is "everything an English pub should be"; it's "great for
after-work drinks" or a "weekend lunch", and the "relaxed
atmosphere" makes it a "pleasant" place to while away a
few hours; N.B. there's even a pianist on Saturdays.

Red Star
▽ | 16 | 17 | 18 | £6 |
319 Camberwell Rd., SE5 (Elephant & Castle/Oval),
020-7703 7779; www.redstarbar.co.uk
☑ "When in the South", stop by this Camberwell sibling to
the Dog Star and Living, suggest some surveyors who say
it's best appreciated for its "good music" ranging from hip-
hop and experimental bands to "'70s and '80s nights" (not to
mention the 4 AM license on a weekend); there's a young,
trendy and arty crowd, and regulars "love it", "sticky
carpets" and all.

Retox Bar
| 12 | 15 | 12 | £5 |
Covent Garden, The Piazza, Russell St., WC2 (Covent Garden),
020-7240 5330; www.retoxbar.com
☑ It "starts off quiet and gets noisier by the hour" at this
"sweaty, intense and fun" bar in the Covent Garden Piazza,
perhaps helped along by the "very good happy hours"
(members get discounted drinks) and the 3 AM closing on
weekends; it's "friendly" and "has a certain something" that
packs 'em in, though some moan it's "more for posing than
drinking" and complain that there are "no pints."

Retro Bar
▽ | 23 | 22 | 21 | £4 |
2 George Ct., WC2 (Charing Cross/Embankment), 020-7321 2811
■ A "trendy", "funky crowd" "keep going back" to this
"brilliant venue" in Covent Garden , a "spacious" bar with
"silver-and-pipes" decor and an "underground" locale
that "somehow makes it more cool"; it's great for "people-
watching" while "having after-work or pre-club drinks", and
nightly activities such as karaoke and a "weekly pop quiz"
ensure that the "atmosphere is friendly."

Revolution
| 17 | 18 | 15 | £5 |
2 St. Anne's Ct., W1 (Tottenham Court Rd.), 020-7434 0330
95 Clapham High St., SW4 (Clapham Common), 020-7720 6642
www.revolution-bars.co.uk
☑ Comrades credit these Soho and Clapham siblings ("part
of a successful [national] chain") for their "young, vibrant"
vibe and large list of cocktails created from some 30
varieties of flavoured vodkas; they get "noisy" and "crowded
at weekends" as the "large groups" descend, but those who
avoid the "meat market" report "a different atmosphere

ʁ", when one can better enjoy the "long couches"
funky music."

Rex Cinema and Bar
– | – | – | E

21 Rupert St., W1 (Piccadilly Circus), 020-7287 0102;
www.rexcinemaandbar.com
"The decor is phenomenal" at this Soho private member's
club, where you can "watch a movie with a beer" in the 75-
seat cinema that shows classic, current and pre-release
pics four times a week; the whole thing is "classy with a
nostalgic, vintage air", and though it's "expensive and
exclusive" it's also "fun"; N.B. closing time is 3 AM.

Richard I
▽ 24 | 14 | 21 | £2

52-54 Royal Hill, SE10 (Greenwich), 020-8692 2996;
www.youngs.co.uk
■ Although it's located in Greenwich, this "classic English
pub" is more a haunt of "locals" than tourists, being a short
walk up the hill; its two bars serve "quality Young's ales", and
though it "always seems to be nearly full", in summer the
crowd can spill out into the nice beer garden.

Rising Sun
– | – | – | I

61 Carter Ln., EC4 (Blackfriars/St. Paul's), 020-7248 4544
A spacious "standard boozer" on a Blackfriars backstreet,
this amenable pub tends to fill up after work; nights can be
busy when football matches are on the big screen, and
it's good in winter when you can sit by the fire; P.S. there's
also a "reasonably priced Thai restaurant upstairs."

RIVOLI BAR AT THE RITZ
24 | 26 | 23 | £11

Ritz Hotel, 150 Piccadilly, W1 (Green Park), 020-7493 8181;
www.theritzlondon.com
■ "Exactly what you would expect from the Ritz", this
"impressive" St. James's cocktail bar with an "art deco
design" is "beautiful", if a little "formal"; the predictably
"elegant and refined" clients are "all turned out" (gents
must wear jackets), but it's a "fun" experience, and the
"outstanding" staff will make "you feel like a million bucks."

Roadhouse
12 | 11 | 11 | £4

Covent Garden, The Piazza, WC2 (Covent Garden),
020-7240 6001; www.roadhouse.co.uk
☑ "Full of suits", "lots of youngsters" and "the occasional
minor celebrity", this Covent Garden club (with a handy 3 AM
license) is a "fun" option that can turn into a "veritable meat
market" of a weekend; "watching the antics" and "flair" of
the "friendly", "cute" bar staff are a bonus, and if you're
lucky you might catch one of the "rocking cover bands."

Rocket, The
– | – | – | M

11-13 Churchfield Rd., W3 (Acton Central), 020-8993 6123
"An oasis in the desert that is Acton", this gastro-pub serves
up the usual Modern European victuals (as well as "a few

unusual dishes") in "an excellent dining room" that "looks great without showing off"; drinkers are also impressed by the "excellent ales", but warn that it "gets full on a Friday – which shows how good it is."

Rockwell, The   20 | 20 | 18 | £8

Trafalgar Hilton, 2 Spring Gardens, SW1 (Charing Cross), 020-7870 2959; www.thetrafalgar.hilton.com

☑ Set in the Trafalgar Hilton, this "hotel lobby bar" has perhaps "the best selection of bourbons in London", with more than 100 available for drinking solo or in "wonderful concoctions"; DJs spinning Wednesdays through Saturdays help make it "trendy" and a "nice pace to lounge and unwind", and those "wanting a nightcap" appreciate its 1 AM closing time most nights; still, some are "annoyed" by the "expense" and "attitude."

RONNIE SCOTT'S   23 | 17 | 17 | £6

47 Frith St., W1 (Leicester Sq.), 020-7439 0747; www.ronniescotts.co.uk

☑ "For anyone who likes jazz, or thinks they want to", this is the "quintessential" venue, with "top-class musicians" playing what is arguably the "best [of its kind] in the UK" and possibly "in Europe" – so "who cares about the service or the food?"; be warned, though, "the crowd are there to appreciate" the "celestial music", and "woe betide you if you speak while the set is on."

Rose & Crown   ▽ 21 | 17 | 20 | £2

55 High St., SW19 (Wimbledon), 020-8947 4713; www.youngs.co.uk

■ This Young's venue in Wimbledon Village is a "nice traditional pub" that's "very popular" for its "lovely terrace" and "conservatory"; the service is "friendly" and the surroundings are "cosy" and "comfortable" – except when a certain tennis tournament goes on in June and things tend to get "lively."

Rosemary Branch   ▽ 19 | 15 | 14 | £3

2 Shepperton Rd., N1 (Old St.), 020-7704 2730; www.rosemarybranch.co.uk

■ At first glance, this "good local pub" in Islington may look "like any other", with the "usual range of drinks", but closer inspection reveals differences – it's "a bit cleaner" than most, it has a theatre upstairs, it hosts constantly changing exhibitions of sculpture, paintings, photographs and mixed media works by local artists and it offers "fun quiz nights" on Mondays and Tuesdays.

Royal Oak   ▽ 19 | 19 | 18 | £4

2 Regency St., SW1 (Pimlico/St. James's Park), 020-7834 7046

■ This straightforward boozer in Westminster is a simple old un-ruined watering hole with wooden floors and a sprinkling of eccentric local types; fans reckon that it's an "ideal" option in an unpromising neighbourhood.

Royal Oak, The
▽ 18 | 14 | 16 | £6

73 Columbia Rd., E2 (Bethnal Green/Liverpool St.), 020-7739 8204

■ With "cheap food, cheap beer and cheap decor", this somewhat "bizarre" but "exceedingly warming" Spitalfields boozer with a largely "gay clientele" is "guaranteed to make you feel" welcome; it opens at 8 AM on a Sunday "for the patrons" and traders on nearby Columbia Road flower market (not to mention "those riding the tail of an all-night boozing session!"), so "definitely pop in if you're in the area!"

ROYAL OAK
28 | 24 | 24 | £2

44 Tabard St., SE1 (Borough), 020-7357 7173

■ It may be "hard to find, but it's worth" the search to locate this "small, neighbourhoody" venue "on a backstreet" in Borough, again voted No. 1 for Appeal and Best Buy in our *Survey*; a true "classic", it also "happens to be the only pub in London" "selling the full range of Harvey's beers", along with "stupendous portions" of "wonderful traditional fare" "warmly" served by "friendly staff"; P.S. unfortunately, it "closes weekends."

Ruby Blue
– | – | – | E

(fka Red Cube Bar & Grill)

1 Leicester Pl., WC1 (Leicester Sq.), 020-7287 8050; www.rubybluebar.co.uk

With leopard skin booths, a slick lounge, bar and dance floor, this Leicester Square club is squarely aimed at those looking for an uncomplicated night of central clubbing; the 3 AM closing time and the location mean it's always going to be a trap for tourists and townies alike, though the focus on food (a mix of Indian, Chinese, Greek and Spanish) adds a civilizing touch and one that's unusual for the area.

Ruby Lounge
▽ 17 | 17 | 16 | £4

34 Lower Marsh, SE1 (Waterloo), 020-7928 9062
33 Caledonian Rd., N1 (King's Cross), 020-7837 9558
www.ruby.uk.com

■ For a "chill-out session", regulars recommend this duo of ruby-hued boozers in Islington and Waterloo where you can settle into a "leather sofa" with a "great cocktail" and some "delicious bar snacks"; resident and guest DJs spin an assortment of music from '80s to hip-hop, but some suggest they're best for "after-work" or just "to pass through."

Running Footman
▽ 14 | 15 | 14 | £4

5 Charles St., W1 (Green Park), 020-7499 2988; www.thespiritgroup.co.uk

◪ Pandering to tourists attracted by the name (taken from the title of a mystery novel), this "average-looking pub" offers T-shirts along with its traditional English beers and lagers; fans feel that its "non-trendiness" makes it a spot where "you can talk and actually be heard", though foes who find it "not very appealing" "only visit when everywhere else is heaving."

Rupert Street
20 | 15 | 15 | £4

50 Rupert St., W1 (Piccadilly Circus), 020-7292 7141; www.mitchellsandbutlers.co.uk

☑ "The place to see and be seen in Soho", this "busy gay hangout" attracts a "hip, good-looking crowd" of "gorgeous boys" mingling with "men in suits"; not surprisingly, it can be a "bit of a cruising ground", and some supporters say it's the closest thing to a "New York bar" this side of the Atlantic, but cynics slam it for having "more attitude than any other bar in London."

Salisbury, The
18 | 21 | 14 | £3

90 St. Martin's Ln., WC2 (Leicester Sq.), 020-7836 5863

■ "A grand gin palace at the centre of Theatreland", this "elegant" old Victorian pub boasts a "splendid interior" of mahogany, "etched mirrors" and an original marble-topped bar; with so much "good atmosphere", it makes a "great post-theatre rendezvous", so "its worth braving the noise and the crowds."

Salisbury Tavern
21 | 20 | 20 | £4

21 Sherbrooke Rd., SW6 (Fulham Broadway/Parsons Green), 020-7381 4005

■ Those who are sweet on this "upmarket pub" owned by Joel Cadbury (of chocolate fame) say it's "a fabulous spot to pass a few hours" relaxing in "cosy leather sofas"; the whole package, complete with 30 wines by the glass and an "amazing" attached restaurant dishing up Modern European nosh, goes down a storm with "a fun crowd of young Fulhamites."

Salmon & Compass
– | – | – | M

58 Penton St., N1 (Angel), 020-7837 3891; www.salmonandcompass.com

Perhaps as close as you can get to the underground in Islington, this "good" venue features "great" live funk and hip-hop some nights and DJs spinning all kinds of eclectic sounds most others; understandably, it attracts folks keen on boogying, but some make use of the extended licence and see it as more of a "late-night bar"; P.S. at press time, a second-floor space was planned.

Salsa!
16 | 14 | 13 | £5

96 Charing Cross Rd., WC2 (Leicester Sq./Tottenham Court Rd.), 020-7379 3277; www.barsalsa.info

■ It's no shock that this large underground joint on Charing Cross Road is "lively at all times", given that the "fun crowd" including "pretty ladies" (and some "old men") gets liberally lubricated with "tequila shots" and "Latin tunes"; though it's certainly "great for dancing" (you can even "learn salsa" at the "nightly lessons"), some warn it can get "sweaty" and "sleazy", so watch that you don't "get groped."

Salt Whisky Bar and Dining Room — | — | — | VE

82 Seymour St., W2 (Marble Arch), 020-7402 1155

A new addition to the Marylebone/Fitzrovia area, this "trendy place" with a chic, sleek, dark-walnut interior is so "intimate" that "the staff get to know your name and drink" – which might be one of the more than 200 whiskies and bourbons or "the best white chocolate martinis anywhere"; some sigh that it's "a bit quiet", but maybe that's what has attracted celebs such as the Coldplay boys.

Sanctuary Soho 18 | 17 | 17 | £6

4-5 Greek St., W1 (Tottenham Court Rd.), 020-7434 3323;
www.sanctuarysoho.com

☑ Catering for a mainly gay crowd, this "trendy-but-not-over-the-top" triple-decker in a "good" Soho location boasts a "real piano bar" where "player Carl Joseph creates a fun, camp atmosphere on Thursday, Friday and Saturday nights" tickling his bright white baby grand (while others "boogie downstairs"); still, some complain that it's too "expensive" and "not as busy as it used to be."

Sand — | — | — | E

156 Clapham Park Rd., SW4 (Clapham Common), 020-7622 3022;
www.sandbarrestaurant.co.uk

An "exclusive gem" round "the back of Clapham" (that's on the way to Brixton down Acre Lane to you and me), this Moroccan-accented venue offers "sublime cocktails", plus the chance to "play chess or backgammon", to the accompaniment of DJs – though for many the late license is attraction enough; there's also a restaurant serving Modern British fare and a members-only bar upstairs.

Scala 21 | 18 | 18 | £4

275 Pentonville Rd., N1 (King's Cross), 020-7833 2022;
www.scala-london.co.uk

■ This "fantastic venue" in King's Cross is "a really cool place to go" "to see hot bands (the sightlines are faultless)", catch an indie film or get busy on the "nice dance floor" to tunes spun by "friendly DJs"; it boasts three "plentiful, well-stocked bars" on multiple levels, all with "different styles", though the "colourful" crowd and "excellent" vibe make for a "fun" night on every floor.

Scarsdale 20 | 18 | 18 | £4

23A Edwardes Sq., W8 (Earl's Court/High St. Kensington),
020-7937 1811

■ A "great little neighbourhood find" in Kensington, this "cute place" offers a "good blend of modern and traditional" according to converts who coo over its "intimate", "woody" interior, "top food" and "amazing wine list"; though two fireplaces make it ideal for winter, many "especially like it during summer", when punters practically fight for the prized "outside space."

Scott's Penguin Bar
– | – | – | VE

20 Mount St., W1 (Bond St./Green Park), 020-7629 5248; www.scottsrestaurant.co.uk

Though it's been serving it up since 1851 (both before and after its 1967 relocation from Piccadilly to Mayfair), this Home House–owned bar impresses modern boozers with its "contemporary" feel; add in "friendly service, good cocktails" by "excellent mixologists" and a "dark, smart ambience" and it's "just what a bar is meant to be about"; P.S. the two "curtained booths" make "great hideaways."

Sekforde Arms
21 | 16 | 23 | £2

34 Sekforde St., EC1 (Angel/Farringdon), 020-7253 3251; www.youngs.co.uk

■ Expect no bells and whistles at this "old-fashioned" "traditional pub" "in a Clerkenwell side street", just a selection of "lively locals" and "excellent Young's beers" at "keen prices"; the "separate dining room upstairs" serves "substantial food" that's "superb in quantity, quality and value", leading admirers to insist that the overall experience is "not really what you'd call nightlife – more London life."

Sequel, The
– | – | – | M

75 Venn St., SW4 (Clapham Common), 020-7622 4222; www.thesequelonline.com

Next door to the Clapham Picture House and opposite Rapscallions (which is owned by the same people), this relaxed "cinema bar" features a selection of 70 wines, as well as a number of Belgian beers in bottles and Bitburger on draught; entertainment comes courtesy of a large video wall playing super-sized but silent versions of flicks.

Seven Stars
21 | 20 | 22 | £3

53 Carey St., WC2 (Holborn/Temple), 020-7242 8521

■ "Tucked directly behind the courts of justice" near Fleet Street, this "wee" "gem" (in business since 1602) is a "magical" place where "cook-proprietor Roxy Beaujolais" serves up some of "the best pub [fare] to be had in London"; "regulars" report it's "best at weekends when it's not so full of lawyers", while wags warn that "the stairs to the loo should be an Olympic event."

79CXR ⌹
13 | 10 | 17 | £3

79 Charing Cross Rd., WC2 (Leicester Sq.), 020-7734 0769

◪ A "great late-night stop for a pint" and some "wonderful people-watching", this "very cruisy", slightly "sleazy" gay haunt on Charing Cross Road is "always popular and busy" with a "decent-looking crowd"; the digs, by contrast, are "not much to look at" attest those who can see in the dark, but thanks to the "friendly" "good vibes", one can "get caught up quite easily in a fun night."

Shadow Lounge   20 | 21 | 16 | £6
5 Brewer St., W1 (Piccadilly Circus), 020-7287 7988;
www.theshadowlounge.co.uk
☑ It's "fun to watch" the "beautiful crowd" of "classy gays",
both garden variety and "celebs", at this Soho members
club where the bar's open to the public; still, some complain
that it's so "packed" it can be "hard to get drinks" (tip: "get
one of the bus boys to look after you"), while others claim
that it's "full of attitude", observing that "all that glitters is
not necessarily nice."

Shepherd's Tavern   ▽ 16 | 15 | 15 | £6
50 Hertford St., W1 (Green Park/Hyde Park Corner), 020-7499 3017
☑ Set on the site of the ancient Shepherd's Market, this
somewhat "plain" pub "brings a sense of history" to the
now rather less than idyllic locale of Mayfair; with its "great
location" well situated for both Hyde Park and Green Park,
it can get "very crowded in the evenings", meaning that
getting served can be a trial.

Sherlock Holmes   19 | 18 | 16 | £5
10 Northumberland St., WC2 (Charing Cross/Embankment),
020-7930 2644
☑ "All decked out with sleuth gear", this "kitschy" and
"slightly seedy" joint "off of Trafalgar Square" is an obvious
"tourist trap", flogging "plenty of souvenirs" related to the
sleuth of 221B and even pulling pints of something called
Sherlock Holmes Fine Ale; still, fans find it "fun" and insist
that you'll "love it if you love" the stories.

Shh... Rooms   18 | 20 | 18 | £10
7-9 Cranbourn St., WC2 (Leicester Sq.), 020-7287 7773
☑ Set in a "nice location" (if you think that Leicester Square
counts as such), this "spacious" bi-level venue with three
DJs who go on until 3 AM on Tuesday–Saturday is certainly
"not a bad spot"; still, surveyors are split over the qualities
of the clientele ("fun" vs. "pretentious").

Ship, The   20 | 14 | 18 | £3
41 Jew's Row, SW18 (Fulham Broadway), 020-8870 9667;
www.theship.co.uk
■ "Always enjoyable in the summer", this "busy" Fulham
boozer with a "riverside location" boasts a "great outside"
seating area (complete with "fantastic barbecues") right
by the Thames; those troubled by "too many people" during
the warm season, though, savour it more "in the winter",
especially for its famous fireworks on Guy Fawkes Night.

Ship & Shovell   18 | 17 | 17 | £2
1-3 Craven Passage, WC2 (Charing Cross/Embankment),
020-7839 1311
■ Below the arches of Charing Cross Station, this "smart"
spot is notable for two reasons – first, it stocks the rarely

spotted Badger ales, and second, it's actually a pair of Siamese twins, with "a bar on each side of the street" connected by an underground passageway (the larger half sporting a "mirrored wall"); given its eccentricity, it's no wonder some see it as "one of the best in Central London."

Shish   − | − | − | M

2-6 Station Parade Willesden Green, NW2 (Willesden Green), 020-8208 9292
313-319 Old St., EC1V (Old St.), 020-7749 0999
www.shish.com

The Willesden original of this gastro duo set the tone of quality eating and drinking, and the new super-trendy Shoreditch venue brings a serious infusion of the East to East London; the menu is a mix of Silk Road cuisines, from Mediterranean to Afghani and Chinese-style kebabs, served in a super-sleek mix of white tables and a funky bar area where bartenders mix cocktails such as the Holy Shish.

Shoreditch Electricity Showroom   19 | 19 | 15 | £4

39 Hoxton Sq., N1 (Old St.), 020-7739 6934

☑ Fans say this "hip bar" in Shoreditch is still "the coolest place to have a drink in Hoxton Square", a "see-and-be-seen spot" where "designer scruffy types" "mix with city slickers" and fashionable young scenies; there's "dancing downstairs" in the evenings, which makes it a "funky space to meet before going clubbing", though some say it "thinks it's cooler than it really is."

Shumi   − | − | − | VE

23 St. James's St., SW1 (Green Park), 020-7747 9380;
www.shumi-london.com

A sibling to Hush, this St James's bar/eaterie is also owned by Jamie Barber and Geoffrey Moore, son of 007 Roger, but it doesn't get as many plaudits as its sister due to "slow bar staff" who are "inattentive at best"; that said, there are "pretty good drinks" on offer, as well as intriguing Italian-Japanese fusion fodder from a former Nobu chef.

6 Degrees   − | − | − | E

56 Frith St., W1 (Piccadilly/Tottenham Court Rd.), 020-7734 8300;
www.6-degrees.co.uk

This Soho spot is a "fun and reliable" option boasting a waterfall, red lighting and burgundy sofas in the main bar, and an upstairs lounge with dark-wood panelling, chaises longues and aquarium fireplaces; in the summer, "drinkers spill out onto the streets" when the doors open onto the sidewalk; N.B. there are live bands Thursdays–Saturdays.

606 Club   21 | 11 | 15 | £5

90 Lots Rd., SW10 (Fulham Broadway), 020-7352 5953;
www.606club.co.uk

■ Admirers are attuned to the "underground vibe" of this "mellow" Chelsea "hideaway" that evokes a "NY jazz cellar" with "fab" acts and a "very real feel" (complete with "arrogant aficionados"); while some grouse that it "forces you to eat" a full meal of "average" Euro fare in order to drink unless you're a member, most agree it's "what a club should be" – "nothing flash, small and focused on the music."

SKETCH
21 | 24 | 17 | £10

9 Conduit St., W1 (Oxford Circus), 087-0777 4488;
www.sketch.uk.com

☑ "Everything breathes coolness" at this "incredibly hip" Mayfair bar/restaurant, "from the newspaperlike drinks menu to the egg-shaped toilet cabins" (which remind some of "*Mork and Mindy*"); unsurprisingly, it pulls in a "stylish crowd with a lot of money", including "Eurotrash", "stars", "supermodels" and assorted "trendies", though "mere mortals" might have "a struggle getting in" – or paying the "exorbitant prices" once they do.

Slug and Lettuce
13 | 13 | 13 | £3

14 Upper St. Martin's Ln., WC2 (Leicester Sq.),
020-7379 4880
19-20 Hanover St., W1 (Oxford Circus), 020-7499 0077
4 St. John's Hill, SW11 (Clapham Jct./rail), 020-7924 1322
474-476 Fulham Rd., SW6 (Fulham Broadway),
020-7385 3209
32 Borough High St., SE1 (London Bridge),
020-7378 9999
5 Chicheley St., SE1 (Waterloo), 020-7803 4790
1 Islington Green, N1 (Angel), 020-7226 3864
25 Bucklersbury, EC4 (Bank), 020-7329 6222
100 Fenchurch St., EC3 (Tower Hill/Bank), 020-7488 1890
30 S. Colonnade, E14 (Canary Wharf), 020-7519 1612
www.slugandlettuce.co.uk
Additional locations throughout London

☑ "City blokes mix with students" and "scrappy jeans" with "miniskirts" at these "chain pubs" that are popular among "antipodeans", "yuppies" and the "late-twentysomething crowd", and equally suited to a "quick drink or a big night"; their "dependable" rep ensures they're "usually fairly busy", and their "modern" atmosphere has some saying they're "classier" than their competitors, but others see them as "sterile", "soulless clone bars."

Smersh
– | – | – | M

5 Ravey St., EC2 (Old St.), 020-7739 0092;
www.smershbar.com

As an original *Goldfinger* poster on the wall suggests, this "fun" Shoreditch "basement venue" takes it name from the Soviet spying organisation James Bond fought in the classic flicks, but the Cold War thawed here long ago thanks to the "friendly" atmosphere and selection of Polish vodkas and Eastern European beers; no wonder spies who love it plead "please don't tell people about it!"

SMITHS OF SMITHFIELD   22 20 17 £5
67-77 Charterhouse St., EC1 (Barbican/Farringdon),
020-7251 7950; www.smithsofsmithfield.co.uk
■ There's plenty to choose from in this "beautiful" "four-floor" former warehouse in Smithfield Market – from a "noisy" ground-level "pre-club hangout" with "loud music" and "fish finger sandwiches" on offer to a "plush [martini-and]-champagne bar" with a "more classy, upscale feel" above; the upper two floors are renowned meat-focused restaurants, the "top" one boasting "views of St Paul's."

Smithy's   – – – E
15-17 Leeke St., WC1 (King's Cross), 020-7278 5949;
www.capitalpubcompany.com
Set in a former blacksmith's stables with cobbled floors and original fittings still in evidence, this sleek bar sports a "good selection of wines" and civilised surroundings, making it a "place to relax" in Clerkenwell; smokers note: there's a cigar vending machine on the premises.

Smollensky's   15 15 16 £5
105 The Strand, WC2 (Charing Cross/Covent Garden),
020-7497 2101
Bradmore House, Queen Caroline St., W6 (Hammersmith),
020-8741 8124
62 Carter Ln., EC4 (St. Paul's), 020-7248 4220
Canary Wharf, 1 Nash Ct., E14 (Canary Wharf), 020-7719 0101
Hermitage Wharf, 22 Wapping High St., E1 (Tower Hill/
Wapping), 020-7680 1818
www.smollenskys.co.uk
◨ Consistently "noisy and busy", these chain American-style bars are located in prime spots that make them "useful watering holes", especially for that "quick drink after work"; big eaters are also pleased that the food is offered in portions large "enough to choke a horse", although the popularity means that they can get "overcrowded" for some tastes.

Social, The   21 20 16 £4
5 Little Portland St., W1 (Oxford Circus), 020-7636 4992
33 Linton St., Arlington Sq., N1 (Angel/Old St.), 020-7354 5809
www.thesocial.com
■ Related but separately run, these venues in fashionable neighbourhoods are both "cool", "noisy places", but in their own distinct ways; the Islingtonian is a "long pine-panelled room" that dishes out "fantastic" gastro-style fodder, while the Fitzrovia version is a "backstreet" DJ bar that's "usually crammed" with trendy sorts.

Soho, The   20 19 20 £9
12-13 Greek St., W1 (Leicester Sq./Tottenham Court Rd.),
020-7025 7844; www.thesohobar.co.uk
■ If you want to "see where the locals go", visit this "chill wine bar in the heart of Soho" that's "elegant yet very hip";

there are "great by-the-glass" choices "and half-price bottles at happy hour", making it a "yummy place" "to hang out, have drinks" and "chat to friends", while an abundance of little nooks offers refuge "for a private drink for two."

Soho Spice
16 | 16 | 15 | £5

124-126 Wardour St., W1 (Piccadilly Circus), 020-7434 0808; www.sohospice.co.uk

■ The 3 AM license on weekends is probably the biggest attraction at this "agreeably dark basement" underneath "one of the few Indian restaurants in Soho"; it has "trendy decor", and the cocktails are cheap for the area, meaning that it's both a "good pre-restaurant bar" and also ideal for those "late-night liaisons."

Sosho
21 | 20 | 19 | £5

2 Tabernacle St., EC2 (Old St./Moorgate), 020-7920 0701; www.sosho3am.com

■ "If you like it loud, you'll love it" at what is in many surveyors' opinions one of the "greatest late-night bars" in town, or at least "one of the best drinks and music venues on the Shoreditch-City fringes"; "brick walls and a warehouse space" give it an edgy feel, while the "supreme cocktails" and "cool music" further contribute to the "appeal"; P.S. it "rocks on Saturdays."

SO.UK
19 | 22 | 16 | £5

93-107 Shaftesbury Ave., W1 (Piccadilly Circus/Leicester Sq.), 020-7494 3040
165 Clapham High St., SW4 (Clapham Common), 020-7622 4004
www.so-uk.co.uk

☑ "Luscious cocktails" are one reason the original branch of this North African–themed duo "is the place to be on Clapham High Street", though some complain that it gets so busy there's "hardly any space to breathe"; the story's similar at the Soho sibling, which is a "nice lounge bar, until the music gets louder at 10 and the place fills up", leading some to suggest that it's "a victim of its own success."

South London Pacific
∇ 21 | 23 | 20 | £7

340 Kennington Rd., SE11 (Kennington/Oval), 020-7820 9189; www.southlondonpacific.com

☑ With a host of special events ranging from 'Hula Boogie' on Wednesdays (complete with dance lessons), 'Cocktail Carnage' on Thursdays (with a live indie band) and a kitsch 'Club Aloha' cabaret on Saturdays, this "Hawaiian-themed" Kennington bar may not be the ideal spot for those in search of a quiet, romantic tête-à-tête, but it's "a good place to spend the evening"; N.B. closed Mondays and Tuesdays.

Southwark Rooms, The
– | – | – | E

60 Southwark St., SE1 (Borough), 020-7357 9301

From the folks who gave us Match and Mint, this Southwark bar and restaurant is a popular after-work bolt-hole for local yuppies and office types to end the day (or start the evening) with an SE1 mai tai or other concoction; the upstairs room is light and white with a huge candelabra, but most of the action is in the darker downstairs Lotus Lounge with its red walls and paper lanterns.

Spaniard's Inn
20 | 17 | 14 | £3

Spaniards Rd., NW3 (Hampstead), 020-8731 6571
■ For a taste of "old England", many tout this "classic" Hampstead watering hole where the main attraction is its "huge" beer garden ("one of the best in the country, never mind London", and "great after a long walk on the Heath"); though it's a favorite "particularly in the summer", a roaring fire also adds to the attraction "on a cold day" in winter.

Spice of Life
15 | 13 | 15 | £4

6 Moor St., W1 (Leicester Sq./Tottenham Court Rd.), 020-7437 7013; www.spiceoflifesoho.com
◪ Located near Cambridge Circus, this Soho boozer is "good for lunch" or "for a quick drink", with "live music" some nights (blues on Tuesdays, jazz on Wednesdays and Thursdays and rock on Fridays and Saturdays); still, some sigh that it's simply your "standard pub."

Spitz
– | – | – | M

109 Commercial St., E1 (Liverpool St), 020-7392 9032; www.spitz.co.uk
Offering a "combination of the funky and the classy", this bar, eaterie, gallery and performance venue "attached to Spitalfields Market" is a "cool location" boasting a "covered outside area"; "with art" exhibits and "great live music" featured almost every night in its "concert venue upstairs", it's a "prime spot" for "chilling" in "laid-back style."

Sporting Page
14 | 15 | 15 | £4

6 Camera Pl., SW10 (Sloane Sq.), 020-7349-0455; www.frontpagepubs.com
■ A "great place to watch Chelsea football" on giant screens, this pub with "tartan-covered walls and sporting regalia" is a fave with the older crowd of enthusiasts ("no under-30s"); it also seems to have become a haunt for the Bollinger classes, leading some to suggest that "the real sport here is resident-watching – fascinating!"

Sports Cafe
12 | 11 | 12 | £4

80 Haymarket, SW1 (Piccadilly Circus), 020-7839 8300; www.thesportscafe.com
■ One hundred and twenty television screens (including two jumbo units) make this Haymarket temple to sport a "home away from home for American sports buffs", and the 2 AM license (3 AM on weekends) means it "stays open until the game finishes"; also, participators can make use of the "pool tables", "arcade games and basketball hoop"; N.B. Friday is, rather optimistically, Ladies' Night.

Spot, The
12 | 10 | 11 | £4

29-30 Maiden Ln., WC2 (Covent Garden), 020-7379 5900;
www.thespot.co.uk

☑ With a full five bars, this "small and trendy" Covent Garden option seems to attract a "lively crowd" thanks to a late (1 AM) license and DJs spinning R&B and garage tunes; though a few sigh that it "tries too hard", it's "popular again after a lull", possibly due to last year's retooling, and fans proclaim it certainly "hits the spot."

Spread Eagle
17 | 12 | 15 | £2

141 Albert St., NW1 (Camden Town), 020-7267 1410;
www.youngs.co.uk

■ Reportedly a location in the British film *Withnail and I,* this unusually shaped Camden classic occupies a building dating from 1858; it's a "traditional" (some say "unexceptional") pub that works as a place to "reminisce over a favourite board game", have a drink "before going clubbing" or "relax" after a wander in "nearby Regent's Park."

STAR TAVERN
23 | 21 | 19 | £3

6 Belgrave Mews W., SW1 (Hyde Park Corner/Knightsbridge),
020-7235 3019

■ Boasting the "authentic" feel of "a country pub in the heart of London", this "popular, well-run" Belgravia boozer offers "more room than most", yet still manages to maintain a "cosy atmosphere"; with "good-quality food upstairs", "Fuller's ales" and some of the "friendliest service to be found", it's no wonder it's "often packed"; P.S. rumour has it this is "where the Great Train Robbery was planned."

Steam
14 | 18 | 15 | £7

Hilton Paddington, 1 Eastbourne Terr., W2 (Paddington),
020-7850 0555

☑ A place to let off steam, this "vast, stylish" venue at the Hilton Paddington is a "trendy and fun spot to have a drink before boarding your train home", and "a must for gin cocktail lovers"; critics concede it's "convenient if you're in the area" but find "no atmosphere", wondering "why would anyone drink here if they weren't a guest of the hotel?"

St. John
19 | 16 | 19 | £4

26 St. John St., EC1 (Barbican/Farringdon),
020-7251 0848
94-96 Commercial St., E1 (Liverpool St.), 020-7247 8724
www.stjohnrestaurant.co.uk

■ "Oozing class", these "super-cool bars" attached to restaurants specialising in all things meaty (offal, pig's face, etc.) attract tipplers with "friendly service" and a "good variety of drinks", including "excellent sherries"; you're sure to have "an interesting night out", though the carnivorous goings on in the adjacent eateries may be "perhaps too close for comfort for vegetarians."

St. Moritz Club

▽ | 18 | 15 | 15 | £6

159 Wardour St., W1 (Oxford Circus/Tottenham Court Rd.), 020-7437 0525

◪ If you're fond of the alternative scene, then this venue in Soho might appeal; the music is the main attraction for the mixed crowd that comes to hear various reggae, R&B, soul, ska and indie bands "banging away" many nights; still, some are "not keen" on it, declaring it merely "ok"; N.B. Heineken is the only beer offered on tap.

Stonemason's Arms

18 | 16 | 16 | £3

54 Cambridge Grove, W6 (Hammersmith), 020-8748 1397

■ "Tucked away" in Hammersmith, this "consistently" "fun" boozer offers "excellent food" and "great drinks", all served by "fantastic bar staff"; even though it's "often quite busy", there's always room "to sit down", something that makes it "a favourite with the locals."

Stringfellows

15 | 13 | 16 | £8

16-19 Upper St. Martin's Ln., WC2 (Leicester Sq.), 020-7240 5534; www.stringfellows.com

◪ "Lap dancers" and "pole"-swinging "women galore" make for quite "an eyeful" at this "entertaining" venue from Peter Stringfellow that's "still going after all these years"; gawpers (including some "famous faces") feel it's a "fun night", even though it's "expensive" and the "decor requires sunglasses", but what some see as "the classiest strip joint on the island" others deem "sad and sleazy."

Studio 6

– | – | – | M

Gabriel's Wharf, 56 Upper Ground, SE1 (Waterloo), 020-7928 6243

Set on the increasingly popular South Bank, this "great gastro-pub" adjacent to the Granada TV studios caters for a mixed bunch of after-workers, tourists and those filling a hole before a show; still, some say that the good reputation of its food and wine means that it's gotten a touch "too popular for its own good."

Sugar Hut

– | – | – | VE

374 North End Rd., SW6 (Fulham Broadway), 020-7386 8950; www.sugarhutfulham.com

"Always busy", this Eastern-themed bar "in the heart of Fulham" attracts the local "beautiful people" – not to mention the odd "celeb" and "overage philanderers" – with its "bedlike settees", "cool cushions" and "fantastic (but not cheap) cocktails"; most call it a "great place to go with a date", though some "could do with less public snogging!"

SULTAN

25 | 19 | 24 | £2

78 Norman Rd., SW19 (Colliers Wood/South Wimbledon), 020-8542 4532; www.hopback.co.uk/sultan.html

■ "Outstanding" beer is the star at London's lone outlet of the Hop Back brewery "hidden away" in South Wimbledon, where you can expect a "friendly welcome" once you enter; it's a small, "plain" pub with a summer beer garden, fireplaces and a dartboard, and for hopsters smitten by the "great choice of ales", it's "just how a local should be"; N.B. there's Wednesday night beer club from 6–9 PM and an annual beer festival in September.

Sun, The
▽ 23 | 16 | 18 | £3

47 Old Town, SW4 (Clapham Common), 020-7622 4980

■ "Trendy" tipsters tout this "spacious, popular" place in the Old Town near the Common, declaring "there's nowhere in Clapham I'd rather be on a sunny day", with a "refreshing beverage" on the "great veranda"; "reasonably priced" drinks and "delicious" Thai fare, a "spacious" interior and a "pleasant" atmosphere are also good for the Sol.

Sun & 13 Cantons
15 | 11 | 13 | £3

21 Great Pulteney St., W1 (Oxford Circus/Piccadilly Circus), 020-7734 0934

■ "May it never stop being scruffy" cry cronies of this lively Soho pub that pours an "honest pint", although be warned that this is lager heaven and there's "often no bitter"; it's always "buzzing" with local "media luvvies", and in summer the crowds spill out onto the pavement; N.B. on Fridays there are DJs in the basement bar.

Sun Inn
19 | 16 | 17 | £3

7 Church Rd., SW13 (Barnes Bridge/rail), 020-8876 5256

■ Quibbles about a renovation and the food at this venerable Barnes pub (circa 1550) are easily forgotten thanks to the "location" and "view of the duck pond"; it's got a "lovely Sunday afternoon atmosphere" and is especially "beautiful on a warm day" when boozers "take their pints to the water's edge" to commune with their feathered friends.

Surprise, The
▽ 18 | 13 | 17 | £3

6 Christchurch Terr., SW3 (Sloane Sq.), 020-7349 1821; www.mbplc.com

■ This Victorian watering hole "in the heart of Chelsea" gets its name from the 17th-century frigate rather than any shock patrons might feel upon finding a "nice local" on a quiet residential street; stained-glass windows and wooden floors figure prominently in the traditional setting.

Swag & Tails, The
22 | 20 | 23 | £6

10-11 Fairholt St., SW7 (Knightsbridge), 020-7584 6926; www.theswagandtails.com

■ Insiders insist "one of London's best little pubs" is this "upmarket" and "adorable" venue "away from the madding crowd" of the Harrod's-going hordes in Knightsbridge; it's "hard to find", but the "delicious", "creative" Eclectic fare, "fantastic wine list" (33 by the bottle and eight by the glass) and "prompt" service make it "well worth the effort to locate"; N.B. open Mondays–Fridays only.

Sway

17 | 17 | 17 | £8

(fka 10 Covent Garden)
61-65 Great Queen St., WC2 (Holborn), 020-7404 6114;
www.swaybar.co.uk

◪ A "relaxed and fun place" "for the more civilised after-work drinking crowd" is how boosters describe this Covent Garden bar with a handy 3 AM license (Wednesdays–Saturdays) and a DJ-driven "sexy groove"; malcontents are merciless, maligning the "cheap" decor, "wanna-be" crowd and "service that stretches the definition of the term."

Swimmer

– | – | – | M

13 Eburne Rd., N7 (Holloway Rd.), 020-7281 4632
It's "not about rowdy boozing" at this Islington oasis on a side street off Holloway Road, where "an interesting selection of beers", including Ridley's, Affligem and various Czechs, is conducive to "an unrushed drink with a good friend"; "comfortable surroundings" with Victorian decor add to the "cosy feel"; N.B. it's closed between 2–5 PM Monday though Thursday.

Taman Gang

– | – | – | VE

141 Park Ln., W1 (Marble Arch), 020-7518-3160
The name of this upmarket Mayfair affair nestled beneath the Marriott Hotel is Balinese for 'Park Lane', a suitably exotic tag for a venue boasting walls of carved limestone from Bali and erotic brass carvings in the gents', staff decked out in designer wear and Asian-themed cocktails and snacks on offer; as you might expect, it's not for the light of wallet, and the door policy can be highly selective.

Tantra Club

– | – | – | VE

62 Kingly St., W1 (Oxford Circus), 020-7434 0888;
www.tantraclub.co.uk

If you're glam enough for the clipboard Stasi at this Soho club you'll enter a scene that resembles an ultramodern Moorish harem, complete with boudoirs and white four-poster beds for lounging, dancers gyrating on an underlit dance floor with a mirrored ceiling and celebs being snapped up by paparazzi; be warned, though, that entrance can run you up to £20 and drinks are breathtakingly steep.

Tattershall Castle

– | – | – | M

King's Reach, Victoria Embankment, SW1 (Embankment),
020-7839 6548; www.thetattershallcastle.co.uk

Originally a ferry that ploughed the waves around Hull, this floating nightspot on the Embankment has recently undergone a revamp and is once again attracting local workers and tourists; below deck is a nightclub where those with sturdy sea legs can try their moves on the (undulating) dance floor, while topside you can take in views of the London Eye, Houses of Parliament and the bright City lights.

Tea Rooms des Artistes
20 | 16 | 14 | £4

697 Wandsworth Rd., SW8 (Clapham Common), 020-7652 6526;
www.tearoomsdesartistes.com

■ A "different" kind of venue, this little Claphamite with comfy sofas and eccentric decor offers art exhibitions, weekend DJs spinning a sophisticated set of soul and funk, and jazz on odd weekends, and it also serves vegetarian and seafood nosh; it's only open on Fridays and Saturdays, but it's available for private parties any day of the week.

Ten Bells, The
19 | 13 | 15 | £4

84 Commercial St., E1 (Liverpool St./Aldgate East), 020-7366 1721;
www.tenbells.com

■ The old days are long gone at this Spitalfields landmark where Jack the Ripper met his victims, for it's now a "trendy", "lively" and "not terribly expensive" DJ bar and after-work hang; though "it's changed a lot" since its days as a grim East End boozer, the listed interior with the "trippy" wallpaper has survived the revolution, adding to its "charm."

10 Room, The
16 | 18 | 14 | £7

10 Air St., W1 (Piccadilly Circus), 020-7734 9990;
www.10-room.co.uk

◪ At this "cosmopolitan" Piccadilly club where "minor celebrities" and a "beautiful" "funky soul" crowd dance to "solid R&B and hip-hop", including live jams on Monday nights; but a "pathetic door policy" and "pretentious" scene have cynics snapping on this "Chinawhites wanna-be."

Thatched House
▽ 17 | 17 | 18 | £3

115 Dalling Rd., W6 (Hammersmith/Ravenscourt Park),
020-8748 6174; www.thatchedhouse.com

■ "From the outside, an old man's pub", but inside this "homely" Young's venue in Hammersmith is a "large, open-plan" space with a "modern spartan" decor; the "emphasis is on food", but it's also "nice for a beer", cocktail or wine; N.B. there's a conservatory for the summer.

Thirst
18 | 17 | 20 | £8

53 Greek St., W1 (Tottenham Court Rd.), 020-7437 1977;
www.thirstbar.com

■ "Not a bad option when you just want quality drinks, tunes and company" advocates aver, this Soho cocktails bar is a "great value for happy hour" and a handy late-night option with a 3 AM closing time; though it's "not the largest of spaces" it's still big enough for a "small group", and with a DJ every night and a "downstairs dance floor", it also works for those who want to boogie.

Three Kings, The ⌂
▽ 19 | 18 | 18 | £3

7 Clerkenwell Close, EC1 (Farringdon), 020-7253 0483

■ An "old and wonderful" venue for a pint, this Clerkenwell boozer attracts a "good crowd", especially after work during the fine weather when it can be "overflowing"; it's a "great scene", with somewhat "odd regulars" and "eccentric decor" that looks almost "LSD"-induced; N.B. it hosts a literary and arts festival in July.

333 Club/Mother Bar   18 | 13 | 14 | £4
333 Old St., EC1 (Old St.), 020-7739 5949; www.333mother.com
◪ Regulars rave this "legendary" Hoxton triple-decker venue is what "East London clubs should be", with a "young", "eclectic crowd" and "great music" creating an "excellent vibe" and an "awesome" bar that resembles a "bordello"; foes, though, find the "long queues" and "crowded" scene "irritating" and feel it's "nowhere near as good as it used to be."

TIGER TIGER   14 | 14 | 12 | £5
29 The Haymarket, SW1 (Piccadilly Circus), 020-7930 1885; www.tigertiger.co.uk
◪ "London's premier meat market" is how many describe this "spacious" Piccadilly pleasuredome that gets "busier than a dockside brothel" on weekends with a "crowd looking to get lucky" in a "dark and sexy" spread that includes five bars, a restaurant and dance club; while grouches growl about "snobby doormen", "ridiculous queues" and a "tacky" scene replete with "bum-pinching old men", for others of a different stripe it's a "fun place to dance" to "standard pop"; N.B. trainers not allowed.

Toast   16 | 17 | 16 | £6
50 Hampstead High St., NW3 (Hampstead), 020-7431 2244
◼ Handily placed above the Hampstead tube station, this "relaxed and very chilled" cocktail bar is a "nice quiet spot before going out to dinner", with "delicious champagne cocktails" and "good service" in a "warm" setting; for some locals, the DJs on Mondays represent the "only worthwhile nightlife" in the area.

Tongue & Groove   ▽ 22 | 18 | 16 | £7
50 Atlantic Rd., SW9 (Brixton), 020-7274 8600; www.tongueandgroove.org
◼ Perfectly placed in Brixton as pre-clubbing warm-up or a destination in its own right, this wee venue aspires to NY style with a lounge atmosphere and leather poufs making the narrow quarters a bit more "cosy", and "hot music" by live bongo and saxophone players and the occasional spoken-word evening making up for the lack of space.

Toucan, The   19 | 15 | 20 | £3
19 Carlisle St., W1 (Tottenham Court Rd.), 020-7437 4123
94 Wimpole St., W1 (Bond St./Oxford Circus), 020-7499 2440
www.thetoucan.co.uk
◼ To a real "Guinness person", a pint of the black stuff paired with "oysters at lunchtime" make these "small", "traditional" pubs with "heaps of atmosphere" the "best

attractions" in Soho and Marylebone; the "friendly, happy staff" are another reason why they're "always busy", with punters often spilling out onto the street at the W1 location.

Townhouse
23 | 21 | 19 | £9

31 Beauchamp Pl., SW3 (Knightsbridge), 020-7589 5080; www.lab-townhouse.com

■ Townies marvel over what some say is "the longest drinks menu I've ever seen" (consisting of 120 "fantastic" libations) at this converted townhouse in Knightsbridge where you can experience "the feel of a private members' club without the pomp"; a crowd of "West End girls" and "hooray Henrys" relax amid "cool", "elegant" surroundings complete with leather banquettes and plasma screens; though claustrophobes carp over how "cramped" it is, most agree that they've "hit the nail squarely on the head" here.

Town of Ramsgate
▽ 20 | 18 | 19 | £2

62 Wapping High St., E1 (Tower Hill/Wapping), 020-7481 8000

■ "Unchanged for generations", this Wapping legend (circa 1545) is where the crew of the Bounty took their last pints before setting sail, and is where the ghost of Captain Kidd, who was hanged nearby, purportedly resides; it's a "great riverside pub" that's probably best to "visit in the summer" when you can sit in the beer garden and watch the Thames roll by.

Trader Vic's
18 | 19 | 19 | £7

Hilton Park Lane, 22 Park Ln., W1 (Green Park/Hyde Park Corner), 020-7208 4113; www.tradervics.com

☑ "Exotic Polynesian drinks", waitresses in "Hawaiian outfits" and "Bali Hai decor" create an air of "superb kitsch" at this long-running theme bar in the cellar of the Park Lane Hilton in Mayfair; the "overdone tropical" motif will "whisk you away from the city for a while" (talk about a "cheap holiday"), but werewolves of London find the "tacky tiki bar" concept altogether "naff."

TRAFALGAR TAVERN, THE
23 | 19 | 20 | £3

Park Row, SE10 (Cutty Sark), 020-8858 2909; www.TrafalgarTavern.co.uk

■ Located near the historic Royal Naval College, this "historic" Greenwich pub "overlooking the Thames" and the Dome makes a "good stopping off point after the boat ride from Westminster", and the "bay window seats" offer "great views" ("get there early" if you want one); it's "scruffy but atmospheric" and literati note it "hasn't lost any of its charm since Dickens alluded to it in *Our Mutual Friend*."

Trailer Happiness
— | — | — | E

177 Portobello Rd., W11 (Nottinghill Gate), 020-7727 2700; www.trailerhappiness.com

"Kitsch and LA '60s stuff", including prints by J. H. Lynch and Vladimir Tretchikoff, decorate this "louche underground bar" in Notting Hill; E-Z boys (and girls) praise the "funky" digs and "superbly made" "fishbowl-sized cocktails for the dedicated booze fiend", though some may balk at the unisex "communal bathrooms."

Troubadour Cafe, The ___ 22 | 20 | 16 | £4
265 Old Brompton Rd., SW5 (Earl's Court), 020-7370 1434;
www.troubadour.co.uk
■ It seems like this "rustic yet groovy", "bohemian gem" of a bar/cafe in Earl's Court has been around "forever" (since 1954, to be precise), and punters report it's "like going back in time" in the "laid-back" setting, notwithstanding the downstairs cabaret and live music venue; you can choose from a wide range of beverages, including a "most excellent selection of shots."

Truckles of Pied Bull Yard ___ ∇ 14 | 12 | 14 | £3
off Bury Pl., WC1 (Holborn/Tottenham Court Rd.), 020-7404 5338;
www.davy.co.uk
■ Close to the British Museum in Bloomsbury and also convenient to Tottenham Court Road, this cafe/bar owned by Davy's sports a "sheltered" flagstone courtyard that's "excellent" for "spring and summer nights"; Old Wallop is on the menu, as well as a "reliable" selection of wines to go with Med menu offerings; N.B. closed on weekends.

Tsar's Bar ___ – | – | – | VE
Langham Hotel, 1 Portland Pl., W1 (Oxford Circus), 020-7636 1000;
www.langhamhotels.com
The "unbelievable selection of vodkas" – 107 at last count – at this temple to all things Russian in the Langham Hotel in Marylebone would keep even Peter the Great busy for a while; there's an extensive cocktail list and "good food" as well, served in stylish panelled-wall surroundings.

Tup ___ 15 | 13 | 15 | £3
2 Savoy St., WC2 (Charing Cross/Covent Garden), 020-7836 9738
93 Marylebone High St., W1 (Baker St./Bond St.), 020-7935 4373
1 Ballantine St., SW18 (East Putney), 020-8877 3766
21 Chestnut Grove, SW12 (Balham), 020-8772 0546
268 Fulham Rd., SW10 (Earl's Court), 020-7352 1859
1 Harwood Terr., SW6 (Fulham Broadway), 020-7610 6131
2-3 Greenland Pl., NW1 (Camden Town), 020-7482 0399
132 Church St., N16 (Angel), 020-7249 1318
80 Liverpool Rd., N1 (Angel), 020-7354 4440
66 Gresham St., EC2 (Bank), 020-7606 8176
www.massivepub.com
■ Though parts of a chain, these "reliable" pubs are the "favourite locals" of many, and with each branch supposedly loyal to a different rugby team, on game days they can get "rowdy" with a "young crowd" of "lads"; "comfortable and friendly", with "no ugly carpets" or "annoying fruit machines", they are a "good value."

Turnmills   18 | 15 | 11 | £4 |
63B Clerkenwell Rd., EC1 (Farringdon), 020-7250 3409;
www.turnmills.co.uk
■ For anyone who wants to experience "the madness of London clubbing" and "dance till dawn" with "trendy" people, this Clerkenwell super-club is a good place to start; when the industrial-looking space is "thumping" with "amazing hard house", it fairly "bubbles with zest" and "subterranean wonderfulness", and while some suggest the "breed is dying", for fans it's still "top-drawer" after nearly 20 years; N.B. closed weeknights.

25 Canonbury Lane   23 | 20 | 19 | £4 |
25 Canonbury Ln., N1 (Highbury & Islington), 020-7226 0955
■ A "welcome change from the bar chains that fill Upper Street", this "intimate and cosy" "neighbourhood bar" in Islington attracts an "affluent but unpretentious", mostly local crowd with 35 cocktails and a tapas menu (with roasts on Saturdays and Sundays) served in a "laid-back" setting that's "nice for gathering with friends"; there's also a courtyard for summertime lounging.

Twentyfour/Vertigo 42   23 | 20 | 18 | £8 |
Tower 42, 25 Old Broad St., 24th & 42nd fls., EC2 (Bank/Liverpool St.), 020-7877 2424; www.vertigo42.co.uk
■ "Awesome" concoctions and "amazing views" are the main draws of these cocktail and champagne bars located on the 24th and 42nd floors, respectively, in the former Natwest Tower in the City; the crowd tends to be "mature" and the libations "expensive", but for a "special occasion" or "showing off the city to friends", they're "perfect spots"; P.S. for champers "beyond the clouds" make sure to "book well in advance."

2 Brewers   16 | 11 | 12 | £3 |
114 Clapham High St., SW4 (Clapham Common), 020-7498 4971;
www.the2brewers.com
◪ Surveyors are split on this "fun gay bar" near the Clapham Common – while some find the cabaret in the front room (with drag acts every night except Mondays and Tuesdays) "hilarious", others sniff that it "gives camp a bad name"; the club in back offers dancing to "loud" music from a high-tech computer-driven system; N.B. open until 3 AM Fridays and Saturdays.

Two Chairmen   ▽ 14 | 12 | 18 | £3 |
39 Dartmouth St., SW1 (St. James's Park), 020-7222 8694
■ Just a short walk from St. James's Park, this "traditional" "old English pub" is popular among workers from the neighbouring offices, serving Courage ales on tap and pub grub "basics" in "intimate" surroundings with a fireplace; there's no live music, no games and most importantly to regulars, scant few tourists.

Two Floors
20 | 17 | 16 | £4

3 Kingly St., W1 (Oxford Circus), 020-7439 1007

■ "For somewhere so trendy", this little venue on the Regent Street side of Soho manages to create a "chilled-out" vibe conducive to a "relaxing drink with friends"; as the name promises, it occupies two floors, with a bar and restaurant on the main floor and a downstairs room with "big sofas", "perfect for lounging and hanging out" and watching the "cool" crowd.

Underworld ⊄
14 | 7 | 12 | £3

174 Camden High St., NW1 (Camden Town), 020-7482 1932; www.theunderworldcamden.co.uk

■ Located beneath the World's End pub in Camden, this "nice alternative" venue is an infernal club and bar straight out of "Dante" showcasing "up and coming bands trying to escape indie hell"; the space is "huge", with "enough levels" for "students", "punks", goths and rockers to "jostle" and "jump."

Vats Wine Bar
▽ 18 | 15 | 18 | £7

51 Lambs Conduit St., WC1 (Holborn/Russell Sq.), 020-7242 8963

■ There's plenty of "value" and "interest" in the "popular wine list" at this retro Covent Garden enoteca that offers 100 labels by the bottle and 17 by the glass, paired with "nice" (but "a bit pricey") food; its "good location", near Bloomsbury and Lincoln's Inn, makes it "great for after-work drinks" for local bacchic barristers.

Vesbar
▽ 16 | 15 | 15 | £3

15-19 Goldhawk Rd., W12 (Goldhawk Rd./Shepherd's Bush), 020-8762 0215

☑ A "good option in Shepherd's Bush", this "smart" Fuller's-owned bar "works" with the usual array of beers and cocktails, as well as a "retro" look and a "comfortable" (though sometimes "noisy") atmosphere; to wet blankets, though, it "feels like a chain" – i.e. "nothing special."

Vespa Lounge
▽ 16 | 13 | 13 | £5

Centre Point Building, Centre Point, 15 St. Giles High St., WC2 (Tottenham Court Rd.), 020-7836 8956; www.vespalounge.com

■ Surveyors smitten by the "lovely view" at this funky Covent Garden lesbian bar aren't talking about the landscape of St. Giles and Centre Point; it's a popular "pre-club" stop for "West End girls" with a happy hour, speed dating and pool competitions, and there's live music and DJs in the mixed bar downstairs, the Conservatory, which has a 1 AM licence.

Via Fossa
15 | 14 | 13 | £4

2 Port East Bldg., Hertsmere Rd., E14 (West India Quay/ Canary Wharf), 020-7515 8549; www.viafossa-canarywharf.co.uk

■ Housed in a century-old National Trust–owned warehouse on West India Quay, this Canary Wharf venue consisting of three bars and a restaurant combines "fabulous" "old-world decor" with modern touches such as fluorescent lighting in the floors; for fans, it's a "great place to meet up and hang out" after work, while pickier pundits faintly praise it as the "best of a bad choice" in "an area beset by chains."

Vibe Bar
21 | 15 | 14 | £3

The Old Truman Brewery, 91-95 Brick Ln., E1 (Aldgate East/Liverpool St.), 020-7377 2899; www.vibe-bar.co.uk
■ Set in the now semi-legendary old Truman Brewery, this "offbeat" DJ bar and club, which played a large role in making Brick Lane "oh-so-cool", is "best in summertime", insiders advise, if you can snaffle a "bench" in the "large courtyard"; if not, you can dance to music by "great DJs" in the club or surf the Net for free in the "living room"—like bar (access comes with the price of a drink).

Vic Naylor
18 | 16 | 17 | £4

38-42 St. John St., EC1 (Farringdon), 020-7608 2181; www.vicnaylor.com
■ A bit of a Cool Britannia hot spot, this "buzzy" Smithfield cocktail bar has appeared in films such as *Lock, Stock and Two Smoking Barrels,* thanks to its "wonderful" dark-wood and brick-walled decor, graced with "nice paintings", and "cosy", "otherworldly" atmosphere; usually "pleasantly busy", it works equally well as a "lunchtime haunt" or a "starting-off point" to an evening.

Village Soho
14 | 14 | 13 | £4

81 Wardour St., W1 (Leicester Sq./Piccadilly Circus), 020-7434 2124
■ "For late-night fun on a Friday it does take a Village" gush groupies of this three-storey gay bar in Soho where male go-go dancers bump and grind and window seats provide choice views of "Old Compton Street"; "good food and drink offers", including a four-hour happy hour, DJs and karaoke nights add allure, and while the scene can be "sometimes cruisy", the vibe is usually "friendly."

Villandry
21 | 18 | 18 | £7

170 Great Portland St., W1 (Great Portland St.), 020-7631 3131; www.villandry.com
■ A "wonderful concept", this Fitzrovia brasserie/bar/deli combination is an "unusual" "neighbourhood hangout" with a "chic yet homey" design", where the selection of wines, flavoured vodkas and rums is "impressive" and the food is "fresh"; while it's "expensive" and caters to a fair share of "suits", it's nonetheless "quaint" in the eyes of many.

Visible
– | – | – | M

229 Portobello Rd., W10 (Notting Hill Gate/Ladbroke Grove), 020-8969 0333
"It's great to settle into the comfy velvet couches" with a cocktail and a plate of mezze at this Notting Hill lounge

behind a blood-red facade that insiders tout as an "excellent launching pad for a night out in the neighbourhood"; it showcases live jazz on Thursdays.

Walkabout Inn   13 | 9 | 14 | £3
11 Henrietta St., WC2 (Charing Cross/Covent Garden), 020-7379 5555; www.walkabout.eu.com
58 Shepherd's Bush Green, W12 (Shepherd's Bush), 020-8740 4339; www.walkabout.eu.com
56 Upper St., N1 (Angel), 020-7359 2097; www.walkaboutinns.com
Hill House, Shoe Ln., EC4 (Blackfriars/Chancery Ln.), 020-7353 7360; www.walkaboutinns.com
☑ "Enter at your own risk" into one of these "loud", "rough 'n' tumble" boozers with "real live Australians" behind and in front of the bar; it's a "wild", "sweaty, packed" scene, especially when there's rugby on, and though some critics chide the "surly" staff and recommend that they "take a trip down under to learn what Aussie hospitality is all about", "young antipodeans and their fans" find the atmosphere simply "awesome."

Warrington Hotel   20 | 22 | 17 | £3
93 Warrington Crescent, W9 (Maida Vale/St. John's Wood), 020-7286 2929
■ A "pretty young set" ("*le tout* Maida Vale") descend on this "fabulous" Victorian pub, but there's no doubting that the "superb interior" is the star with its ornate tiles and columns and "wonderful naked ladies"; for those who find it "too smoky", the "beer garden in summer" offers a good escape, as does the option of sampling the "tasty Thai" food in the restaurant upstairs.

Wax   – | – | – | M
(fka Bar Madrid)
4 Winsley St., W1 (Oxford Circus), 020-7436 4650; www.wax-bar.co.uk
The funky house, classic and modern cocktails, swish modern design spread over two floors give this Soho bar/club a few yards north of Oxford Street a female-friendly feel; the happy hours prove a popular draw and night-owls are waxing lyrical over the 3 AM closing time.

Waxy O'Connor's   17 | 19 | 14 | £3
14-16 Rupert St., W1 (Leicester Sq./Piccadilly Circus), 020-7287 0255; www.waxyoconnors.co.uk
■ With an enormous preserved beech tree stuck inside, this "labyrinthine" "monster" of a pub is possibly "the biggest Irish bar in the world", and attracts a fair share of "Americans" and "Europeans", though there's plenty of "room to escape" even when it's "crowded"; "Irish music" and a "great variety of beers" add to the "lively" air, and even leery locals allow that it's "not bad for a tourist trap."

WELL, THE
23 | 19 | 16 | £5

180 St. John St., EC1 (Angel/Farringdon), 020-7251 9363;
www.downthewell.com

■ A "nice local gastro-pub with an edge", this Clerkenwell venue is "well worth the trip" for a "constantly changing menu" of Modern British fare and a large international selection of beers (10 on draught and 11 by the bottle, including one from Zimbabwe); the "casual" ambience, "outdoor seating" and "good music" all sit well with a somewhat "eccentric crowd of regulars."

WENLOCK ARMS ∉
26 | 18 | 24 | £2

26 Wenlock Rd., N1 (Old St.), 020-7608 3406;
www.wenlock-arms.co.uk

■ Serving six guest ales from around the country at any one time (and Adnams all the time), at "sensible prices", this "hidden gem" in Shoreditch is a hit with hard-core "CAMRA types"; "friendly" service, "wedges to die for", "superb jazz at the weekends" and a "roaring fire" add allure, and fans lament that there are "not enough establishments like this is London."

WESTBOURNE, THE
23 | 18 | 15 | £4

101 Westbourne Park Villas, W2 (Royal Oak/Westbourne Park),
020-7221 1332

☑ A "tragically hip" crowd of "rockers, artists and American bankers" gravitates to this Notting Hill gastro-pub for "nice food and drinks" in a "casual chic" setting that's "paradise in springtime" on the patio, and "cosy in winter" as well; the interior is "modern, but not overbearingly so", though "horrendous" service prompts the jaded to jeer that it's "so full of itself it's almost unbearable."

Westminster Arms
18 | 14 | 19 | £3

9 Storey's Gate, SW1 (St. James's Park/Westminster),
020-7222 8520

☑ This Westminster pub is handy for Parliament Square and a stone's throw from St. James's Park, but its main attraction for many seems to be that it's "next door to my office"; there's hearty food from the top-floor restaurant and "good" real ale on offer, but some despair that it just "should be better, given its location."

Wheatsheaf, The
∇ 20 | 15 | 19 | £2

6 Stoney St., SE1 (London Bridge), 020-7407 7242;
www.youngs.co.uk

☑ A "local" with a beer garden in the "heart of Borough Market", this Young's pub serves home-cooked grub, including "doorstop sandwiches", and real ales in a "no-frills" setting that was refurbished when it came under the brewery's banner; traditionalists complain that the owners "re-varnished anything that didn't move" and accuse it of undue "pretensions because of its location."

Whisky Bar, The

▽ 23 | 20 | 21 | £9

Athenaeum Hotel, 116 Piccadilly, W1J , 020-7499 3464;
www.athenaeumhotel.com

■ "Lovely in every sense", this bar in the Athenaeum Hotel in Mayfair is an oasis for fans of scotch, offering 157 varieties from what may be the biggest collection in London; there's also a full cocktail menu and "nice" complimentary snacks, and while the atmosphere is a bit "businesslike", it's still "fun to go with friends."

White Cross, The

▽ 23 | 20 | 18 | £3

Water Ln., Riverside, Richmond (Richmond), 020-8940 6844;
www.youngs.co.uk

■ With a "great location" by Richmond Bridge and a "nice garden next to the river" this "unpretentious" Young's pub gets "extremely crowded on summer evenings" when there's an "open air bar"; some feel there's "not much to stay inside for", though the two fireplaces can be inviting on a "winter's Sunday night", and you can also keep an eye on Old Man Thames from the upstairs bar.

White Horse

19 | 17 | 17 | £5

94 Brixton Hill, SW2 (Brixton), 020-8678 6666;
www.whitehorsebrixton.com

■ Just a little way up the hill from Coldharbour Lane and the clubs in Brixton's heart, this revamped gastro-pub is a popular opening act for "trendies" who drop in for DJs spinning soul, funk and hip-hop before moving on (or staying put – happy hour lasts all night on Mondays and Tuesdays); it's also "great on Sunday" with its traditional roasts.

White Horse, The

21 | 16 | 16 | £3

1-3 Parson's Green, SW6 (Parsons Green), 020-7736 2115;
www.whitehorsesw6.com

■ The "happy sound of contented drinkers" fills the "Sloany Pony", as this Fulham "institution" is known, a "real ale mecca" with 20 "well-kept, tasty" draughts and 88 bottled beers, including five Belgians, that are showcased at the "excellent winter festival"; the "summertime barbies" are also a must "when the garden is open" (remember to wear your "rugby shirt and cords"), and though the brews are the story here, the "crowds" and atmosphere may "make you want a Bloody Mary."

White House, The

▽ 19 | 18 | 14 | £4

65 Clapham Park Rd., SW4 (Clapham Common), 020-7498 3388;
www.thewhitehouselondon.co.uk

◪ Those who don't often "venture south of the river" may be taken aback by this "fab venue" located between Clapham and Brixton sporting a small private room and brand-new roof terrace; though foes fault the "cool, aloof" service and "pretentious" crowd, the "fantastic scenery" and "great vibe" compensate.

White Swan, The
20 | 18 | 17 | £4

25-26 Old Palace Ln., Richmond (Richmond), 020-8940 0959;
www.fluidpubs.com

■ A "charming atmosphere" pervades at this "smart and comfortable" Richmond boozer with a "secluded garden at the back" that makes it popular in summer, though it's never "swamped with people"; while it may be true that there's "no excitement" here, save the "experimental" Med- and Asian-accented British fare and occasional "celeb spotting", for many it's "what a good local should be."

White Swan, The
∇ 15 | 15 | 17 | £3

14 Vauxhall Bridge Rd., SW1 (Pimlico), 020-7821 8568

■ Unless you're local or a "civil servant", you're probably only likely to find yourself at this Pimlico boozer after the Tate Britain; regulars have "no complaints" about the Belgian beers, lagers and ales, or the "standard pub grub fare."

Windmill, The
18 | 14 | 17 | £5

6-8 Mill St., W1 (Oxford Circus), 020-7491 8050;
www.thewindmill.info

■ Food is the emphasis of this Mayfair boozer with two restaurants – one smoking and one smoke-free – dishing out award-winning steak and kidney pies and other "nice" fare, as well as three bars (one nonsmoking); it's a "friendly and unpretentious" option in an area that doesn't boast many great pubs, and a good place for an "after-work drink."

Windmill on the Common
20 | 15 | 15 | £3

Clapham Common Southside, SW4 (Clapham Common),
020-8673 4578; www.youngs.co.uk

◪ There's "no better place when the sun's out" than this ancient "classic" pub (circa 1500) where you can "sunbathe on Clapham Common" and "chat with friends" as you "sink your teeth into a pint of bitter"; inside it's "comfortable", though critics are "unsure about the decor", and feel it also "could do better" with the beer and "unimaginative food."

WINDOWS BAR
23 | 20 | 19 | £10

Hilton Park Lane, 22 Park Ln., 28th fl., W1K (Hyde Park Corner),
020-7493 8000; www.hilton.co.uk

■ The "best nighttime view of the West End" and other "incredible and rare" vistas are the selling points of this aptly named bar on the 28th floor of Mayfair's Hilton Park Lane hotel; a piano player and "old-fashioned" decor appeal to an "older" clientele, but young turks find it plenty "cool" for the "start of a glam evening" or a "romantic" occasion; P.S. a drink doesn't come cheap, so "make it last."

Windsor Castle
19 | 18 | 16 | £3

27-29 Crawford Pl., W1 (Edgware Rd.), 020-7723 4371

■ Formerly a servants' watering hole dating back to the 19th century, this "fun" Marylebone pub "sitting in a mews" is most notable for its hand-drawn beers and photos and artefacts that adorn the walls, most of them royalist in tenor; in contrast to its "country" feel, it serves a menu of Thai fare from the restaurant upstairs.

Windsor Castle, The   23 | 20 | 18 | £4

114 Campden Hill Rd., W8 (High St. Kensington/Notting Hill Gate), 020-7243 9551; www.windsor-castle-pub.co.uk

■ The rights of man and woman to a "well-kept real ale" in a "congenial" atmosphere are unaffected by the ghost of Thomas Paine, who's supposedly buried in the basement of this "wonderful" Kensington boozer that punters proclaim is "everything a proper English pub should be"; you can quaff Hoegaarden and tuck into fresh oysters at one of two "low-ceilinged, wood-panelled bars" heated by "roaring fires", and there's also a beer garden that gets "ridiculously packed" in summer.

Wine Library, The   ▽ 21 | 18 | 22 | £10

43 Trinity Sq., EC3 (Tower Hill), 020-7481 0415

■ At this "unique" wine bar located on a former skittles alley in Tower Hill, oenophiles are in rapture over an "amazing selection" of "perfectly served" wines (650 by the bottle); they can be purchased at retail plus a £3.50 corkage if you partake of the all-you-can-eat spread of "delicious meats, pâtés and cheese" that'll run you a touch over a tenner.

WKD   14 | 13 | 14 | £3

(aka Mint)

18 Kentish Town Rd., NW1 (Camden Town), 020-7267 1869

■ "Groovy music" by live acts and nightly DJs attract a "fun crowd" of "posh studenty types" to this Kentish Town club with a handy 2 AM license; "cheap drinks", a balcony bar overlooking the dance floor and theme nights such as the Wonderful World of Beautiful People on Fridays and Saturday '70s night are all part of the "funky" scene.

Woody's Club   18 | 17 | 15 | £6

41-43 Woodfield Rd., W9 (Westbourne Park), 020-7266 3030; www.woodysclub.com

■ A "nice mixture of London" converges on this converted four-storey Notting Hill townhouse with a "different type of bar" on each level, resulting in a "handy mix of booths and dance floors" that allow you to "dance or chat" depending on your whim; music varies from chart pop to spaced out punk funk to Afro-Latin house, and "no matter what day you drop by", the tunes are "unbelievably good."

World's End ⊅   13 | 11 | 13 | £3

174 Camden High St., NW1 (Camden Town), 020-7482 1932; www.theworldsend.co.uk

☑ Yet another former Dickens haunt (how did he get any writing done?), this "dark and dingy" Camden venue is a "crowded and sweaty" "adventure playground with beers", a "dodgy clientele" and, some gripe, "too much rock music"; as long as your expectations aren't too great, though, it's "good for meeting up" before heading to the Underworld club downstairs.

Yard Bar, The
20 | 16 | 16 | £4

57 Rupert St., W1 (Leicester Sq./Piccadilly Circus), 020-7437 2652; www.theyardbar.com

■ Not your average Soho gay bar, this "classy", "pleasant" place is a real find on a summer's day, with a rare "great courtyard"; though it gets "very busy" there's still "a chilled out fun vibe" and the "tunes are good for the weekend"; P.S. cognoscenti consider the upstairs Lost Bar a "bit more classy" than downstairs.

Yauatcha
– | – | – | E

15 Broadwick St., W1 (Piccadilly Circus/Oxford St.), 020-7494-8888

Two and a half years in the making, restaurateur Alan Yau's (Hakkasan, Wagamama) Soho dim sum specialist is quickly turning heads with its unique basement dining room highlighted by modernistic neon lighting, grey slate tables, frosted glass and a bar-length fish tank; but the most audacious feature may be the elegant ground-level tearoom serving 50 types of *cha* and patisserie – unheard of in beery old W1.

Ye Grapes
19 | 18 | 18 | £4

16 Shepherd Mkt., W1 (Green Park), 020-7499 1563

◪ In summer at this "friendly" Mayfair pub, the crowd "spills out" into Shepherd's Market and you can "rest your pint on the window ledge" under the "blooming bougainvillaea"; it's an "old-fashioned" kind of place that attracts a "great cross-selection of life", although some describe the interior as a "smoke-filled pit."

Ye Olde Cheshire Cheese
21 | 21 | 17 | £3

145 Fleet St., EC4 (Blackfriars), 020-7353 6170; www.yeoldecheshirecheese.com

■ "A true London institution" serving Sam Smith's beers at "give-away prices", this "ancient pub" was rebuilt after the Great Fire and is famed for its passageways, "alcoves, dark corners and winding staircases" ("watch your head!"); "full of character", it's catered to virtually every old-time London literati, though now the clientele consists mainly of barristers and "tourists."

YE OLDE MITRE
25 | 24 | 20 | £2

1 Ely Ct., EC1 (Chancery Ln./Farringdon), 020-7405 4751

■ "Small, historic, comfortable" and "almost impossible to find", this "wonderful" City pub dating back to 1546 is officially in Cambridgeshire due to an ancient law; those who do locate it describe it as "too cool for words", a "great place to take visitors" or "stealing away with a small group", though some find the trek to the "outdoor gents'" a bit "annoying", especially "in the cold."

Ye Olde Watling ▽ 18 | 19 | 18 | £3

29 Watling St., EC4 (Mansion House), 020-7653 9971

■ "Doctor Johnson could be propping up the bar" at this "old, historic" Blackfriars boozer, the site of Christopher Wren's office when he was overseeing the rebuilding of St. Paul's; while some feel it's become a "bit of a barn" with the addition of a separate restaurant upstairs, others insist it's retained its "real pub" character.

Yo! Below 19 | 18 | 16 | £4

52 Poland St., W1 (Oxford Circus), 020-7439 3660; www.yosushi.com

☒ At this Soho bar attached to Yo! Sushi restaurant, "you pour your own beer" from taps at the table, something that's guaranteed to lead to "fun and frivolity", if sake cocktails, bright lights or "manga animation" don't; regulars recommend it "when you fancy a change" from the "dark and intimate", though the karaoke-singing staff "can be a little too much", and sceptics suggest something's getting "lost in translation."

Zander Bar 17 | 19 | 16 | £6

45 Buckingham Gate, SW1 (St. James's Park), 020-7379 9797; www.bankrestaurants.com

☒ An "atmospheric" "oasis" in a nightspot-challenged area, this "bubbling" Victoria venue is endowed with the "longest bar in London", a mack daddy that stretches for 48 metres; sometimes, though, there seems to be "too few bar staff" to man it say critics who feel that it's "past its prime", although admirers insist that it's always "worth a pint if you're stuck" in the neighbourhood.

Zd Bar – | – | – | E

289 Kilburn High Rd., NW6 (Kilburn), 020-7372 2544

With DJs four nights a week, live blues on Thursdays and a restaurant serving Japanese and Thai food, this Kilburn bar is "one of the best in the area" groupies gush, while cynics point out that that's "not difficult on the High Road"; still, "friendly" service and a late license go a long way in any postal code.

Zebrano 19 | 19 | 16 | £6

14-16 Ganton St., W1 (Oxford Circus), 020-7287 5267; www.freedombrewery.com

☒ Sophisticates may shrug at this bar as a "standard Soho effort", with its "padded walls", "cacti", "red booths and "animal prints" and a restaurant upstairs, but the less jaded find it a "terrific", "loungey" kind of place that comes alive when "the pace and music pick up as the night progresses"; the drinks are "reasonably priced", and to encourage repeat visits, it allows you to buy a bottle of spirits, and then store it "in a locker" until you return.

Zerodegrees   17 | 17 | 18 | £4

29-31 Montpelier Vale, SE3 (Blackheath/rail), 020-8852 5619; www.zerodegrees-microbrewery.co.uk

■ No barrels, beards or basements at this "bright" brewpub in Blackheath pouring "great original beers" in a modern space that's often "very crowded with wealthy youngsters in the evening"; the "bangers and mash" are recommended, and they also do "decent" pizzas and Belgian dishes.

Zeta Bar   20 | 20 | 16 | £8

35 Hertford St., W1 (Green Park/Hyde Park Corner), 020-7208 4067; www.zeta-bar.com

■ This "hip", "NY-style" bar owned by the Mayfair Hilton makes a "nice stop after Nobu" for a "fashionable crowd" (and slightly "dodgy out-of-town businessmen"); the strains of "commercial dance music" with "live percussion" fill the "spacious, well-decorated" surroundings, and ease the sting of the "extraordinarily expensive" cocktails somewhat.

Zig-Zag   20 | 19 | 18 | £7

12 All Saints Rd., W11 (Westbourne Pk.), 020-7243 2008

☑ A "trippy" decor of pinks and reds sets the tone of this "cool, hip" "out-of-the-way" Notting Hill spot where DJs play four nights a week and there are art exhibitions from local artists; "oh-so-yesterday" sniff cynics who advise you to "zig-zag in another direction."

Zilli Bar   17 | 14 | 19 | £6

40 Dean St., W1 (Leicester Sq./Piccadilly Circus), 020-7734 1853

■ While it's no longer part of the Aldo empire, this Soho old-timer is still a "firm favourite" of "locals" and a "good place to start" an evening with some Italian wine or a cocktail; though it "packs 'em in" year-round, it's especially popular in summer with its outdoor tables.

Zinc Bar & Grill   17 | 16 | 15 | £6

21 Heddon St., W1 (Oxford Circus/Piccadilly Circus), 020-7255 8899; www.conran.com

☑ In a "great location to meet up just off Regent Street", this Conran bar/brasserie is a popular stop for many to get the night started with a "tasty cocktail" before plunging on into Mayfair or Soho; foes, though, find it too "middle of the road" and "more of a restaurant", appealing to "advertising and marketing" types; N.B. there's live jazz on Wednesdays.

Zoo Bar   15 | 14 | 13 | £5

13-17 Bear St., WC2 (Leicester Sq.), 020-7839 4188; www.zoobar.co.uk

☑ "One of the most touristy bars in London", this Covent Garden nightclub with a 3.30 AM closing time is "tacky, cheap and nasty", but the mix of "exchange students" and "pretentious locals" can be undeniably "fun", "if you know what you're getting yourself into"; the "noisy", "crowded" "meat-market" scene is exacerbated by an "annoying layout", and zoologists observe "you really need to be young for this place."

ZUMA

24   24   20   £10

5 Raphael St., SW7 (Knightsbridge), 020-7584 1010;
www.zumarestaurant.com
■ "So hip it hurts", this "exotic yet relaxed" Knightsbridge bar and restaurant has "survived the initial hype" and is still a "must" for a "sexy" crowd that includes "heavy hitters" and "wanna-bes" alike, who mingle over "lovely cocktails" with a "Japanese touch" and "fab sushi"; a "fantastic", "modern" interior adds to the "trendy, buzzy, colourful" atmosphere, while the "friendly" staff help keep the vibe "stylish but not overbearing."

Indexes

LOCATIONS
SPECIAL APPEALS

LOCATIONS

CENTRAL LONDON

Belgravia
Antelope
Grenadier
Grouse & Claret
Library
Nag's Head
Plumbers Arms
Star Tavern

Bloomsbury/Fitzrovia
Bradley's
Bricklayer's Arms
Cock Tavern
Crazy Bear
Crown & Sceptre
Duke of York
Eagle Bar
Enterprise
Firevault
First Out
Fitzroy
Ha!Ha! Bar
Jamies
Jerusalem
Lamb
La Perla
Ling Ling
Long Bar
Market Place
Mash
Matchbar
Museum Tavern
mybar
No. 5
Office
O'Neill's
Oscar
Perseverance
Princess Louise
Purple Bar
Queen's Larder
Social
Truckles of Pied
Villandry

Chinatown
Bar Room Bar
De Hems

Covent Garden/Holborn
Africa Bar
AKA

American Bar
Angel
Bank
Bar des Amis
Bar 38
Belgo
Belushi's
Blend
Box
Browns
Bünker Bar
Cirque/Hippodrome
Coach & Horses
Coal Hole
Cross Keys
Davy's
Denim
Detroit
Dial
East@West
End
Fine Line
Freud
Fuel
Gardening Club
Ha!Ha! Bar
hog's head
Knights Templar
Kudos
Lamb & Flag
Langley
La Perla
Light Bar
Lobby Bar
Lowlander
Lyceum Tavern
Maple Leaf
Marquess/Anglesey
Marquis/Granby
Navajo Joe's
Na Zdrowie
O'Neill's
Opera Tavern
Pitcher & Piano
Porterhouse
Porters Bar
Punch & Judy
Queen Mary
Retox Bar
Retro Bar
Roadhouse
Salisbury, The

EAST/SOUTH EAST LONDON

Blackfriars/City
All Bar One
Artillery Arms
Auberge
Balls Brothers
Barcelona Tapas
Black Friar
Bonds
Cittie of Yorke
Corney & Barrow
Counting House
Davy's
Digress
Dirty Dick
El Vino
Evangelist
Fine Line
Fishmarket
George Bar
George Inn
Glasshouse
hog's head
Jamaica Wine
Jamies
La Grande Marque
Lamb Tavern
Leadenhall
Lime
Nylon
Old Bank
Old Bell
115 @ Hodgsons
O'Neill's
1 Lombard St.
Pacific Oriental
Pitcher & Piano
Prism
Punch Tavern
Rising Sun
Slug & Lettuce
Smollensky's
Tup
Twentyfour
Walkabout
Wine Library
Ye Olde Cheshire
Ye Olde Mitre
Ye Olde Watling

Bow/Mile End/Hackney/Bethnal Green
Approach Tavern
Black Horse
Cat & Mutton

Crown, The
Florist
Jongleurs/Bar Risa

Canary Wharf/Docklands
Bar 38
City Pride
Corney & Barrow
Davy's
1802
Fine Line
Slug & Lettuce
Smollensky's
Via Fossa

Clerkenwell/Smithfield/Farringdon
Abbaye
All Bar One
Al's Bar
Anexo
Bar 38
Beduin
Bishops Finger
Bleeding Heart Tav.
Café Lazeez
Café Med
Cellar Gascon
Charterhouse
Cicada
Clerkenwell Hse.
$
Dust
Eagle
Easton, The
Fabric
Fluid
Fox & Anchor
hog's head
Jerusalem Tavern
Kick
Lifthouse
Match ec1
Medcalf
19:20
O'Hanlon's
Peasant
Play
Potemkin
Sekforde Arms
Smiths/Smithfield
Smithy's
St. John
Three Kings
Turnmills

NORTH/NORTH WEST LONDON

Camden Town/Chalk Farm/Kentish Town/Primrose Hill

Adelaide
Arizona Bar
Bar Gansa
Bar Solo
Bartok
Bar Vinyl
Belgo
Belushi's
Black Cap
Camden Brewing
Dublin Castle
Edinboro Castle
Electric Ballroom
Engineer
Forum
Good Mixer
Head of Steam
Henry J Bean's
Highgate
Hill
hog's head
Jazz Cafe
Jongleurs/Bar Risa
Jorene Celeste
Junction Tavern
Lansdowne
Monkey Chews
Oh! Bar
Positively 4th St.
Purple Turtle
Quinns
Spread Eagle
Tup
Underworld
WKD
World's End

Hampstead/Kilburn/Swiss Cottage

Bar Room Bar
Café Rouge
Flask, The
Freemasons Arms
Holly Bush
King William IV
Magdala
Shish
Spaniard's Inn
Toast
Zd Bar

Highgate/Muswell Hill/Crouch End/Tufnell Park

All Bar One
Flask
Ha!Ha! Bar
Lord Palmerston
O'Neill's

Islington

Albion
Almeida
Babushka
Barnsbury
Bierodrome
Camden Head
Chapel, The
Compton Arms
Crown
Cuba Libre
Draper's Arms
Duke of Cambridge
Elbow Room
Filthy MacNasty's
Garage
Hen & Chickens
hog's head
Hope & Anchor
House, The
Island Queen
Jorene Celeste
King's Head Theatre
La Finca
Medicine
Narrow Boat
Old Red Lion
Pitcher & Piano
Rosemary Branch
Ruby Lounge
Salmon & Compass
Slug & Lettuce
Social
Swimmer
Tup
25 Canonbury Ln.
Walkabout

King's Cross

Backpacker
Cross
Lincoln Lounge
Scala

St. John's Wood

Abbey Road Pub
Café Med

Café Rouge
Clifton
Duke of York
Lord's Tavern
Otto
Warrington

Stoke Newington
Bar Lorca
Fox Reformed
Tup

SOUTH/SOUTH WEST LONDON

Barnes
Bull's Head
Coach & Horses
Porterhouse
Sun Inn

Battersea
Duke of Cambridge
Dusk
Holy Drinker
Inigo
Jongleurs/Bar Risa
Lavender
Mason's Arms

Brixton/Clapham
Alexandra Pub
Arch635
Atlantic 66
Bar Local
Belle Vue
Bierodrome
Bread & Roses
Brixton B & G
Brixtonian
Bug
Café Rouge
Calf
Dogstar
Fine Line
Fridge Bar
Frog/Forget-Me-Not
Grand, The
Infernos
Iniquity
Kazbar
Lavender
Living
Lounge
Mistress P's
Oblivion
Plan B
Prince of Wales
Rapscallion
Revolution
Sand
Sequel, The

Slug & Lettuce
SO.UK
Sun
Tea Rooms/Artistes
Tongue & Groove
2 Brewers
White Horse
White House
Windmill on Common

Camberwell/Dulwich/Herne Hill
Barcelona Tapas
Crown & Greyhound
Funky Munky
Red Star

Chelsea
ad lib
Anglesea Arms
Apartment 195
Bluebird
Builder's Arms
Cadogan Arms
Chelsea Potter
Chelsea Ram
Coopers Arms
Cross Keys
Eclipse
Fox & Hounds
Henry J Bean's
Imperial
Jim Thompson's
Kosmopol
mybar
Orange Brewery
Phene Arms
PJ's Bar/Grill
Po Na Na
606 Club
Sporting Page
Surprise

Earl's Court
Nam Long
O'Neill's
Troubadour Cafe

Cafeteria
Churchill Arms
Cuba
Scarsdale
Windsor Castle

Notting Hill/Holland Park/ Ladbroke Grove/ Westbourne Grove
Babushka
Beach Blanket
Bed
blagclub
Café Med
Castle
e&o
Eclipse
Elbow Room
Gate
Grand Union
Ground Floor
Harlem
Julie's
Ladbroke Arms
Lonsdale Hse.

Market Bar
Mook
Paradise/Kensal
Portobello Gold
Portobello Star
Prince Bonaparte
Trailer Happiness
Visible
Westbourne
Woody's Club
Zig-Zag

Paddington
Cubana
Low Life
Steam

Shepherd's Bush
Anglesea Arms
Belushi's
Bush B&G
Havelock
O'Neill's
Vesbar
Walkabout

SPECIAL APPEALS

(Indexes list the best of many within each category. For multi-location nightspots, the availability of index features may vary by location. For some categories, schedules may vary; call ahead or check Web sites for the most up-to-date information.)

After Work

Abbey Road Pub (NW8)
Akbar (W1)
All Bar One (multi. loc.)
Alphabet (W1)
Al's Bar (EC1)
Antelope (SW1)
Archduke (SE1)
Argyll Arms (W1)
Artillery Arms (EC1)
Auberge (multi. loc.)
Audley (W1)
Babble (W1)
Balham Kitchen/Bar (SW12)
Balls Brothers (multi. loc.)
Baltic (SE1)
Bank (WC2)
Bar Chocolate (W1)
Bar 38 (W6)
Belgo (WC2)
Bierodrome (multi. loc.)
Bishops Finger (EC1)
Black Friar (EC4)
Blue Posts (W1)
Bonds (EC2)
Cantaloupe (EC2)
Chandos (WC2)
Chapel (NW1)
Cittie of Yorke (WC1)
Coach & Horses (W1)
Coal Hole (WC2)
Cock Tavern (W1)
Cork & Bottle (WC2)
Corney & Barrow (multi. loc.)
Davy's (multi. loc.)
De Hems (W1)
Dirty Dick (EC2)
Dog & Duck (W1)
1802 (E14)
Fenchurch Colony (EC3)
Fishmarket (EC2)
Fitzroy (W1)
Frog/Forget-Me-Not (multi. loc.)
George Bar (EC2)
Gordon's (WC2)
Griffin (EC2)
Henry J Bean's (multi. loc.)
hog's head (multi. loc.)
Jamaica Wine (EC3)
Jamies (multi. loc.)
Jerusalem (W1)
Jerusalem Tavern (EC1)
John Snow (W1)
Kick (multi. loc.)
Knights Templar (WC2)
La Grande Marque (EC4)
Lamb (WC1)
Lamb Tavern (EC3)
Langley (WC2)
Leadenhall (EC3)
Ling Ling (W1)
Lowlander (WC2)
Mash (W1)
Mulligans Mayfair (W1)
19:20 (EC1)
Nylon (EC2)
Office (W1)
Old Bank (EC4)
Old Bell (EC4)
115 @ Hodgsons (WC2)
O'Neill's (multi. loc.)
1 Lombard St. (EC3)
Pillars of Hercules (W1)
Pitcher & Piano (multi. loc.)
Porterhouse (multi. loc.)
Porters Bar (multi. loc.)
Princess Louise (WC1)
Queen Mary (WC2)
Rising Sun (EC4)
Scott's Penguin (W1)
Seven Stars (WC2)
Ship & Shovell (WC2)
Slug & Lettuce (multi. loc.)
Smersh (EC2)
Smiths/Smithfield (EC1)
Smollensky's (multi. loc.)
Spice of Life (W1)
Studio 6 (SE1)
Sun & 13 (W1)
Tattershall Castle (SW1)
Three Kings (EC1)
Toucan (W1)

Wax (W1)
Ye Grapes (W1)
Ye Olde Cheshire (EC4)
Zebrano (W1)

Beautiful People

ad lib (SW10)
Admiral Codrington (SW3)
Alphabet (W1)
American Bar (WC2)
American Bar (W1)
Annabel's (W1)
Apartment 195 (SW3)
Atlantic B&G (W1)
Attica (W1)
Aura (SW1)
Avenue (SW1)
Baltic (SE1)
Beach Blanket (W11)
Bluebird (SW3)
Box (WC2)
Browns (WC2)
Bush B&G (W12)
Café de Paris (W1)
Cafeteria (W10)
Chinawhite (W1)
Cinnamon Club (SW1)
Circus (W1)
Click (W1)
Crazy Bear (W1)
Dukes Hotel Bar (SW1)
e&o (W11)
Elysium (W1)
Embassy (W1)
Fifth Floor (SW1)
G-A-Y Bar (W1)
Harlem (W2)
Heaven (WC2)
Hush (W1)
ICA Bar (SW1)
Isola (SW1)
Jewel (W1)
Kemia Bar (W1)
Kingly Club (W1)
Ku De Ta (W1)
Light Bar (WC2)
Ling Ling (W1)
Long Bar (W1)
Lonsdale Hse. (W11)
Medicine (multi. loc.)
Met Bar (W1)
Milk & Honey (W1)
Millbank Lounge (SW1)
Mint Leaf (SW1)
Nam Long (SW5)
noble rot. (W1)
190 Queensgate (SW7)

Paparazzi (SW3)
Purple Bar (W1)
Quaglino's (SW1)
Rockwell (SW1)
Salt Whisky Bar (W2)
Sanctuary Soho (W1)
Shadow Lounge (W1)
Sketch (W1)
Taman Gang (W1)
Tantra Club (W1)
Vibe Bar (E1)
Village Soho (W1)
Zeta Bar (W1)
Zuma (SW7)

Beer Specialists

(* Microbreweries)
Abbaye (EC1)
Anchor and Hope (SE1)
Archery Tavern (W2)
Ashburnham Arms (SE10)
Atlas (SW6)
Auberge (multi. loc.)
Barley Mow (W1)
Barnsbury (N1)
Belgo (multi. loc.)
Bierodrome (multi. loc.)
Bishops Finger (EC1)
Bread & Roses (SW4)
Buckingham Arms (SW1)
Bünker Bar (WC2)*
Cantaloupe (EC2)
Castle (W11)
Chapel (NW1)
Cittie of Yorke (WC1)
City Barge (W4)
Clifton (NW8)
Coach & Horses (SW13)
Coach & Horses (WC2)
Counting House (EC3)
Cow (W2)
Crown (N1)
Crown, The (E3)
De Hems (W1)
Dog & Duck (W1)
Dove (W6)
Dover Castle (W1)
Draper's Arms (N1)
Duke of Cambridge (SW11)
Duke of Cambridge (N1)
1802 (E14)
Filthy MacNasty's (EC1)
Fire Station (SE1)
Flask (N6)
Fox & Hounds (SW1)
George Inn (SE1)
Greenwich Union (SE10)

Cocktail Experts

Woody's Club (W9)
Zander Bar (SW1)
Zebrano (W1)
Zeta Bar (W1)
Zig-Zag (W11)
Zinc B&G (W1)
Zuma (SW7)

Comedy Clubs
(Call ahead to check nights,
times, performers and covers)
Bar Code (W1)
Bedford (SW12)
Comedy Café (EC2)
Comedy Store (SW1)
Jongleurs/Bar Risa (multi. loc.)
Madame JoJo's (W1)
Troubadour Cafe (SW5)
Tup (N16)

Commuter
Blackfriars
   Black Friar (EC4)
   El Vino (EC4)
   Evangelist (EC4)
Canary Wharf
   Corney & Barrow (E14)
   1802 (E14)
   Via Fossa (E14)
Cannon St.
   El Vino (EC4)
Charing Cross
   Coal Hole (WC2)
   Gordon's (WC2)
   Ship & Shovell (WC2)
City Thameslink
   Corney & Barrow (EC4)
   La Grande Marque (EC4)
   Punch Tavern (EC4)
Euston
   Head of Steam (NW1)
Farringdon
   All Bar One (EC1)
   Jerusalem Tavern (EC1)
   19:20 (EC1)
   Smiths/Smithfield (EC1)
Fenchurch St.
   Balls Brothers (EC3)
   Corney & Barrow (EC3)
   Lamb Tavern (EC3)
   Pitcher & Piano (EC3)
   Slug & Lettuce (EC3)
King's Cross
   Lincoln Lounge (N1)
   Smithy's (WC1)

Liverpool St.
   All Bar One (EC2)
   Balls Brothers (EC3)
   Corney & Barrow (EC2)
   Dirty Dick (EC2)
   Hamilton Hall (EC2)
   Pitcher & Piano (EC2)
London Bridge
   Market Porter (SE1)
   Slug & Lettuce (SE1)
Paddington
   Steam (W2)
Tower Gateway
   Fenchurch Colony (EC3)
   Fine Line (EC3)
   Smollensky's (E1)
   Wine Library (EC3)
Victoria
   Plumbers Arms (SW1)
   Zander Bar (SW1)
Waterloo
   All Bar One (SE1)
   Archduke (SE1)
   Fire Station (SE1)
   King's Arms (SE1)
   Studio 6 (SE1)

DJ Bars
ad lib (SW10)
AKA (WC1)
Anexo (EC1)
Babushka (multi. loc.)
Bar Rumba (W1)
Bar Sia (SW19)
Bar Soho (W1)
Bar Sol Ona (W1)
Bed (W10)
Bedroom Bar (EC2)
blagclub (multi. loc.)
Bluu (N1)
Brixton B & G (SW9)
Brixtonian (SW9)
Bug (SW2)
Camden Brewing (NW1)
Candy Bar (W1)
Cargo (EC2)
Cocomo (EC1)
Comptons of Soho (W1)
Cross (N1)
Cru (N1)
Denim (WC2)
Detroit (WC2)
Dogstar (SW9)
Dragon (EC2)

dreambagsjaguar (E2)
Dusk (SW11)
Dust (EC1)
Eagle Bar (W1)
Edge (W1)
Elbow Room (multi. loc.)
Elysium (W1)
First Out (WC2)
Fluid (EC1)
Forum (NW5)
Freedom (W1)
Fridge Bar (SW2)
Fuel (WC2)
Funky Munky (SE5)
Garage (N5)
Gate (W11)
G-A-Y Bar (W1)
Glasshouse (EC4)
Gossips (W1)
Grand Central (E1)
Harlem (W2)
Heaven (WC2)
Herbal (E2)
Home (EC2)
Hoxton Sq. Bar (N1)
Inigo (SW8)
Iniquity (SW11)
Jerusalem (W1)
Jewel (W1)
Ku De Ta (W1)
Lifthouse (EC1)
Light (E1)
Lime (EC2)
Lincoln Lounge (N1)
Living (SW9)
Low Life (W1)
Madame JoJo's (W1)
Market Bar (W11)
Market Place (W1)
Matchbar (W1)
Match ec1 (EC1)
Medicine (multi. loc.)
Metro Club (W1)
Millbank Lounge (SW1)
Monkey Chews (NW5)
93 Feet East (E1)
noble rot. (W1)
Nylon (EC2)
Office (W1)
Oh! Bar (NW1)
Otto (W9)
Oxygen (WC2)
Plan B (SW9)
Player (W1)
Po Na Na (multi. loc.)
Pool (EC2)

Positively 4th St. (NW1)
Prince Bonaparte (W2)
Purple Night (SW6)
Q Bar (W1)
Red Star (SE5)
Retro Bar (WC2)
Ruby Blue (WC1)
Ruby Lounge (multi. loc.)
Salmon & Compass (N1)
Sand (SW4)
Shadow Lounge (W1)
Shoreditch Electricity (N1)
Sketch (W1)
Smersh (EC2)
Social (multi. loc.)
Sosho (EC2)
Sun & 13 (W1)
Sway (WC2)
Tantra Club (W1)
Tea Rooms/Artistes (SW8)
Ten Bells (E1)
Thirst (W1)
333 Club/Mother (EC1)
Tiger Tiger (SW1)
Toast (NW3)
Tongue & Groove (SW9)
Two Floors (W1)
Vibe Bar (E1)
Yauatcha (W1)
Zd Bar (NW6)

Dramatic Interiors
Akbar (W1)
American Bar (WC2)
American Bar (W1)
Annabel's (W1)
Artesian Well (SW8)
Attica (W1)
Aura (SW1)
Avenue (SW1)
Baltic (SE1)
Bar Sia (SW19)
Beach Blanket (W11)
Bedroom Bar (EC2)
Black Friar (EC4)
Blue Bar (SW1)
Bonds (EC2)
Chinawhite (W1)
Cinnamon Club (SW1)
Circus (W1)
Claridge's Bar (W1)
Click (W1)
Collection (SW3)
Crazy Bear (W1)
Cross Keys (SW3)
Detroit (WC2)
Dorchester Bar (W1)

1802 (E14)
Elysium (W1)
Fiesta Havana (W1)
Firevault (W1)
Fluid (EC1)
Garlic & Shots (W1)
George Bar (EC2)
Grand Central (E1)
Hamilton Hall (EC2)
Highgate (NW5)
Hush (W1)
Island Queen (N1)
Isola (SW1)
Jim Thompson's (SW6)
Kosmopol (SW10)
Ku De Ta (W1)
La Grande Marque (EC4)
Light (E1)
Light Bar (WC2)
Lime (EC2)
Ling Ling (W1)
Long Bar (W1)
Market Bar (W11)
Mash (W1)
Match ec1 (EC1)
Milk & Honey (W1)
Millbank Lounge (SW1)
Monkey Chews (NW5)
Narrow Boat (N1)
93 Feet East (E1)
noble rot. (W1)
Nylon (EC2)
115 @ Hodgsons (WC2)
1 Lombard St. (EC3)
190 Queensgate (SW7)
Oscar (W1)
Oxo Tower (SE1)
Paxton's Head (SW1)
Perseverance (WC1)
Po Na Na (W6)
Pop (W1)
Positively 4th St. (NW1)
Prince of Wales (SW4)
Prism (EC3)
Purple Bar (W1)
Retro Bar (WC2)
Rivoli Bar/Ritz (W1)
Rockwell (SW1)
Ruby Lounge (N1)
Salisbury, The (WC2)
Salt Whisky Bar (W2)
Sanctuary Soho (W1)
Scott's Penguin (W1)
Sketch (W1)
Soho (W1)
Sway (WC2)
Taman Gang (W1)

Tantra Club (W1)
Ten Bells (E1)
10 Room (W1)
Thirst (W1)
Townhouse (SW3)
Via Fossa (E14)
Vic Naylor (EC1)
Warrington (W9)
Yauatcha (W1)
Zig-Zag (W11)

Expense-Accounters
Akbar (W1)
American Bar (WC2)
American Bar (W1)
Annabel's (W1)
Apartment 195 (SW3)
Atlantic B&G (W1)
Attica (W1)
Avenue (SW1)
Baltic (SE1)
Blue Bar (SW1)
Bonds (EC2)
Bush B&G (W12)
Café de Paris (W1)
Cafeteria (W10)
Chinawhite (W1)
Cinnamon Club (SW1)
Circus (W1)
Claridge's Bar (W1)
Collection (SW3)
Dorchester Bar (W1)
Dukes Hotel Bar (SW1)
Elysium (W1)
Embassy (W1)
Fenchurch Colony (EC3)
Fifth Floor (SW1)
Fishmarket (EC2)
Isola (SW1)
Kettner's (W1)
Kingly Club (W1)
Ku De Ta (W1)
Library (SW1)
Ling Ling (W1)
Long Bar (W1)
Met Bar (W1)
115 @ Hodgsons (WC2)
Opium (W1)
Oxo Tower (SE1)
Prism (EC3)
Purple Bar (W1)
Purple Night (SW6)
Quaglino's (SW1)
Red Bar (W1)
Rockwell (SW1)
Scott's Penguin (W1)
Sketch (W1)

Yauatcha (W1)
Yo! Below (W1)
Zilli Bar (W1)
Zinc B&G (W1)

First Date
ad lib (SW10)
Akbar (W1)
American Bar (WC2)
Apartment 195 (SW3)
Atlantic B&G (W1)
Atlas (SW6)
Aura (SW1)
Avenue (SW1)
Bartok (NW1)
Beach Blanket (W11)
Bleeding Heart Tav. (EC1)
Blend (WC2)
Blue Bar (SW1)
Bluebird (SW3)
Blues Bistro (W1)
Bonds (EC2)
Bush B&G (W12)
Cantaloupe (EC2)
Cinnamon Club (SW1)
Circus (W1)
City Barge (W4)
Claridge's Bar (W1)
Clerkenwell Hse. (EC1)
Cork & Bottle (WC2)
Cross Keys (SW3)
Dorchester Bar (W1)
Eagle Bar (W1)
Firevault (W1)
Fox Reformed (N16)
Freemasons Arms (NW3)
Freud (WC2)
Highgate (NW5)
Holly Bush (NW3)
Hush (W1)
Julie's (W11)
Kettner's (W1)
Leadenhall (EC3)
Light Bar (WC2)
Long Bar (W1)
Mandarin Bar (SW1)
mybar (multi. loc.)
Narrow Boat (N1)
115 @ Hodgsons (WC2)
Oxo Tower (SE1)
Paradise/Kensal (W10)
Purple Bar (W1)
Putney Bridge (SW15)
Quaglino's (SW1)
Rivoli Bar/Ritz (W1)
Rockwell (SW1)
Scott's Penguin (W1)

Sequel, The (SW4)
Sketch (W1)
Smiths/Smithfield (EC1)
Smithy's (WC1)
Soho (W1)
Soho Spice (W1)
Sun (SW4)
Troubadour Cafe (SW5)
25 Canonbury Ln. (N1)
Twentyfour (EC2)
Warrington (W9)
Windows Bar (W1K)
Ye Olde Mitre (EC1)
Zilli Bar (W1)

Foreign Feeling
Eastern
ad lib (SW10)
Akbar (W1)
Bar Bollywood (W1)
Chinawhite (W1)
Cicada (EC1)
Cinnamon Club (SW1)
Crazy Bear (W1)
e&o (W11)
Elysium (W1)
Fluid (EC1)
Jim Thompson's (SW6)
Ling Ling (W1)
Opium (W1)
Positively 4th St. (NW1)
Sugar Hut (SW6)
Taman Gang (W1)
Tantra Club (W1)
Yauatcha (W1)
Yo! Below (W1)
Zd Bar (NW6)
Zuma (SW7)

French/Belgian
Auberge (multi. loc.)
Belgo (multi. loc.)
Bierodrome (multi. loc.)
Café Boheme (W1)
Café Rouge (multi. loc.)
Lowlander (WC2)

Irish
Filthy MacNasty's (EC1)
Mulligans Mayfair (W1)
O'Conor Don (W1)
O'Hanlon's (EC1)
O'Neill's (multi. loc.)
Porterhouse (multi. loc.)
Quinns (NW1)
Toucan (W1)
Waxy O'Connor's (W1)

Latin

(Call to check nights and times)

Amber (W1)
Arizona Bar (NW1)
Barcelona Tapas (multi. loc.)
Bar Gansa (NW1)
Bar Lorca (N16)
Bar Sol Ona (W1)
Brixtonian (SW9)
Cactus Blue (SW3)
Cuba (W8)
Cuba Libre (N1)
Cubana (multi. loc.)
Fiesta Havana (W1)
Kick (EC1)
La Finca (multi. loc.)
La Mancha (SW15)
La Perla (multi. loc.)
Leadenhall (EC3)
Lomo (SW10)
Navajo Joe's (WC2)
Salsa! (WC2)

Moroccan

Bed (W10)
Beduin (EC1)
Duke of York (NW8)
Kemia Bar (W1)
Po Na Na (SW19)
SO.UK (multi. loc.)

Russian

Potemkin (EC1)
Tsar's Bar (W1)

Gastro-Pubs

Abingdon (W8)
Anchor and Hope (SE1)
Anglesea Arms (W6)
Anglesea Arms (SW7)
Approach Tavern (E2)
Atlas (SW6)
Barnsbury (N1)
Bull's Head (SW13)
Bull's Head (W4)
Calf (SW4)
Cantaloupe (EC2)
Castle (W11)
Cat & Mutton (E8)
Clifton (NW8)
Couch (W1)
Cow (W2)
Crown (N1)
Crown, The (E3)
Cru (N1)
Draper's Arms (N1)
Drayton Arms (SW5)
Duke of Cambridge (N1)

Duke of York (NW8)
Eagle (EC1)
Easton, The (WC1)
Edinboro Castle (NW1)
Engineer (NW1)
Fire Station (SE1)
Gate (W11)
Grand Union (W9)
Hartley Bar (SE1)
Havelock (W14)
Highgate (NW5)
Hill (NW3)
Ifield (SW10)
Jim Thompson's (SW6)
Jolly Gardeners (SW15)
Junction Tavern (NW5)
Ladbroke Arms (W11)
Lansdowne (NW1)
Lord Palmerston (NW5)
Magdala (NW3)
Mason's Arms (SW8)
Medcalf (EC1R)
North Star (N1)
Paradise/Kensal (W10)
Peasant (EC1)
Perseverance (WC1)
Phene Arms (SW3)
Rocket, The (W3)
Salisbury Tavern (SW6)
St. John (multi. loc.)
Stonemason Arms (W6)
Studio 6 (SE1)
Swimmer (N7)
Well (EC1)
Westbourne (W2)

Gay

(See also Lesbian; * certain nights only)

Admiral Duncan (W1)
Astoria (WC2)*
Bar Code (W1)*
Black Cap (NW1)
Black Horse (E1)
Box (WC2)
Comptons of Soho (W1)
Edge (W1)
First Out (WC2)
Freedom (W1)
G-A-Y Bar (W1)
Heaven (WC2)
King William IV (NW3)
Ku Bar (WC2)
Kudos (WC2)
Office (W1)*
Retro Bar (WC2)
Royal Oak (E2)

Rupert St. (W1)
Sanctuary Soho (W1)
79CXR (WC2)
Shadow Lounge (W1)
2 Brewers (SW4)
Vespa Lounge (WC2)
Village Soho (W1)
Yard Bar (W1)

Group-Friendly

Albion (N1)
All Bar One (multi. loc.)
Alphabet (W1)
Amber (W1)
Astoria (WC2)
Babble (W1)
Babushka (multi. loc.)
Backpacker (N1)
Balls Brothers (multi. loc.)
Bar Code (W1)
Barley Mow (EC2)
Bar Lorca (N16)
Bar Room Bar (multi. loc.)
Bar Rumba (W1)
Bar Soho (W1)
Bar 38 (W6)
Beach Blanket (W11)
Belgo (multi. loc.)
Belushi's (multi. loc.)
Bünker Bar (WC2)
Cactus Blue (SW3)
Café de Paris (W1)
Cargo (EC2)
Charterhouse (EC1)
Chelsea Ram (SW10)
Cuba Libre (N1)
Cubana (multi. loc.)
Drayton Arms (SW5)
Eclipse (multi. loc.)
Elbow Room (multi. loc.)
Equinox (WC2)
Fabric (EC1)
Fiesta Havana (W1)
Fire Station (SE1)
Fridge Bar (SW2)
Frog/Forget-Me-Not (multi. loc.)
Fuel (WC2)
Gardening Club (WC2)
Glasshouse (EC4)
Ha!Ha! Bar (multi. loc.)
Halfmoon (SW15)
Hanover Grand (W1)
Henry J Bean's (multi. loc.)
hog's head (multi. loc.)
Jazz Cafe (NW1)
JD Wetherspoons (SW1)
Langley (WC2)

Loop (W1)
Maple Leaf (WC2)
Mean Fiddler (WC2)
Ministry of Sound (SE1)
Moonlighting (W1)
Navajo Joe's (WC2)
On Anon (W1)
O'Neill's (multi. loc.)
Paparazzi (SW3)
Pitcher & Piano (multi. loc.)
Play (EC1)
Po Na Na (multi. loc.)
Pool (EC2)
Pop (W1)
Porterhouse (multi. loc.)
Princess of Wales (SE3)
Punch & Judy (WC2)
Red Star (SE5)
Retox Bar (WC2)
Revolution (multi. loc.)
Roadhouse (WC2)
Ruby Blue (WC1)
Salsa! (WC2)
Scala (N1)
Shh... Rooms (WC2)
Slug & Lettuce (multi. loc.)
South London (SE11)
Spice of Life (W1)
Sports Cafe (SW1)
Spot (WC2)
Sun & 13 (W1)
Sway (WC2)
333 Club/Mother (EC1)
Turnmills (EC1)
Walkabout (multi. loc.)
Wax (W1)
Waxy O'Connor's (W1)
Windmill on Common (SW4)
World's End (NW1)
Zoo Bar (WC2)

Grown-Ups

Abigail's Party (W1)
Abingdon (W8)
Albion (N1)
Almeida (N1)
American Bar (WC2)
American Bar (W1)
Anchor and Hope (SE1)
Angel (WC2)
Anglesea Arms (W6)
Anglesea Arms (SW7)
Annabel's (W1)
Archduke (SE1)
Artillery Arms (EC1)
Ashburnham Arms (SE10)
Atlantic B&G (W1)

Audley (W1)
Australian (SW3)
Balham Kitchen/Bar (SW12)
Bar des Amis (WC2)
Bartok (NW1)
Bluebird (SW3)
Bonds (EC2)
Browns (WC2)
Bull's Head (SW13)
Cadogan Arms (SW3)
Calf (SW4)
Cantina Vinopolis (SE1)
Cinnamon Club (SW1)
Circus (W1)
Claridge's Bar (W1)
Davy's (multi. loc.)
Dial (WC2)
Dorchester Bar (W1)
Dove (W6)
Dukes Hotel Bar (SW1)
El Vino (multi. loc.)
Fenchurch Colony (EC3)
Firevault (W1)
French House (W1)
George Bar (EC2)
George Inn (SE1)
Gordon's (WC2)
Hare & Billet (SE3)
Highgate (NW5)
Hill (NW3)
Jazz Cafe (NW1)
Kemia Bar (W1)
Kettner's (W1)
Kingly Club (W1)
Ling Ling (W1)
Lord's Tavern (NW8)
Milk & Honey (W1)
Nag's Head (SW1)
Old Ship (Richmond)
115 @ Hodgsons (WC2)
Oscar (W1)
Oxo Tower (SE1)
Phene Arms (SW3)
Porters Bar (multi. loc.)
Quaglino's (SW1)
Queen's Head (E14)
Rapscallion (SW4)
Ronnie Scott's (W1)
Royal Oak (SW1)
Scott's Penguin (W1)
Ship & Shovell (WC2)
606 Club (SW10)
Sketch (W1)
Smithy's (WC1)
Surprise (SW3)
Swimmer (N7)
Taman Gang (W1)

Wenlock Arms (N1)
Westminster Arms (SW1)
Wheatsheaf (SE1)
White Swan (Richmond)
Yauatcha (W1)
Ye Grapes (W1)
Ye Olde Cheshire (EC4)
Ye Olde Mitre (EC1)
Zig-Zag (W11)

Hen Party

Abigail's Party (W1)
Alexandra Pub (SW4)
Alexandra/Smart (SW19)
Amber (W1)
Arizona Bar (NW1)
Artesian Well (SW8)
Babble (W1)
Backpacker (N1)
Bar Gansa (NW1)
Bar Rumba (W1)
Bar Soho (W1)
Beduin (EC1)
Belushi's (multi. loc.)
Cactus Blue (SW3)
CC Club (W1)
Cheers (W1)
Cirque/Hippodrome (WC2)
Cross (N1)
Cuba (W8)
Eclipse (multi. loc.)
Equinox (WC2)
Fiesta Havana (W1)
Fuel (WC2)
Gardening Club (WC2)
Glasshouse (EC4)
Hanover Grand (W1)
Inigo (SW8)
Jongleurs/Bar Risa (multi. loc.)
Julie's (W11)
La Finca (multi. loc.)
La Perla (multi. loc.)
Lonsdale Hse. (W11)
Loop (W1)
Madame JoJo's (W1)
Ministry of Sound (SE1)
Monkey Chews (NW5)
Moonlighting (W1)
Nam Long (SW5)
Navajo Joe's (WC2)
noble rot. (W1)
O Bar (W1)
Office (W1)
On Anon (W1)
Oxygen (WC2)
Paparazzi (SW3)
Pitcher & Piano (multi. loc.)

Player (W1)
Point 101 (WC1)
Po Na Na (multi. loc.)
Pop (W1)
Prince Bonaparte (W2)
Q Bar (W1)
Quaglino's (SW1)
Retox Bar (WC2)
Retro Bar (WC2)
Revolution (multi. loc.)
Roadhouse (WC2)
Ruby Blue (WC1)
Salsa! (WC2)
Sand (SW4)
Scala (N1)
Shh... Rooms (WC2)
Shoreditch Electricity (N1)
Slug & Lettuce (multi. loc.)
Smollensky's (multi. loc.)
Sosho (EC2)
SO.UK (multi. loc.)
South London (SE11)
Spot (WC2)
Steam (W2)
Sway (WC2)
Tattershall Castle (SW1)
Tea Rooms/Artistes (SW8)
10 Room (W1)
Thirst (W1)
Tiger Tiger (SW1)
25 Canonbury Ln. (N1)
Wax (W1)
Waxy O'Connor's (W1)
World's End (NW1)
Zander Bar (SW1)
Zoo Bar (WC2)

Historic Interest
(Year opened; * building)
1430 Cittie of Yorke (WC1)*
1474 City Barge (W4)*
1500 Pillars of Hercules (W1)
1500 Windmill on Common
       (SW4)*
1522 Prospect/Whitby (E1)*
1542 George Inn (SE1)
1545 Town of Ramsgate (E1)*
1550 Market Porter (SE1)*
1550 Sun Inn (SW13)*
1583 Grapes (E14)
1585 Spaniard's Inn (NW3)*
1598 Hoop & Grapes (EC3)*
1600 Grenadier (SW1)*
1602 Seven Stars (WC2)*
1633 Flask (N6)*
1652 Jamaica Wine (EC3)*
1659 Rose & Crown (SW19)*

1667 Ye Olde Cheshire (EC4)*
1668 Old Bell (EC4)*
1695 Cutty Sark (SE10)*
1700 Flask, The (NW3)*
1700 Jerusalem Tavern (EC1)*
1720 Lamb (WC1)*
1735 Old Ship (Richmond)*
1735 Shepherd's Tavern (W1)*
1740 Argyll Arms (W1)
1740 Ship & Shovell (WC2)
1750 Green Man (SW15)*
1750 Ye Olde Mitre (EC1)*
1753 Ten Bells (E1)*
1756 Captain Kidd (E1)*
1800 Old Thameside (SE1)*
1800 Princess Louise (WC1)*
1800 Red Lion (SW1)
1800 Ye Olde Watling (EC4)*
1835 White Cross (Richmond)*
1837 Trafalgar Tavern (SE10)*
1850 John Snow (W1)
1867 Morpeth Arms (SW1)*
1870 Lamb Tavern (EC3)*
1870 Royal Oak (SE1)
1882 Red Lion (SW1)
1882 Ye Grapes (W1)
1884 Ship (SW18)
1888 Old Bank (EC4)*
1889 Coal Hole (WC2)*
1890 Old Red Lion (EC1)*
1890 Punch Tavern (EC4)*
1892 Salisbury, The (WC2)
1898 Cock Tavern (W1)*
1900 French House (W1)
1931 Dorchester Bar (W1)

Hotel Bars
Athenaeum Hotel
    Whisky Bar (W1J)
Berkeley Hotel
    Blue Bar (SW1)
Charlotte Street Hotel
    Oscar (W1)
Claridge's Hotel
    Claridge's Bar (W1)
Connaught Hotel
    American Bar (W1)
Dorchester Hotel
    Dorchester Bar (W1)
Dukes Hotel
    Dukes Hotel Bar (SW1)
Gore Hotel
    190 Queensgate (SW7)
Great Eastern Hotel
    Fishmarket (EC2)
    George Bar (EC2)

Jazz Clubs

Late Licence

(Serves alcohol after 11PM;
call ahead to check times and
days of the week)

Met Bar (W1)
Metro Club (W1)
Millbank Lounge (SW1)
Ministry of Sound (SE1)
Nam Long (SW5)
93 Feet East (E1)
Nylon (EC2)
O Bar (W1)
Oh! Bar (NW1)
On Anon (W1)
Oxygen (WC2)
Paparazzi (SW3)
Plan B (SW9)
Play (EC1)
Player (W1)
Point 101 (WC1)
Pop (W1)
Purple Night (SW6)
Quinns (NW1)
Red Star (SE5)
Roadhouse (WC2)
Ruby Blue (WC1)
Ruby Lounge (N1)
Sanctuary Soho (W1)
Sand (SW4)
Scala (N1)
Shoreditch Electricity (N1)
Shumi (SW1)
6 Degrees (W1)
Sketch (W1)
Social (W1)
Soho (W1)
Sosho (EC2)
Spot (WC2)
Sway (WC2)
Thirst (W1)
333 Club/Mother (EC1)
Tiger Tiger (SW1)
Tsar's Bar (W1)
Turnmills (EC1)
Vespa Lounge (WC2)
Vibe Bar (E1)
Zander Bar (SW1)
Zoo Bar (WC2)
Zuma (SW7)

Lesbian
(* certain nights only)
Astoria (WC2)*
Candy Bar (W1)
First Out (WC2)
Kudos (WC2)
Office (W1)*
Retro Bar (WC2)
Sanctuary Soho (W1)
Vespa Lounge (WC2)

Live Entertainment
(See also Comedy Clubs, DJ Bars and Jazz Clubs)
Africa Bar (WC2) (world music)
Ain't Nothin' But (W1) (blues)
Astoria (WC2) (rock)
Bartok (NW1) (classical)
Bedford (SW12) (varies)
Café de Paris (W1) (cabaret)
Camden Head (N1) (comedy)
Cargo (EC2) (varies)
Comedy Café (EC2) (comedy)
Comedy Store (SW1) (comedy)
De Hems (W1) (comedy)
Dragon (EC2) (varies)
Drayton Arms (SW5) (rock)
Electric Ballroom (NW1) (rock)
End (WC1) (rock)
Fabric (EC1) (hip-hop/rock)
Filthy MacNasty's (EC1) (varies)
Fire Station (SE1) (jazz)
Halfmoon (SW15) (varies)
Hen & Chickens (N1) (varies)
Kabaret (W1) (varies)
Kemia Bar (W1) (world music)
Kettner's (W1) (varies)
Ku Bar (WC2) (cabaret)
Kudos (WC2) (varies)
La Mancha (SW15) (guitar)
Lamb & Flag (WC2) (jazz)
La Perla (SW6) (rock)
Library (SW1) (piano)
Lomo (SW10) (guitar)
Mean Fiddler (WC2) (varies)
Retro Bar (WC2) (karaoke)
Turnmills (EC1) (rock)
Underworld (NW1) (rock/indie)
Vic Naylor (EC1) (jazz)
Wenlock Arms (N1) (blues/jazz)
Walkabout (multi. loc.) (rock)
World's End (NW1) (rock)

Meat Markets
All Bar One (multi. loc.)
Amber (W1)
Arizona Bar (NW1)
Artesian Well (SW8)
Astoria (WC2)
Atlantic B&G (W1)
Attica (W1)
Babble (W1)
Babushka (N1)
Backpacker (N1)
Bank (WC2)
Bar Code (W1)
Bar Rumba (W1)

Bar Soho (W1)
Belushi's (multi. loc.)
Box (WC2)
Cactus Blue (SW3)
Candy Bar (W1)
Castle (W11)
CC Club (W1)
Cheers (W1)
Chinawhite (W1)
Cirque/Hippodrome (WC2)
Click (W1)
Comptons of Soho (W1)
Dogstar (SW9)
Eclipse (multi. loc.)
Edge (W1)
Equinox (WC2)
Fiesta Havana (W1)
First Out (WC2)
Freedom (W1)
Gardening Club (WC2)
G-A-Y Bar (W1)
Glasshouse (EC4)
Hanover Grand (W1)
Heaven (WC2)
Inigo (SW8)
Jamies (multi. loc.)
Jolly Gardeners (SW15)
Jongleurs/Bar Risa (multi. loc.)
Kazbar (SW4)
Kosmopol (SW10)
Ku Bar (WC2)
Kudos (WC2)
La Finca (multi. loc.)
Loop (W1)
Mean Fiddler (WC2)
Ministry of Sound (SE1)
Moonlighting (W1)
Navajo Joe's (WC2)
noble rot. (W1)
O Bar (W1)
On Anon (W1)
Oxygen (WC2)
Paparazzi (SW3)
PJ's Bar/Grill (SW3)
Player (W1)
Point 101 (WC1)
Po Na Na (SW19)
Pop (W1)
Prince Bonaparte (W2)
Retro Bar (WC2)
Roadhouse (WC2)
Ruby Blue (WC1)
Rupert St. (W1)
Salsa! (WC2)
Sanctuary Soho (W1)
Scala (N1)
79CXR (WC2)

Shadow Lounge (W1)
Shh... Rooms (WC2)
South London (SE11)
Spot (WC2)
Sway (WC2)
Tantra Club (W1)
Tiger Tiger (SW1)
2 Brewers (SW4)
Vespa Lounge (WC2)
Village Soho (W1)
Wax (W1)
WKD (NW1)
Woody's Club (W9)
Yard Bar (W1)
Zd Bar (NW6)
Zoo Bar (WC2)

Noteworthy Newcomers

Anchor and Hope (SE1)
Atlantic 66 (SW9)
Balham Kitchen/Bar (SW12)
Bar Bollywood (W1)
Baroque Rooms (SW7)
Bar Sia (SW19)
Brixton B & G (SW9)
Bünker Bar (WC2)
Cafeteria (W10)
Cat & Mutton (E8)
Crazy Bear (W1)
Destino (W1)
$ (EC1)
Dusk (SW11)
Easton, The (WC1)
Harlem (W2)
Hartley Bar (SE1)
Iniquity (SW11)
Jolly Gardeners (SW15)
Junction Tavern (NW5)
Legion, The (EC1)
Lounge (SW9)
Loungelover (E1)
Medcalf (EC1R)
Millbank Lounge (SW1)
Mint Leaf (SW1)
NYT (WC2)
Opal (SW7)
Pasha (SW7)
Rex Cinema (W1)
Rocket, The (W3)
Salt Whisky Bar (W2)
Shish (EC1V)
Shumi (SW1)
6 Degrees (W1)
Southwark Rooms (SE1)
Taman Gang (W1)
Trailer Happiness (W11)
Tsar's Bar (W1)

White Horse (SW2)*
White Horse (SW6)*
White Swan (Richmond)*
Windmill on Common (SW4)*
Windsor Castle (W8)*
Yard Bar (W1)

People-Watching

Abigail's Party (W1)
Abingdon (W8)
ad lib (SW10)
Admiral Codrington (SW3)
Almeida (N1)
Alphabet (W1)
Amber (W1)
American Bar (WC2)
American Bar (W1)
Anexo (EC1)
Angel (WC2)
Annabel's (W1)
Apartment 195 (SW3)
Artesian Well (SW8)
Astoria (WC2)
Atlantic B&G (W1)
Attica (W1)
Aura (SW1)
Babushka (W11)
Bluebird (SW3)
Blues Bistro (W1)
Bluu (N1)
Café de Paris (W1)
Chinawhite (W1)
Claridge's Bar (W1)
Click (W1)
Coach & Horses (W1)
Cocomo (EC1)
Couch (W1)
Dial (WC2)
Dover St. (W1)
dreambagsjaguar (E2)
e&o (W11)
Elysium (W1)
Fifth Floor (SW1)
Freedom (W1)
Freud (WC2)
Gate (W11)
Herbal (E2)
Hoxton Sq. Bar (N1)
Hush (W1)
ICA Bar (SW1)
Intrepid Fox (W1)
Isola (SW1)
Jewel (W1)
Kabaret (W1)
Kazbar (SW4)
Kemia Bar (W1)
Kingly Club (W1)

Kosmopol (SW10)
Ku De Ta (W1)
Lime (EC2)
Ling Ling (W1)
Long Bar (W1)
Lonsdale Hse. (W11)
Mandarin Bar (SW1)
Match ec1 (EC1)
Met Bar (W1)
Nam Long (SW5)
19:20 (EC1)
noble rot. (W1)
Nylon (EC2)
1 Lombard St. (EC3)
Opium (W1)
Paparazzi (SW3)
Play (EC1)
Pop (W1)
Purple Bar (W1)
Quaglino's (SW1)
Retro Bar (WC2)
Sanctuary Soho (W1)
Shh... Rooms (WC2)
Sketch (W1)
SO.UK (multi. loc.)
Sun (SW4)
Taman Gang (W1)
Tantra Club (W1)
Thirst (W1)
Townhouse (SW3)
Vibe Bar (E1)
Village Soho (W1)
Villandry (W1)
Westminster Arms (SW1)
Yard Bar (W1)
Zig-Zag (W11)
Zilli Bar (W1)

Sleepers

(Good to excellent ratings, but
little known)
Approach Tavern (E2)
Ashburnham Arms (SE10)
Clifton (NW8)
Coach & Horses (SW13)
Cru (N1)
Draper's Arms (N1)
1802 (E14)
Firevault (W1)
Fox & Anchor (EC1)
Fox & Grapes (SW19)
Just Oriental (SW1)
Lincoln Lounge (N1)
Living (SW9)
Lobby Bar (WC2)
Loungelover (E1)
Monkey Chews (NW5)

Na Zdrowie (WC1)
Plan B (SW9)
Positively 4th St. (NW1)
Red Lion (SW1)
Red Lion (W1)
Retro Bar (WC2)
Richard I (SE10)
Sultan (SW19)
Sun (SW4)
Tongue & Groove (SW9)
Well (EC1)
Whisky Bar (W1J)
White Cross (Richmond)

Stag Party

Alexandra Pub (SW4)
Alexandra/Smart (SW19)
Amber (W1)
Arizona Bar (NW1)
Babble (W1)
Backpacker (N1)
Bar Rumba (W1)
Bar Soho (W1)
Bedford (SW12)
Beduin (EC1)
Belgo (WC2)
Belushi's (multi. loc.)
Bünker Bar (WC2)
Cactus Blue (SW3)
CC Club (W1)
Cheers (W1)
Cirque/Hippodrome (WC2)
Comedy Store (SW1)
Cross (N1)
Equinox (WC2)
Fuel (WC2)
Gardening Club (WC2)
Glasshouse (EC4)
Hanover Grand (W1)
Inigo (SW8)
Jongleurs/Bar Risa (multi. loc.)
Loop (W1)
Maple Leaf (WC2)
Ministry of Sound (SE1)
Moonlighting (W1)
Navajo Joe's (WC2)
noble rot. (W1)
O Bar (W1)
Office (W1)
On Anon (W1)
Pitcher & Piano (multi. loc.)
Player (W1)
Point 101 (WC1)
Po Na Na (multi. loc.)
Pop (W1)
Porterhouse (multi. loc.)
Prince Bonaparte (W2)

Racing Page (TW9)
Retox Bar (WC2)
Revolution (multi. loc.)
Roadhouse (WC2)
Ruby Blue (WC1)
Sand (SW4)
Scala (N1)
Shh... Rooms (WC2)
Shoreditch Electricity (N1)
Slug & Lettuce (multi. loc.)
Sosho (EC2)
South London (SE11)
Spice of Life (W1)
Sports Cafe (SW1)
Spot (WC2)
Stringfellows (WC2)
Sway (WC2)
Tattershall Castle (SW1)
10 Room (W1)
Thirst (W1)
Tiger Tiger (SW1)
Walkabout (multi. loc.)
Waxy O'Connor's (W1)
World's End (NW1)
Zoo Bar (WC2)

Suits

Abingdon (W8)
Akbar (W1)
All Bar One (multi. loc.)
American Bar (WC2)
American Bar (W1)
Anglesea Arms (SW7)
Annabel's (W1)
Antelope (SW1)
Argyll Arms (W1)
Artillery Arms (EC1)
Atlantic B&G (W1)
Auberge (SE1)
Avenue (SW1)
Babble (W1)
Balls Brothers (multi. loc.)
Baltic (SE1)
Bank (WC2)
Bar 38 (W6)
Black Friar (EC4)
Bleeding Heart Tav. (EC1)
Boisdale (SW1)
Bonds (EC2)
Cantina Vinopolis (SE1)
Chapel (NW1)
Cinnamon Club (SW1)
Coal Hole (WC2)
Corney & Barrow (multi. loc.)
Counting House (EC3)
Davy's (multi. loc.)
Digress (EC2)

Dirty Dick (EC2)
1802 (E14)
El Vino (multi. loc.)
Evangelist (EC4)
Fenchurch Colony (EC3)
Fine Line (multi. loc.)
Firevault (W1)
Fishmarket (EC2)
Gordon's (WC2)
Jamaica Wine (EC3)
Jamies (multi. loc.)
JD Wetherspoons (SW1)
La Grande Marque (EC4)
Leadenhall (EC3)
Milk & Honey (W1)
19:20 (EC1)
Old Bank (EC4)
Old Coffee Hse. (W1)
115 @ Hodgsons (WC2)
1 Lombard St. (EC3)
Pacific Oriental (EC2)
Pitcher & Piano (multi. loc.)
PJ's Bar/Grill (SW3)
Plumbers Arms (SW1)
Princess Louise (WC1)
Prism (EC3)
Quaglino's (SW1)
Rising Sun (EC4)
Scott's Penguin (W1)
Seven Stars (WC2)
Slug & Lettuce (multi. loc.)
Smiths/Smithfield (EC1)
Smollensky's (multi. loc.)
St. John (multi. loc.)
Tup (multi. loc.)
Vats Wine Bar (WC1)
Villandry (W1)
Westminster Arms (SW1)
Wine Library (EC3)

Tourist Favourites

Anchor Bankside (SE1)
Archduke (SE1)
Argyll Arms (W1)
Audley (W1)
Backpacker (N1)
Bar Room Bar (W1)
Bar Rumba (W1)
Belgo (multi. loc.)
Belushi's (multi. loc.)
Black Friar (EC4)
Blue Anchor (W6)
Bluebird (SW3)
Bunch of Grapes (SW3)
Café de Paris (W1)
Café Rouge (W1)
Camden Head (N1)

Cheers (W1)
Churchill Arms (W8)
Cirque/Hippodrome (WC2)
Coal Hole (WC2)
Counting House (EC3)
Cutty Sark (SE10)
De Hems (W1)
Equinox (WC2)
Fitzroy (W1)
Flask (N6)
Founder's Arms (SE1)
Freemasons Arms (NW3)
French House (W1)
Gardening Club (WC2)
George Inn (SE1)
Gipsy Moth (SE10)
Grapes (E14)
Greenwich Union (SE10)
Henry J Bean's (multi. loc.)
Holly Bush (NW3)
Hope & Anchor (N1)
Jamaica Wine (EC3)
Lord Moon (SW1)
Lowlander (WC2)
Lyceum Tavern (WC2)
Maple Leaf (WC2)
Marquess/Anglesey (WC2)
Marquis/Granby (WC2)
Museum Tavern (WC1)
Narrow Street (E14)
Navajo Joe's (WC2)
O Bar (W1)
Old Bell (EC4)
Old Thameside (SE1)
On Anon (W1)
Opera Tavern (WC2)
Oxygen (WC2)
Paxton's Head (SW1)
Pillars of Hercules (W1)
Point 101 (WC1)
Princess Louise (WC1)
Prospect/Whitby (E1)
Punch & Judy (WC2)
Q Bar (W1)
Queen Mary (WC2)
Queen's Larder (WC1)
Ruby Blue (WC1)
Running Footman (W1)
Salisbury, The (WC2)
Salsa! (WC2)
Sherlock Holmes (WC2)
Ship (SW18)
Smollensky's (multi. loc.)
Spaniard's Inn (NW3)
Spice of Life (W1)
Sporting Page (SW10)
Spot (WC2)

Town of Ramsgate (E1)
Trafalgar Tavern (SE10)
Walkabout (multi. loc.)
White Cross (Richmond)
Windows Bar (W1K)
Windsor Castle (W1)
Ye Olde Cheshire (EC4)
Ye Olde Mitre (EC1)
Zoo Bar (WC2)

Traditional/Local

Albion (N1)
Anchor Bankside (SE1)
Angel (WC2)
Anglesea Arms (SW7)
Antelope (SW1)
Approach Tavern (E2)
Archery Tavern (W2)
Argyll Arms (W1)
Artillery Arms (EC1)
Ashburnham Arms (SE10)
Barley Mow (W1)
Bedford (SW12)
Bishops Finger (EC1)
Blind Beggar (E1)
Blue Posts (W1)
Bricklayer's Arms (W1)
Bricklayer's Arms (EC2)
Buckingham Arms (SW1)
Builder's Arms (SW3)
Bunch of Grapes (SW3)
Cadogan Arms (SW3)
Calf (SW4)
Camden Brewing (NW1)
Camden Head (N1)
Captain Kidd (E1)
Castle (W11)
Chandos (WC2)
Chelsea Potter (SW3)
Chelsea Ram (SW10)
Churchill Arms (W8)
City Barge (W4)
Clachan (W1)
Clifton (NW8)
Coach & Horses (SW13)
Coach & Horses (W1)
Coach & Horses (W1)
Coach & Horses (WC2)
Coal Hole (WC2)
Coat & Badge (SW15)
Cock Tavern (W1)
Compton Arms (N1)
Coopers Arms (SW3)
Cross Keys (WC2)
Cross Keys (SW3)
Crown (N1)
Crown & Greyhound (SE21)

Dog & Duck (W1)
Dove (W6)
Dover Castle (W1)
Duke of Devonshire (SW12)
Duke of York (WC1)
Enterprise (WC1)
Fitzroy (W1)
Flask (N6)
Flask, The (NW3)
Founder's Arms (SE1)
Fox & Anchor (EC1)
Fox & Grapes (SW19)
Fox & Hounds (SW1)
Freemasons Arms (NW3)
George Inn (SE1)
Gipsy Moth (SE10)
Golden Heart (E1)
Grapes (E14)
Grenadier (SW1)
Griffin (EC2)
Guinea (W1)
Hand in Hand (SW19)
Havelock (W14)
Holly Bush (NW3)
Hoop & Grapes (EC3)
Ifield (SW10)
John Snow (W1)
Ladbroke Arms (W11)
Lamb (WC1)
Lamb & Flag (WC2)
Lamb Tavern (EC3)
Lyceum Tavern (WC2)
Magdala (NW3)
Market Porter (SE1)
Marquess/Anglesey (WC2)
Marquis/Granby (WC2)
Morpeth Arms (SW1)
Nag's Head (SW1)
Narrow Street (E14)
Old Bell (EC4)
Old Coffee Hse. (W1)
Old Red Lion (EC1)
Old Ship (Richmond)
Old Ship (W6)
Paxton's Head (SW1)
Perseverance (WC1)
Phene Arms (SW3)
Plumbers Arms (SW1)
Portobello Star (W11)
Prince of Wales (SW4)
Princess Louise (WC1)
Red Lion (SW1)
Red Lion (SW1)
Richard I (SE10)
Rose & Crown (SW19)
Royal Oak (SE1)
Royal Oak (E2)

Trendy

Shish (EC1V)
Shoreditch Electricity (N1)
Sketch (W1)
Smersh (EC2)
Social (multi. loc.)
Sosho (EC2)
Taman Gang (W1)
Tantra Club (W1)
333 Club/Mother (EC1)
Toast (NW3)
Tongue & Groove (SW9)
Townhouse (SW3)
Turnmills (EC1)
Two Floors (W1)
Vibe Bar (E1)
White Horse (SW2)
White House (SW4)
Yauatcha (W1)
Yo! Below (W1)
Zeta Bar (W1)
Zinc B&G (W1)

Views of London

Anchor Bankside (SE1)
Founder's Arms (SE1)
JD Wetherspoons (SW1)
Narrow Street (E14)
Oxo Tower (SE1)
Rockwell (SW1)
Smiths/Smithfield (EC1)
Tattershall Castle (SW1)
Trafalgar Tavern (SE10)
Twentyfour (EC2)
Windows Bar (W1K)

Water Views

Anchor Bankside (SE1)
Babushka (N1)
Blue Anchor (W6)
Bull's Head (W4)
City Barge (W4)
City Pride (E14)
Cutty Sark (SE10)
Dove (W6)
Duke's Head (SW15)
1802 (E14)
Fine Line (E14)
Founder's Arms (SE1)
Grand Union (W9)
Grapes (E14)
Narrow Boat (N1)
Narrow Street (E14)

Old Ship (W6)
Old Thameside (SE1)
Pitcher & Piano (Richmond)
Prospect/Whitby (E1)
Putney Bridge (SW15)
Queen Mary (WC2)
Ship (SW18)
Sun Inn (SW13)
Tattershall Castle (SW1)
Town of Ramsgate (E1)
Trafalgar Tavern (SE10)
Via Fossa (E14)
White Cross (Richmond)

Wine Bars

Abingdon (W8)
Alexandra/Smart (SW19)
Archduke (SE1)
Balls Brothers (multi. loc.)
Bar Bollywood (W1)
Bar des Amis (WC2)
Bartok (NW1)
Bleeding Heart Tav. (EC1)
Cantina Vinopolis (SE1)
Cellar Gascon (EC1)
Coal Hole (WC2)
Cork & Bottle (WC2)
Corney & Barrow (multi. loc.)
Cru (N1)
Davy's (multi. loc.)
Dover St. (W1)
El Vino (multi. loc.)
Fenchurch Colony (EC3)
Fox Reformed (N16)
Gordon's (WC2)
Isola (SW1)
Jamaica Wine (EC3)
Jamies (multi. loc.)
Julie's (W11)
Kettner's (W1)
La Grande Marque (EC4)
Leadenhall (EC3)
Lupo (W1)
115 @ Hodgsons (WC2)
Smithy's (WC1)
Soho (W1)
Tea Rooms/Artistes (SW8)
Truckles of Pied (WC1)
Vats Wine Bar (WC1)
Wine Library (EC3)

Wine Vintage Chart

This chart is designed to help you select wine to go with your meal. It is based on the same 0 to 30 scale used throughout this *Survey*. The ratings (prepared by our friend **Howard Stravitz,** a law professor at the University of South Carolina) reflect both the quality of the vintage and the wine's readiness for present consumption. Thus, if a wine is not fully mature or is over the hill, its rating has been reduced. We do not include 1987, 1991–1993 vintages because they are not especially recommended for most areas. A dash indicates that a wine is either past its peak or too young to rate.

	'85	'86	'88	'89	'90	'94	'95	'96	'97	'98	'99	'00	'01	'02
WHITES														
French:														
Alsace	24	18	22	28	28	26	25	24	24	26	24	26	27	–
Burgundy	26	25	–	24	22	–	29	28	24	23	25	24	21	–
Loire Valley	–	–	–	–	24	–	20	23	22	–	24	25	23	–
Champagne	28	25	24	26	29	–	26	27	24	24	25	25	26	–
Sauternes	21	28	29	25	27	–	21	23	26	24	24	24	28	–
California (Napa, Sonoma, Mendocino):														
Chardonnay	–	–	–	–	–	–	25	21	25	24	24	22	26	–
Sauvignon Blanc/Semillon	–	–	–	–	–	–	–	–	–	25	25	23	27	–
REDS														
French:														
Bordeaux	24	25	24	26	29	22	26	25	23	25	24	27	24	–
Burgundy	23	–	21	24	27	–	26	28	25	22	28	22	20	24
Rhône	25	19	27	29	29	24	25	23	24	28	27	26	25	–
Beaujolais	–	–	–	–	–	–	–	–	22	21	24	25	18	20
California (Napa, Sonoma, Mendocino):														
Cab./Merlot	26	26	–	21	28	29	27	25	28	23	26	23	26	–
Pinot Noir	–	–	–	–	26	23	23	25	24	26	25	27	–	–
Zinfandel	–	–	–	–	–	25	22	23	21	22	24	–	25	–
Italian:														
Tuscany	26	–	24	–	26	22	25	20	29	24	28	26	25	–
Piedmont	26	–	26	28	29	–	23	27	27	25	25	26	23	–